OUTLINE

OF THE

HISTORY OF ETHICS

A Reprinting of the Fifth Edition
Published in 1902 by Macmillan and Company Ltd.

OUTLINES
OF THE
HISTORY OF ETHICS
FOR ENGLISH READERS

HENRY SIDGWICK

Hackett Publishing Company
Indianapolis/Cambridge

For further information, please address

Hackett Publishing Company, Inc.
P.O. Box 44937
Indianapolis, Indiana 46204

Library of Congress Cataloging-in-Publication Data

Sidgwick, Henry, 1838–1900.
Outlines of the history of ethics for English readers / Henry Sidgwick.
p. cm.
Reprint. Originally published: London : Macmillan, 1902.
Includes index.
ISBN 0-87220-061-2 : $24.50. ISBN 0-87220-060-4 (pbk.) : $7.95
1. Ethics–History. I. Title.
BJ71.S55 1988
170′.9–dc19

88-10986
CIP

PREFACE

THE nucleus of this little book is formed by an article on "Ethics" which I wrote some years ago for the *Encyclopædia Britannica.* I found that, in the opinion of persons whose judgment had weight with me, this article appeared likely to meet the needs of English students desirous of obtaining a general knowledge of the history of ethical thought: I have, therefore, by the permission of Messrs. Black, the publishers of the *Encyclopædia Britannica*, reprinted it in this separate form. In so doing, I have considerably altered and enlarged it: but, after some hesitation, I determined to adhere to the main outlines of the original article, according to which the chapter (IV.) dealing with the modern period is mainly confined to English Ethics, and only deals with foreign ethical systems in a subordinate way, as sources of influence on English thought. I adopted this resolution, partly because it seemed to me that the merit of my article—if it had any—lay in a certain compact unity of movement which would inevitably be lost if I tried to include a treatment of French and German moralists on a scale corresponding to my treatment of English moralists: while at the same time a considerable portion[1] of what I thus omitted appeared to me to have a distinctly subordinate interest for English readers as compared with what I included. I ought further to explain that, for somewhat similar reasons, I have taken pains to keep Ethics as separate as I conveniently could from Theology and Metaphysics, and also from Politics: this separation, however, is naturally less complete in some parts of the subject than in others;—*e.g.* in dealing with the mediæval period the relations of Ethics to Theology are necessarily more prominent than in the modern period. Finally, I may perhaps say that I have aimed throughout at the greatest possible impartiality and "objectivity" of treatment; and in order better to attain this result I have not attempted to deal with contemporary modes of ethical thought—with which I have been engaged controversially—except in a very brief and summary way.

In the greater part of the book—*i.e.* in by far the larger part of Chapter II., in almost all Chapter IV.,

[1] I draw attention to the words "a considerable portion" because they were overlooked by a reviewer who selected this sentence for severe criticism. The omission of them substitutes an opinion which I should regard as indefensible for one which I still think almost incontrovertible.

and in some of Chapter III.—my exposition is primarily based on my own study of the original authors. Where this is not the case I have tried to guard myself from error by comparing different historians of philosophy, and referring to the original authors whenever this comparison left me doubtful. And throughout I have endeavoured to correct and supplement the results of my own study by comparing them with the views expressed in other historical works. I am especially indebted, as regards Chapter II., to Zeller's *Geschichte der Griechischen Philosophie;* but, in revising the chapter, I have also derived useful suggestions from Ziegler, *Geschichte der Ethik*, and from an excellent little book on Epicureanism by Mr. Wallace. The account of Christian morality in Chapter III. was naturally derived from sources too numerous to mention; but for one or two statements in it I am certainly indebted to Lecky's *History of European Morals.* The account of mediæval ethics in the same Chapter was mainly composed, in the original article, by the aid of Neander and Wuttke; but in revising it I have had the valuable aid of Gass's *Christliche Ethik.*[1] In the modern period I have derived suggestions from Jödl, *Geschichte der Ethik*, from the *Principles of Morals* by Wilson and Fowler, from a little book

[1] I ought also to have mentioned Stöckl's *Geschichte der Philosophie des Mittelalters* as a book from which I have derived occasional assistance.

by Mr. Fowler on Shaftesbury and Hutcheson, from another of the same kind on Hobbes by Mr. Croom Robertson, and from Mr. Sully's *Pessimism;* as well as from the comprehensive histories of philosophy by Ueberweg and Erdmann. I must also express my acknowledgment to friends and correspondents for advice that they have given me on various parts of the work: especially to Lord Acton; to R. D. Hicks, Esq., Fellow of Trinity College, Cambridge; and to the Rev. Alexander Stewart, of Mains, Dundee, who has kindly aided me by reading through the proofs of the book.

In revising this book for a second edition I have endeavoured to profit by all the criticism that has come under my notice; and have, in consequence, made several minor modifications in my statements. These have been chiefly in Chapter II. ("Greek and Greco-Roman Ethics"); but I have also rewritten a large part of the account of Kant's doctrine in Chapter IV. To avoid misunderstanding, I ought perhaps to explain that my changes do not necessarily imply an admission that my previous statements were erroneous; I have tried to avoid even objections that appeared to me unfounded, if I thought that I could do this without sacrificing anything that was in my own view important.

Two different criticisms have been passed on the

"General Account of the Subject" in Chapter I. by writers whose views deserve respectful consideration. An American critic—Mr. H. M. Stanley—says that "the chapter is not characterised by that objectivity of treatment which the writer has stated to be his method. Its spirit is dogmatic rather than historical. One who is simply a historian should not give his own conception of the science of Ethics and discuss his subject accordingly, as Professor Sidgwick appears to do." On the other hand, Professor Wallace (*Mind*, vol. xi. p. 471) speaks of this chapter as being "little else than an abstract *résumé* of the facts presented elsewhere in the book under their historical aspect." What I aimed at in this chapter was something intermediate between these two descriptions of what I have actually done. I aimed at giving not "my own conception," but a conception which would be generally accepted as adequately impartial and comprehensive by thinkers of different schools at the present day : while, in order to make this introductory definition more useful to historical students of ethics, I endeavoured to indicate briefly the order and manner in which the different elements in our present conception of the subject were historically developed.

In conclusion, I must again express my obligations to Mr. R. D. Hicks for the valuable assistance that he has given me in the revision of Chapter II.

In the third edition the chief alteration that I have made has consisted in enlarging materially my accounts of the doctrines of Hume and Adam Smith. I have also changed my opinion on a point of some importance in the history of Utilitarianism: I am now disposed to accept the posthumously published *Deontology* of Bentham, as giving a generally trustworthy account of his view as to the relation of Virtue to the virtuous agent's Happiness. Further—besides correcting some misprints and clerical errors, and endeavouring to remove some awkwardnesses of expression—I have modified or explained a few statements which correspondents have criticised as obscure or misleading. I am grateful for such criticisms, to which I wish always to pay respectful attention.

In the fourth edition I have made only verbal alterations; for several of which I am indebted to Miss Jones of Girton College, who has kindly assisted me in the revision.

H. SIDGWICK.

CONTENTS

CHAPTER I

GENERAL ACCOUNT OF THE SUBJECT

CHAPTER II

GREEK AND GRECO-ROMAN ETHICS

CHAPTER III

CHRISTIANITY AND MEDIÆVAL ETHICS

CHAPTER IV

MODERN, CHIEFLY ENGLISH, ETHICS

INTRODUCTION

In order to assist the reader in grasping and arranging the somewhat compressed historical matter presented to him in this book, I have thought it desirable to prefix a brief conspectus of the three periods treated in Chapters II. III. and IV. respectively.

I.—Greek and Greco-Roman Ethics

The first of the three great divisions of my subject—the history of Greek and Greco-Roman Ethics—is most naturally subdivided again into Pre-Socratic Ethics, Socratico-Platonic-Aristotelian Ethics, and Post-Aristotelian Ethics. If we use these as definite chronological divisions, the first period may be taken to extend till somewhere about 430 B.C., when the new dialectic of Socrates began to impress the Athenian public: the second may be taken to end either with the death of Aristotle (322 B.C.), or with the approximately simultaneous appearance of Zeno and Epicurus as teachers at Athens, near the end of the 4th century; the third may be extended, if we like, to the suppression of the schools of philosophy at Athens by the orthodox zeal of Justinian, 529 A.D.; but I have not tried to carry the reader's interest, in this last stage, beyond the 3rd century A.D. In dealing with the first division, however, I have not thought it desirable to observe a strictly chronological line of demarcation; as I have included in it Democritus, a younger contemporary of Socrates, on the ground that the teaching of Democritus stands in close positive relation to the pre-Socratic philosophy, and has not been influenced by any of the new lines of thought which find their common point of departure in Socrates.

1. Pre-Socratic Ethics (550-430 B.C.)

In any case the three periods above distinguished are of very unequal importance. The leading characteristic of the first or pre-Socratic period of Greek philosophy is, that philosophic inquiry is mainly concentrated on the explanation of the external world; the interest in human conduct occupies a secondary and subordinate place. It is in and through the teaching of Socrates that moral philosophy came to occupy in Greek thought the central position which it never afterwards lost: Socrates is the main starting-point from which all subsequent lines of Greek ethical thought diverge: speculations on conduct before Socrates are, to our apprehension, merely a kind of prelude to the real performance. Further, the three thinkers of this period, to whom I have directed attention—Pythagoras, Heraclitus, and Democritus—are only known to us at second-hand, or through fragmentary passages quoted by other writers. On both grounds we cannot afford to spend much time in examining their doctrines. It is, however, interesting—and it may assist the student in fixing their chief characteristics in his mind—to note the relations of affinity in which these three Pre-Socratic thinkers stand respectively to three important lines of post-Socratic thought: Pythagoras to Platonism, Heraclitus to Stoicism, and Democritus to Epicureanism.

2. Socrates, Plato, and Aristotle (430-322 B.C.)

The second period, though very much shorter in time than the third, occupies, as the reader will see, a much larger space in my chapter. This is partly because the actual works of Plato and the most important part of the works of Aristotle have come down to us, whereas the books of the leading post-Aristotelian thinkers have almost entirely perished. But this is not the whole explanation: rather, this fact is itself an indication of the pre-eminent and permanent interest attaching to the writings of these earlier masters. For us, at any rate, Socrates, Plato, and Aristotle, taken together, hold a unique place in the history of moral philosophy: and in order to understand the men and their work we should contemplate them as much as possible in relation to each other. Considered apart from Plato and Aristotle, Socrates would indeed be a most interesting historical figure; but the deepest significance of his dialectical method would inevitably be lost. Plato's work is, as he himself presents it, essentially the prosecution of an inquiry started by Socrates; and Aristotle's work, in ethics at least, is in the main a systematic restatement of the definite results gradually worked out by the untiring and continually renewed research of Plato, supplemented by further applications of what is essentially the method of Socrates formalised.

Cynics and Cyrenaics.

A subordinate share of attention is due to the development of the Cynic and Cyrenaic schools within this period: it is chiefly interesting as presenting to us in an earlier and cruder form that uncompromising opposition between Virtue and Pleasure, which afterwards, in the post-Aristotelian period, is continued between Stoicism and Epicureanism. Both Cynic and Cyrenaic schools linger for a time, after the founding of the later and more important schools of Zeno and Epicurus; but we cannot trace Cyrenaic doctrine beyond the middle of the third century B.C.; and by the end of this century Cynicism, as an independent school, seems to become extinct, though it revives later as an offshoot or modification of Stoicism.

3. Post-Aristotelian Ethics, from 300 B.C. to (say) 300 A.D.

The third and concluding period of Greek and Greco-Roman Ethics may be taken to extend, roughly speaking, over six centuries—half before and half after the Christian era. But the philosophic interest of the period is very unequally distributed over it. The most interesting point in it is the very beginning; since Zeno and Epicurus appear to have founded the Stoic and Epicurean schools respectively about the same time, just before the end of the 4th century B.C. No event at all equal in importance to this double origination of doctrine occurs in the history of moral philosophy for the subsequent six centuries,—at any rate until the founding of Neo-Platonism in the 3rd century A.D.; and even this is of less importance in the history of ethics than it is in the history of philosophy generally. Hence, in studying this period, it is convenient to divide it—if I may so say—*longitudinally* rather than *transversely*; first considering separately each of the four schools founded by Plato, Aristotle, Zeno, and Epicurus respectively, and then examining their mutual relations. Stoicism in this period takes the lead, and throughout claims the first and largest share of our attention until the close of the 2nd century A.D., when the interest is transferred to the later developments of Platonism. The antithetical relation of Stoicism to Epicureanism is simple, permanent, and easily apprehended; while the attitude of the Peripatetic or Aristotelian school, overlooking minor changes, may be briefly characterised as that of "moderate orthodoxy," endeavouring to maintain the paramount claims of Virtue adequately, yet so as to avoid the Stoic extravagances. The earlier history of Stoicism itself is an obscure subject, into which I have entered no further than just to note the importance of the work of Chrysippus, the "second founder" of Stoicism (*circ.* 280–206 B.C.); after this, the chief points to observe in its development are the tendency to Eclecticism or Syncretism towards the end of the 2nd century B.C., represented by Panætius, the influence of Stoicism on Roman thought as traced in Cicero's writings, and the characteristics of the later Roman Stoicism that we know from the writings of Seneca and Marcus Aurelius. The variations in Plato's school are the most marked: speaking broadly, we may distinguish three principal transitions in its history; the first change is to a period of philosophic scepticism (*circ.* 250-100 B.C.) in which its ethical teaching is dubious; then scepticism dies out during the 1st century B.C., and the predominant view of the school becomes broadly similar to the moderate orthodoxy of the Peripatetics—until, in the 2nd century A.D., a tendency to Mysticism appears, which reaches its fullest development in the Neo-Platonism of Plotinus in the 3rd century.

II.—Christianity and Mediæval Ethics

When, at the close of the 3rd century A.D., we turn our attention from Neo-Platonism, we find Christianity already dominant in European thought: accordingly, I commence my second chapter with a brief characterisation of the distinctive features of Christian morality, and then proceed to a summary sketch of the development of ethical

1. Pre-Scholastic Period to 1100 A.D. Augustine (354-430 A.D.)

doctrine in the Western Church. If the reader should be startled by the rapidity with which he is carried over more than six centuries, from Augustine to Anselm, he must bear in mind the long suspension of the higher intellectual activities that took place during these ages of social dissolution and reconstruction; and he may note that the one original thinker who claims our attention during these

Erigena (*circ.* 810-877 A.D.)

"dark ages," Johannes Erigena, is connected indirectly with the partial gleam of light and order which Europe owed to Charles the Great; since the only part of Erigena's life of which we have any accurate knowledge is that which he spent as head of the Court school (*Schola Palatina*) under Charles the Bald, from 843 onward. Further, it is note-

2. Scholasticism grows and culminates (1100-1274 A.D.)

worthy that the important development of mediæval philosophy, which begins with Anselm, and which is called Scholasticism, nearly coincides with the great effort to establish social and political order in Western Europe on the basis of ecclesiastical supremacy, which begins with Hildebrand; and that Scholasticism, like the power of the papacy, culminates in the 13th century with Thomas Aquinas—the only writer whose doctrines I have thought it desirable to expound at any length in this chapter. In the

3. Decay of Mediæval Philosophy and transition to Modern Thought (*circ.* 1300-1600 A.D.)

14th century Scholasticism has passed its prime, though its method still dominates educated Europe; in the 15th century the sway of mediæval thought is assailed and undermined by the Renaissance; in the 16th the Reformation and the growth of physical science combine to shatter it; with the 17th century the period of modern thought has effectively begun.

III.—Modern, chiefly English, Ethics

The concluding chapter is principally occupied with the process of English ethical thought from Hobbes to J. S. Mill: but, to explain Hobbism, it seemed desirable to begin by describing the previous view of Natural Law from which Hobbism is formed by antithesis, and which had been taken as the basis of International Law in the epoch-making work of Grotius, some fifteen years before Hobbes's view took written shape. For the century and a half that intervenes between Hobbes and Bentham the development of English ethics proceeds without receiving any material influence from foreign sources. This process may be conveniently divided into parts, as follows; but the reader must observe that the divisions cannot altogether be treated as chronologically successive.

1. Hobbes (1640 and 1651).

In the first period, the aspect of Hobbism which orthodox moralists oppose is the dependence of social morality on the establishment of political order. Overlooking minor differences, we may distinguish broadly two lines of opposition: (1) that of the "Cambridge moralists" and Clarke, which laid stress on the self-evidence of moral principles viewed abstractly, and their intrinsic cogency for rational wills as such, apart from any consideration of them as laws laid down for men by an omnipotent ruler; (2) that of Cumberland and Locke, which treats morality as a code of Divine Legislation to be ascertained by considering the relations of human beings as designed and created by God. The former line I may call that of the Earlier Rational Intuitionists, to distinguish it from a somewhat similar line of thought introduced in the next century by Price and

2. Independent Morality. Rational and Jural (1651-1711).

Reid; while the Jural moralists, Cumberland and Locke, are perhaps most instructively viewed as precursors of the later Utilitarianism of Paley—although, as I have shown, Locke's method of determining the laws of nature is rather intuitional than utilitarian. It should be added, however, that these two lines of thought are not definitely opposed to each other in this period: Cumberland, especially, is regarded by Clarke as altogether an ally, and is in some ways nearer to him than he is to Locke.

3. Psychological Anti-Egoism. Naturalness of disinterested Benevolence and Conscience (1711-1747).

In the second period the reply to Hobbism takes a new departure, and penetrates to its basis of Psychological Egoism. This line of thought is initiated by Shaftesbury, and developed in different ways by Butler and Hutcheson: all three agree in maintaining against Hobbes (*a*) that disinterested Benevolence and the moral Sense or Conscience are natural springs of action not reducible to Self-love; and (*b*) that they prompt, always, or for the most part, to the conduct that enlightened self-interest would dictate, and are therefore *harmonious* with, though *distinct* from, Self-love. I say "always *or* for the most part"; for on this point the greater caution of Butler leads him into a manner of thought sufficiently different from that of Shaftesbury or Hutcheson to constitute a new departure. In the view of Shaftesbury and Hutcheson the Moral Sense, Comprehensive Benevolence, and Enlightened Self-interest combine in a triple band to draw us, if we only see empirical facts as they are, to good conduct: in Butler's view it is needful (1) to face the possibility of an apparent conflict between conscience and Self-love, and therefore lay stress on the authority of the former; and (2) to note that the dictates of Conscience diverge importantly from the directions which a mere regard for general happiness would give. On the first of these

4. Butler (1726 and 1736). Dualism of Governing Principles. Divergence of Conscience and Benevolence.

points he lays stress in the preface to his *Sermons* (1726); the second only became perfectly clear to him later, and is emphasised in the dissertation *On the Nature of Virtue* appended to the *Analogy* (1736); this latter date accordingly may be taken as the starting-point of the controversy between Intuitional and Utilitarian Ethics, which becomes prominent afterwards. The next division of the subject is characterised by the preponderance of Psychology over Ethics: the question that is both most originally and most effectively treated is not (*a*) How right conduct is to be determined, but (*b*) How moral sentiments are to be scientifically explained. Three lines of explanation—all of which supply elements to the later Associationism of James and John Mill and others—are developed by Hume, Hartley, and Adam Smith respectively. Of these, Hume's, which resolves moral sentiment into sympathy with the pleasurable and painful effects of action, leads naturally to a utilitarian solution of the strictly ethical question (*a*): but Hume's concern is primarily with psychological explanation, not ethical construction.

5. Psychology predominant over Ethics. Explanation of Moral Sentiments (1740-1759).

Finally, when the main interest turns again to the systematic determination of right conduct, we find the opposition between the plain man's Conscience and comprehensive Benevolence, which Butler noted in 1736, developed into the antithesis between Intuitional and Utilitarian morality, which has lasted on into our own time. My historical sketch was intended to end with the Utilitarianism of Mill; but I have thought it well to include a brief notice of two current modes of thought not represented in the historical sketch, which I have called "Evolutional" and "Transcendental" Ethics. Further, before the end of the last century, we have to note a reintroduction of foreign influence: the Utili-

6. Later Intuitionism and Common Sense, from 1757 (Price) or 1788 (Reid).

7. Fully developed Utilitarianism, from 1785 (Paley) or 1789 (Bentham).

tarian systems of Bentham and Mill show the influence respectively of the French writers Helvetius and Comte: while, again, the influence of Kantism has partly blended, partly contrasted with the Common Sense Intuitionism of what is commonly known as the Scottish[1] School, represented by Reid and Stewart; and later, in the third quarter of the present century, a new form of ethical thought which I have called Transcendentalism has been developed under the influence of Kant and Hegel combined: and the pessimism[2] faintly discernible in current English thought may be partially traced to a German origin. I have accordingly concluded the chapter with a brief account of certain French and German systems of ethics, regarded in relation to English thought.

[1] This term is liable to mislead, as the intellectual activity of Scotland plays a prominent part in the movement of English ethical thought from Hutcheson onward; but what is most widely known as the Scottish school was founded by Reid.

[2] I use the term pessimism in its popular sense, to denote the view that the world is so bad that its non-existence would be preferable to its existence—not necessarily that it is the worst possible world.

CHAPTER I

GENERAL ACCOUNT OF THE SUBJECT

THERE is some difficulty in defining the subject of Ethics in a manner which can fairly claim general acceptance; since its nature and relations are variously understood by writers of different schools, and are in consequence conceived somewhat indefinitely by educated persons in general. It has therefore seemed to me best, in this introductory chapter, first to develop gradually the different views which the human mind has been led to take of the objects of ethical inquiry, and its relations to cognate subjects such as Theology, Politics, and Psychology; and then to conclude with a statement on these points, and an account of the chief divisions of the subject, which I shall aim at making at once as neutral and as comprehensive as possible.

§ 1. Ethics; the study of the Ultimate Good of man.

The derivation of the term is to some extent misleading; for Ethics (ἠθικά) originally meant what relates to character as distinct from intellect; but the qualities of character which we call virtues and vices constituted only one element in the subject of the treatise of Aristotle which this term was used to denote. According to the Aristotelian view—which is that of Greek philosophy generally, and has been widely taken in later times—the primary subject of ethical investigation is all that is included under the notion of what is ultimately good or desirable for man; all that is reasonably chosen or sought by him, not as a means to some ulterior end, but for itself. The qualification "for man" is important to distinguish the subject-matter of Ethics from that Absolute Good or Good of the Universe, which may be stated as the subject-matter of Theology—taking "Theology" in a wide sense, as involving only the assumption of some ultimate end or Good, to the realisation of which the whole process of the world, as empirically known to us, is somehow a means, but not necessarily connecting Personality with this end or Good. This distinction between Ethics and Theology was not, however, reached at once and without effort in the development of Ethical reflection; indeed in Platonism, as we shall see, Ethics and Theology were indissolubly blended. Nor, again, must the distinction be taken to imply a complete separation of the two subjects; on the contrary, in almost every philosophical system in which the universe is contemplated as having an ultimate end or Good, the good of human beings is conceived as either identical with, or included in, this Universal Good—or at any rate closely related to it in the way of resemblance or derivation.

distinguished from Theology, the study of Absolute Good.

§ 2. Ethics partially distinguished from Politics.

But further, in the definition above given, Ethics is not yet clearly distinguished from Politics; for Politics is also concerned with the Good or Welfare of men, so far as they are members of states. And in fact the term Ethics is sometimes used, even by modern writers, in a wide sense, so as to include at least a part of Politics—viz. the consideration of the ultimate end or Good of the state, and the general standard or criterion for determining the goodness or badness of political institutions. It is, however, also current in a narrower sense—equivalent to the qualified term "Private Ethics," which is sometimes preferred—as a study of the Good or Wellbeing of man, so far as this is attainable by the rational activity of individuals as such. This latter is the meaning to which the term is, in the main, restricted in the historical sketch that follows; at the same time I have not tried to draw a sharp division between the two subjects, the connection of which, in many at least of the systems with which we have to deal, is conceived as very close and intimate. The difficulty of separating them is easily seen, whether we approach the boundary between them from the ethical or from the political side. On the one hand, individual men are almost universally members of some political or governed community; what we call their virtues are chiefly exhibited in their dealings with their fellows, and their most prominent pleasures and pains are derived in whole or in part from their relations to other human beings: thus most of those who consider either Virtue or Pleasure to be the sole or chief constituent of an individual's highest good would agree that this good is not to be sought in a life of monastic isolation, and without regard to the wellbeing of his community; they would admit that private ethics has a political department. On the other hand, it would be generally agreed that a statesman's main ultimate aim should be to promote the wellbeing of his fellow-citizens, present and to come, considered as individuals: so that the investigation of the particulars of this wellbeing must be an integral part of Politics. Still we may, to a great extent, study the elements and conditions of the good of individual men, so far as it is attainable by the rational activity of themselves or other individuals acting as private persons, without considering the manner in which the structure and functions of government should be determined with a view to the same end; it is, then, to the former of these subjects, as distinct from the latter, that attention will be primarily directed in the following pages.

§ 3. Ethics and Psychology.

When, however, we thus as far as possible isolate in thought the individual man for the purposes of ethical contemplation, a different relation of Ethics comes prominently into view—its relation, namely, to Psychology, the study of the human soul or mind. Reflection soon makes it appear that the chief good of man cannot consist in anything external and material, such as wealth; nor even in mere bodily health, which experience shows to be compatible with extreme badness and wretchedness. It would seem, indeed, that we commonly judge men to be good or bad —courageous, just, temperate, or their opposites—from a consideration of the external effects of their actions; still, in the first place, reflective persons generally are agreed that such judgments are liable to be superficial and erroneous, and that a certain state of the agent's mind, a certain quality of intention, purpose, motive, or disposition, is required to constitute an act morally good; and secondly, when we analyse in their turn the external consequences above mentioned, we find that what are really judged to be ultimately good or bad are almost always either effects on the feelings of men or other sentient beings, or effects on human character and volition. Hence almost all ethical schools would agree that the main object of their investigation must belong to the psychical side of human life; whether (1) they hold that man's ultimate end is to be found in psychical existence regarded as merely sentient and emotional, identifying it with some species of desirable feeling or Pleasure, or the genus or sum of such feelings; or whether (2) they rather maintain that the wellbeing of the mind must lie solely or chiefly in the quality of its activity—its Virtue. And when we attempt to work out either view into a clear and complete system, we are led inevitably to further psychological study, either (1) in order to examine different kinds and degrees of pleasure and pain, or (2) to determine the nature and mutual relations of the different virtues or good qualities of character, and their opposites. Again, I have spoken of man's good as being the object of rational choice or aim; meaning thereby to distinguish it from the objects of merely sensual and emotional impulses, which are liable to prompt to action opposed to the agent's true good, as he conceives it. But this conception of "Reason choosing" or "impelling" is found on reflection to be involved in difficulties; it appears to some that the ultimate impulse to action is always given, not by Intellect, but by Feeling; hence careful psychological analysis is found to be necessary to make clear the normal operation of Intellect in the action which we call reasonable, and especially its relation to the desires and aversions that arise—at least in part—independently of reason, and appear to conflict with it. Further, in the course of the controversy that moralists have carried on as to what is truly good or desirable—the fundamental nature of which has already been indicated—appeal has continually been made to experience of men's actual desires; on the assumption that what is truly desirable for a man may be identified with what he desires naturally, or permanently, or on the whole. Thus in various ways ethical questions lead inevitably to psychological discussions; in fact, we may say that all important ethical notions are also psychological; except perhaps the fundamental antitheses of "good" and "bad," "right" and "wrong," with which psychology, as it treats of what is and not of what ought to be, is not directly concerned.

§ 4. Ethics; the study of Duty or Right Conduct.

The two antitheses just mentioned are frequently regarded as identical. And in fact it does not matter for ordinary purposes whether we speak of "right" or "good" conduct, "wrong" or "bad" motives. Reflection, however, will show that the common notion of what is Good for a human being—even if we restrict it to what is "ultimately" good, or "good in itself," and not merely as a means to some further end—includes more than the common notion of what is Right for him, or his Duty: it includes also his Interests or Happiness. No doubt it is commonly believed that it will be ultimately best for a man to do his duty, and that this will promote his real Interest or Happiness; but it does not follow that the notions of duty and interest are to be identified, or even that the inseparable connection between the two may be scientifically known and demonstrated. This connection, indeed, is often, by modern thinkers, regarded rather as a matter of faith;—as something providentially left obscure, in order that duty may be done as duty, and not from a mere calculation of self-love. Thus we arrive at another conception of Ethics, in which it is thought to be concerned primarily with the general rules of Duty or Right Action—sometimes called the Moral Code—viewed as absolutely binding on every man, and properly to be obeyed by him without regard to his personal interests; the relation of duty to the agent's private happiness being regarded as a matter of secondary concern from an ethical point of view. On this view the study connects itself in a new way with theology, so far as the rules of duty are regarded as a code of divine legislation.

Further, as we shall see, it has a close affinity to abstract jurisprudence, so far as this is conceived to treat of rules of Law cognisable by reason as naturally and universally valid, and accordingly not dependent on human legislation for their claim to be enforceable by judicial punishment; since such jural rules must always constitute an important part —though not the whole—of the Moral Code. We might contrast this as a modern view of ethics with the view before given, which was that primarily taken in ancient Greek philosophy generally[1]—the transition from the one to the other being due chiefly to the influence of Christianity, but partly also to that of Roman jurisprudence. It is true that the thought of "the gods' unwritten and unfaltering law" was not by any means absent from the moral reflection of Greece; still, the idea of Law was not taken as the ultimate and fundamental notion in the ancient ethical systems. These proceed on the assumption that man, as a reasonable being, must seek his own highest good in this earthly life, and therefore that any laws he has to obey must be shown to be means to the attainment of this good, or particulars in which it is realised. On this point the change produced by Christianity is more striking if we consider its effects on mankind generally, than if we only regard its influence on the minds that were most completely penetrated by its religious spirit. For the true Christian saint lived even on earth, no less than the pagan philosopher, a life which he regarded as intrinsically preferable to all other modes of earthly exist-

[1] This statement requires some qualification as applied to Stoicism; through which, in fact, as will presently appear, the transition was partly made from the ancient to the modern manner of thought. See ch. ii. §§ 15 and 19, and ch. iv. § 1.

ence; and, like the Platonic philosopher, a life of which practical virtue was not so much the essence as the outward expression. Still even for the saint this earthly life afforded but an imperfect foretaste of the bliss for which he hoped; and in the view of more ordinary Christians, the ultimate good of man vanished from the scrutiny of mere ethical speculation into the indefinite brightness of a future life of happiness, supernaturally bestowed by God as a reward for obedience to His laws. Or rather, perhaps, by the mass of Christians, the moral code was more commonly regarded, in still closer analogy to human legislation, as supported by penal sanctions; since in all ages of Christianity the fear of the pains of hell has probably been a more powerful motive to draw men from vice than the hope of the pleasures of heaven. On either view the ultimate weal or ill of human beings became something that might be imagined and rhetorically described, but not definitely known or scientifically investigated; and thus the subject-matter of Ethics defined itself afresh as Moral Law, a body of rules absolutely prescribed, and supplying a complete guidance for human conduct, though not claiming to contain an exhaustive statement of human good.

§ 5. Ethics and Jurisprudence.

Within the Christian Church, through the earlier ages of its history, the rules of morality were commonly held to be known—in the main, if not altogether—by Revelation and not by mere Reason; and hence it naturally fell to theologians to expound, and to priests to administer, this code of divine legislation. But when a more philosophical treatment of ethics was introduced by the schoolmen, the combination in the code of two elements—one distinctively Christian, and the other cognisable by natural reason, and binding on all men apart from revelation—began to be clearly seen; and an adequate theory of this second element seemed to be supplied by the development of theoretical jurisprudence that followed on the revival, in the 12th century, of the study of Roman law. In the later treatment of legal principles in Rome, the notion of a law of nature had become prominent; and this notion was naturally and easily adapted to represent the element in morality that was independent of revelation. It is true that the natural law with which the philosophical jurists were concerned did not relate to right conduct generally, but only to such right actions (or abstinences) as are required to satisfy the rightful claims of others; hence it could not properly be identified with more than a portion of the moral code. This portion, however, is of such fundamental importance that the distinction just noticed was often overlooked or treated as subordinate by mediæval and early modern thinkers; the notion of Natural Law was taken as coincident with Morality generally so far as cognisable by Reason and regulative of outward conduct.

Origin of Moral Faculty.

It is chiefly in connection with this jural view of morality that the inquiry into the origin of the moral faculty has occupied a prominent place in the modern treatment of Ethics. So long as the principle in man that governs or ought to govern is regarded merely as the faculty of knowing our true good, together with its main causes or conditions, it hardly seems important to inquire how this faculty originated, any more than it is important for a geometer to investigate the origin of the spatial faculty. But when the moral faculty had come to be conceived as Conscience, *i.e.* as a faculty cognisant of rules absolutely binding, to be obeyed without reference to the agent's apparent interest—a kind of legislator within the man that claims unquestioned and unconditional supremacy over all other springs of action—it was to be expected that the legitimacy of its claim would be challenged and seriously investigated; and it is not hard to understand how this legitimacy is thought to depend on the "originality" of the faculty—that is, on its being a part of the plan or type according to which human nature was originally constructed. Hence investigations into the moral condition of children and savages, and even animals, and more or less conjectural theories of the soul's growth and development, have been commonly regarded as necessary appendages or introductions to modern ethical discussion.

Free Will.

So again, it is through the jural conception of Ethics that the controversy on free will chiefly becomes important. A plain man does not naturally inquire whether he is "free" or not to seek his own good, provided only he knows what it is, and that it is attainable by voluntary action. But when his conduct is compared with a code to the violation of which punishments are attached, the question whether he really could obey the rule by which he is judged is obvious and inevitable, since if he could not, it seems contrary to justice to punish him.

Summary view of Ethics.

To sum up: the subject of Ethics, most comprehensively understood, includes (1) an investigation of the constituents and conditions of the Good or Wellbeing of men considered individually, which chiefly takes the form of an examination into the general nature and particular species of (*a*) Virtue or (*b*) Pleasure, and the chief means of realising these ends; (2) an investigation of the principles and most important details of Duty or the Moral Law (so far as this is distinguished from Virtue); (3) some inquiry into the nature and origin of the Faculty by which duty is recognised and, more generally, into the part taken by Intellect in human action, and its relation to various kinds of Desire and Aversion; (4) some examination of the question of human Free Will. It is connected with Theology, in so far as a Universal Good is recognised, inclusive of Human Good, or analogous to it; and again, so far as morality is regarded as a Code of Divine appointment. It is connected with Politics, so far as the wellbeing of any individual man is bound up with the wellbeing of his society; and again with Jurisprudence —if this is separated from Politics—so far as morality is identified with Natural Law. Finally, almost every branch of ethical discussion belongs at least in part to Psychology; and the inquiries into the origin of the moral faculty and the freedom of the Will are entirely psychological;—except that if Psychology is distinguished from Metaphysics, and taken as a purely empirical science, the discussion of Free Will may perhaps be relegated to the latter subject.

We will now proceed to trace briefly the course of ethical speculation from its origin in Europe to the present day; confining our attention, during the latter part of this period, to such modes of thought as have been developed in England, or have exercised an important influence there.

I may observe that the term "moral" is commonly used as synonymous with "ethical" (*moralis* being the Latin translation of ἠθικός), and I shall so use it in the following pages.

CHAPTER II

GREEK AND GRECO-ROMAN ETHICS

§ 1. Pre-Socratic Philosophy.

THE ethical speculation of Greece, and therefore of Europe has not, any more than other elements of European civilisation, an abrupt and absolute commencement. The naive and fragmentary utterances of sage precepts for conduct, in which nascent moral reflection everywhere first manifests itself, supply a noteworthy element of Greek literature in the "gnomic" poetry of the 7th and 6th centuries before Christ; their importance in the development of Greek civilisation is strikingly characterised by the traditional enumeration of the "seven sages" of the 6th century; and their influence on ethical thought is sufficiently shown in the references that Plato and Aristotle make to the definitions and maxims of poets and sages. But from such utterances as these to moral philosophy there was still a long step; for though Thales (*circ.* 640-560 B.C.), one of the seven sages, was also the first physical philosopher of Greece, we have no ground for supposing that his practical wisdom had anything of a philosophical character; and a general concentration of interest on physical or metaphysical—as distinct from moral—questions is characteristic of Greek philosophy generally, in the period between Thales and Socrates: so that, in the series of original thinkers who are commonly classed as pre-Socratic philosophers, there are only three—if we omit the Sophists—whose ethical teaching demands our attention. These three are Pythagoras, Heraclitus, and Democritus. It is noteworthy that each of them anticipates, in an interesting way, an important element in post-Socratic thought.

Pythagoras (*circ.* 580-500 B.C.)

The first of these, Pythagoras, would probably be the most interesting of all, if we could trace with any definiteness even the outlines of his work through the thick veil of legend that has overgrown the historical tradition of it. The most trustworthy testimony, however, represents Pythagoras rather as the founder of an order or brotherhood with moral and religious aims—based on a belief in the transmigration of souls—than as the originator of a school of ethical philosophy. In his precepts of moderation, courage, loyalty in friendship, obedience to law and government, his recommendation of daily self-examination—even in the rules of abstinence and ceremonial observance, which we may believe him to have delivered—we may discern an effort, striking in its originality and earnestness, to mould the lives of men as much as possible into the "likeness of God"; but these precepts seem to have been announced much more in a dogmatic, or even prophetic, than in a philosophic manner; and, whether sound or arbitrary, to have been accepted by his disciples with a decidedly unphilosophic reverence for the *ipse dixit*[1] of the master. Still we can trace a genuinely philosophical element in some of the fragmentary traditions of Pythagorean doctrine which have come down to us. Thus the—at first startling—proposition of the Pythagoreans, that the essence of justice

[1] This well-known phrase was originally attributed to the Pythagoreans.

(conceived as equal retribution) is a square number, indicates a serious attempt to extend to the region of conduct that mathematical view of the universe which was the fundamental characteristic of Pythagoreanism; the notion of "squareness" being doubtless used to express that exact proportionment of requital to desert which is commonly felt to be the essence of retributive justice. Similarly in the propositions that Virtue and Health are "harmonies," that Friendship is a "harmonic equality," and in the Pythagorean classification of good with unity, limit, straightness, etc., and of evil with the opposite qualities, we may find at least the germ of Plato's view that goodness in human conduct, as in external nature and works of art, depends on certain quantitative relations of elements in the good result, exactly proportioned so as to avoid excess or defect.

Heraclitus (*circ.* 530-470 B.C.)

If Pythagoras partially anticipates certain features of Platonism, Heraclitus may be regarded as a forerunner of Stoicism. We have no reason, indeed, to suppose that the moral element in his "dark" philosophisings was worked out into anything like a complete ethical system. But when he bids men obey the "divine law from which all human laws draw their sustenance," the Justice to which even the heavens are subject; when he enjoins on them to abide firmly by the Reason that is in truth common to all men, though most surrender themselves to the deceptions of sense, and reduce happiness to the satisfaction of the most grovelling appetites; when he tells them that "Wisdom is to . . . act according to nature with understanding";—we recognise a distinctly Stoical quality in this uncompromising reverence for an objective law, recognised in a threefold aspect as Rational, Natural, and Divine. So again, in his optimistic view of our world of battle and strife as in the sight of God all "good and fair and just"—the apparent injustice in it being only relative to human apprehension—we may find a simple anticipation of the elaborate proof of the world's perfection which the Stoics afterwards attempted. It was, we may believe, in the surrender of his soul to this divine or universal view of things that Heraclitus chiefly attained the "complacency" (*εὐαρέστησιν*) which he is said to have regarded as the highest good; and we find the same term used by the later Stoics to express a similar attitude of cheerful acquiescence in the decrees of Providence.

Democritus (*circ.* 460-370 B.C.)

Democritus—whose philosophical system, as a whole, stands to Epicureanism in a relation somewhat resembling that which Heraclitus holds in respect to Stoicism—is usually and properly classed with "pre-Socratic" thinkers, as his doctrine shows no trace of the influence of Socrates, from whose teaching all the great schools of ethical thought in Greece take their main departure; chronologically speaking, however, Democritus is a somewhat younger contemporary of Socrates. His anticipation of the Epicurean system is more clearly marked in the department of physics—where, indeed, he supplied Epicurus with the main part of his doctrine—than it is in ethics; still, a certain number of the fragments that remain of his ethical treatises have a decidedly Epicurean character. Thus he seems to have been the first thinker to declare expressly that "delight" or "good cheer" (*εὐθυμία*) is the ultimate or highest good; and his identification of this with an equable and unperturbed temper of mind (*συμμετρία*, *ἀταραξία*), the stress laid by him on moderation and limitation of desires as a means to obtaining the greatest pleasure, his preference of the delights of the soul to those of the mere body, the importance he attaches to insight or Wisdom, especially as releasing from the fear of death and what comes after death,—these have all their counterpart in the Epicurean doctrine. The main part, however, of the moral teaching of Democritus—so far as we can judge of it from the mere fragments handed down to us—seems to have been of the unsystematic kind that belongs to the pre-Socratic period; and many of his utterances—as, *e.g.* that it is worse to do than to suffer injustice, that not only wrong-doing but wrong-wishing is bad and hateful,—seem the naive expression of an elevated strain of moral sentiment which has not been reduced to any rational coherence with his view of ultimate Good. On the whole, we may say that what remains of the moral treatises of Democritus is sufficient to enable us to conjecture how the turn of Greek philosophy in the direction of ethics, which was actually due to Socrates, might have taken place without him; but it does not justify us in attributing to their author more than a rudimentary apprehension of the formal conditions which moral teaching must fulfil before it can lay claim to be treated as scientific.

The truth is that a moral system could not be satisfactorily constructed until attention had been strongly directed to the vagueness and inconsistency of the common moral opinions of mankind; until this was done, the moral counsels of the philosopher, however supreme his contempt for the common herd, inevitably shared these defects. For this purpose there was needed the concentration of a philosophic intellect of the first order on the problems of practice. In Socrates, for the first time, we find the required combination of a paramount interest in conduct, and an ardent desire for knowledge; a desire, at the same time, that was repelled from the physical and metaphysical inquiries which had absorbed the main attention of his predecessors, by a profound dissatisfaction with the results of their speculations, and a consequent disbelief in the possibility of penetrating the secret of the physical universe. The doctrines of these thinkers, he said, were at once so extravagant and so mutually contradictory, that they were "like madmen disputing." A similar negative attitude towards the whole antecedent series of dogmatic philosophers had already found expression in the sweeping scepticism of Gorgias, who declared that the essential nature of things which the philosophers investigated did not exist, or at any rate could not be known, or if known, could not be stated; and also in the famous proposition of Protagoras, that human apprehension is the only standard of what is and what is not. In the case of Socrates, however, such a view found further support in a naive piety that indisposed him to search into things of which the gods seemed to have reserved the knowledge to themselves. The regulation of human action, on the other hand (except on occasions of special difficulty, for which omens and oracles might be vouchsafed), they had left to human reason; on this accordingly Socrates concentrated his efforts.

§ 2. The age of the Sophists (*circ.* 450-400 B.C.)

The demand for a reasoned theory of good conduct was not, however, original in Socrates, though his conception of the requisite knowledge was so in the highest degree. The thought of the most independent thinker is conditioned by that of his age; and we cannot disconnect the work of Socrates from the professional instruction in the art of conduct—given by a group of persons who have since been commonly described as "Sophists"—which is so striking a phenomenon of this period of Greek civilisation. Of the professional "teachers of virtue"[1] or "human excellence," to whom this name was applied, the most brilliant and impressive appears to have been Protagoras of Abdera, to whose philosophic doctrine I just now referred; and it is not improbable that the original notion of imparting instruction in virtue by means of lectures was due to this vigorous and enterprising thinker, whom we may suppose to have been turned, like Socrates, to the study of human affairs in consequence of his negative attitude towards current ontological speculation. The instruction, however, that was actually given by Protagoras, Prodicus, Hippias, and other sophists, does not seem to have been based on any philosophical system, and was in fact of too popular a quality to be of much philosophical importance. It seems to have combined somewhat loosely the art of getting on in the world with the art of managing public affairs, and to have mingled encomiastic expositions of different virtues with prudential justifications of virtue, as a means of obtaining pleasure and avoiding pain; of these latter the best example that has come down to us is the fable of the Choice of Hercules, attributed to Prodicus. But however commonplace the teaching of the "sophists" may have been, the general fact of the appearance of this new profession to meet a new

[1] οἱ φάσκοντες παιδεύειν ἀνθρώπους εἰς ἀρετήν (Plato, *Gorg.*, p. 519), cf. Xenophon, *Memorabilia*, I., ch. ii. ἀρετὴν ἐπαγγελλόμενος. It must not be supposed that this profession was made by all the popular lecturers to whom the name "Sophist" was currently given; but it was evidently made, in a marked and impressive manner, by an important group among them.

As I afterwards explain, the word ἀρετή has a somewhat wider meaning than our "virtue"; I have therefore added "human excellence" as an alternative translation: still the term as applied to human beings would most prominently suggest the moral excellences which we call "virtues."

social need is sufficiently remarkable. In order to understand the originality of this work and the social impression produced by it, we have to conceive of a society full of eager intellectual activity, and with æsthetic sensibility stimulated and cultivated by works of contemporary art that have remained the wonder of the world, but entirely without any official or established teaching of morality: a society in which Homer, one may say, occupied the place of the Bible. Now Homer supplies nothing like the ten commandments; but he does supply more or less impressive notions of human excellences and defects of various kinds—qualities of conduct and character that drew strong utterances of liking and aversion from those who took note of them. And in the vigorous and concentrated social life developed since Homer's time in the city-states of Greece—and especially intense in Athens in the 5th century—the praise and blame attached to such qualities would naturally grow in fulness of expression and fineness of discrimination. In the genus of human excellence, Virtues or moral excellences would constitute the most prominent group; though not yet clearly distinguished from intellectual skills and gifts, and graces of social behaviour. And no well-bred Greek gentleman—no one deserving the name of "fair and good" (καλοκἀγαθός)—would doubt that the different species of moral excellence were qualities to be desired, objects that a man should aim at possessing. He might indeed have no very definite notion of their rank or place in the class of good or desirable things; he might be more or less troubled by the apparent incompatibility occasionally perceived between the exercise of virtue and the attainment of pleasure, wealth, or power; he might even doubt how far virtue, though admittedly good and desirable, was always worth the sacrifice of other goods. Still such doubts would only occur transiently and occasionally to the few; in the view of impartial spectators the beauty of virtue would only be made more manifest by its triumphing over seductive desires directed to other objects; thus an ordinary well-trained Athenian would be as simply confident that it was good for a man to be virtuous—and the more virtuous the better—as that it was good for him to be wise, healthy, beautiful, and rich.

When, therefore, Protagoras or any other sophist came forward to teach Virtue or excellence of conduct, he would not find in his audience any general recognition of a possible divergence between Virtue and self-interest properly conceived. They would understand that in professing to show them "how to live well and manage well one's own affairs," he was claiming to guide them to the best way of living, from the points of view of both Virtue and Self-interest at once. It may, however, be asked how the need and advantage of such guidance came to be so generally recognised, as the success of the sophists shows it to have been. How came it that after so many centuries, in which the Greeks must have applied their moral notions in distributing praise and blame, with unhesitating confidence,—and must have attributed to any cause rather than imperfect knowledge the extensive failure of men to realise virtue,—they should suddenly become persuaded that good conduct was something that could be learned from lectures? The answer to this question is partly to be found in that very fusion of the moral view of life with the prudential view, which I have just described, in consequence of which the virtues which the sophists professed to impart by teaching were not sharply distinguished by them from other acquirements that sustain and enrich life. In this age, as in more modern times, most men would suppose that they had sufficient knowledge of justice and temperance; but they would not be equally confident that they possessed the art of making the best of life generally. Further, we must remember the importance of the civic or public side of life, to a free-born leisured Greek in the small town-communities of this age. The art of conduct as professed and taught to him would mean to a great extent the art of public life; indeed, Plato's *Protagoras* defines his function to be that of teaching "civic excellence"—the art of managing public no less than private affairs. It is more natural that a plain man should think scientific training necessary in dealing with affairs of state than in the ordering of his own private concerns.

Still this emergence of an art of life with professional teachers cannot thoroughly be understood, unless it is viewed as a crowning result of a general tendency at this stage of Greek civilisation to substitute technical skill for traditional procedure and empirically developed faculty. In the age of the sophists we find, wherever we turn, the same eager pursuit of knowledge, and the same eager effort to apply it directly to practice. The method of earth-measurement was rapidly becoming a science; the astronomy of Meton was introducing precision into the computation of time; Hippodamus was revolutionising architecture by building towns with straight broad streets; and old-fashioned soldiers were grumbling at the new pedantries of "tactics" and "hoplitics." Again, the art of music had recently received a great technical development; and a still greater change had been effected in that training of the body which, along with music, constituted ordinary Greek education. If bodily vigour was no longer to be left to nature and spontaneous exercise, but was to be attained by the systematic observance of rules laid down by professional trainers, it was natural to think that the same might be the case with excellences of the soul. The art of rhetoric, again, which was developed in Sicily in the second half of the 5th century, is a specially striking example of the general tendency we are here considering; and it is important to observe that the profession of rhetorician was commonly blended with that of sophist. Indeed throughout the age of Socrates sophists and philosophers were commonly regarded, by those who refused to recognise their higher claims, as teaching an "art of words." It is easy to see how this came about; when the demand for an art of conduct made itself felt, it was natural that the rhetoricians, skilled as they were in handling the accepted notions and principles of practice, should come forward to furnish the supply. Nor is there any reason to regard them as conscious charlatans for so doing, any more than the professional journalist of our own day, whose position as a political instructor of mankind is commonly earned rather by a knack of ready writing than by any special depth of political wisdom. As Plato's *Protagoras* says, the sophists in professing to teach virtue only claimed to do somewhat better than others what all men are continually doing; and similarly we may say that, when tried by the touchstone of Socrates, they only exhibited somewhat more conspicuously than others the deficiencies which the great questioner found everywhere.

§ 3. Socrates (*b.* about 470 B.C.; *d.* 399 B.C.)

The charge that Socrates brought against the sophists and his fellow-men generally may be viewed in two aspects. On one side it looks quite artless and simple; on the other it is seen to herald a revolution in scientific method, and to contain the germ of a metaphysical system. Simply stated, the charge was that they talked about justice, temperance, law, etc., and yet could not tell what these things were; the accounts of them which they gave when pressed were, as Socrates forced them to admit, inconsistent with their own judgments on particular instances of justice, legality, etc. This "ignorance" of the real meaning of their terms was not, indeed, the only lack of knowledge that Socrates discovered in his contemporaries, but it was the most striking; and its exposure was a philosophic achievement of profound importance. For the famous "dialectic," by which he brought this ignorance home to his interlocutors, at once exhibited the scientific need of exact definitions of general notions, and suggested that these definitions were to be attained by a careful comparison of particulars. Thus, we can understand how, in Aristotle's view, the main service of Socrates to philosophy consisted in "introducing induction and definitions." This description, however, is too technical for the naive character of the Socratic dialectic, and does not adequately represent its destructive effects. For that the results of these resistless arguments were mainly negative is plain from those (earlier) Platonic dialogues in which the impression of the real Socrates is to be found least modified. The pre-eminent "wisdom" which the Delphic oracle attributed to him was held by himself to consist in a unique consciousness of ignorance. And yet it is equally plain, even from Plato, that there was a most important positive element in the teaching of Socrates; had it been otherwise, the attempt of Xenophon to represent his discourses as directly edifying, and the veneration felt for him by the most dogmatic among subsequent schools of philosophy, would be quite inexplicable.

The union of these two elements in the work of Socrates has caused historians no little perplexity; and certainly we cannot quite save the philosopher's consistency, unless we regard some of the doctrines attributed to him by Xenophon as merely tentative and provisional. Still the positive pronouncements of Socrates that are most important in the history of ethical thought are not only easy to harmonise with his avowal of ignorance, but even render it easier to understand his unwearied cross-examination of common opinion. For they are all involved in or derived from his exalted estimate of the efficacy of this knowledge that was so hard to find, his profound conviction that men's ignorance of their true good was the source of all their wrong-doing. If his habitual inquiries were met by the reply, "We do know what justice and holiness are, though we cannot say," he would rejoin, "Whence, then, these perpetual disputes about what is just and holy?" True knowledge, he urged, would settle these quarrels, and produce uniformity in men's moral judgments and conduct. To us, no doubt, it seems an extravagant paradox to treat men's ignorance of justice as the sole cause of unjust acts; and to the Greek mind also the view was paradoxical; but if we would understand the position, not of Socrates only, but of ancient ethical philosophy generally, we must try to realise that this paradox was also a nearly unanswerable deduction from a pair of apparent truisms. That "every one wishes for his own good, and would get it if he could," an arguer would hardly venture to question; and he would equally shrink from denying that justice and virtue generally were goods, and of all goods the finest. It thus became difficult for him to refuse to admit that "those who knew what were just and righteous acts would prefer nothing else, while those who did not know could not do them if they would,"[1] which would land him at once in the conclusion of Socrates that justice and all other virtues were summed up in wisdom or knowledge of good.

This view of virtue, to most modern minds, would seem incompatible with moral freedom; but to Socrates it appeared, on the contrary, that knowledge alone could really make men free. Only good conduct, he maintained, is truly voluntary; a bad man is constrained by ignorance to do what is contrary to his real wish, which is always for his own greatest good: only knowledge can set him free to realise his wish.

Thus, we may say, in spite of the conflict between Socrates and the sophists, that we find him in essential agreement with the fundamental assumption on which their novel claims were based—the assumption that the right manner of life for human beings was a result attainable through knowledge, and capable of being imparted by adequate instruction to properly qualified intellects. And this fundamental assumption is maintained throughout all the development and variations of the post-Socratic schools. Greek philosophy, after Socrates, always makes a prominent claim to impart the true art of life; however differently its scope and method may be defined by different schools, it is always conceived as the knowledge through which the best life is to be lived.[2] It may be added that Socrates, as Plato

[1] Cf. Xenophon, *Memorabilia*, III., ch. ix. 5, where Xenophon fully confirms what Plato's dialogues abundantly illustrate.

[2] It should be observed that this statement has to be understood in a peculiar sense as applied to Aristotle: since Aristotle separates philosophy, conceived as the contemplation of eternal truth, from the study of the good and evil in human life, which he regards as an inferior exercise of intellect. In Aristotle's view, Philosophy does not show us the way to the best mode of life: but it is itself this best mode.

after him, asserted the supremacy of knowledge in a no less uncompromising manner in the sphere of politics. "The true general," he says, "is he who knows the art of strategy, whether he be elected or not; the votes of all mankind cannot turn an ignorant man into a general deserving of the name." It was no peculiar flight of Plato's idealising imagination that made him place the absolute control of his ideal state in the hands of philosophers; it was an immediate application of his master's cardinal doctrine that no one can be fit to govern men who does not know man's true end or good.

Observe that the "knowledge of good" at which Socrates aims is misconceived if we think of it as knowledge of Virtue as distinct from Interest. The force of his argument depends upon an inseparable union of the conceptions of Virtue and Interest in the single notion of Good. This union Socrates did not, of course, invent—he found it, as the sophists did, in the common thought of his age—; but it was the primary moral function of his dialectic to draw out and drive home its practical consequences. The kernel of the positive moral teaching that Xenophon attributes to him is his profound conviction of the reality and essential harmony of the different constituents of human good, as commonly recognised; especially his earnest belief in the eminent value for the individual of those "goods of the soul," which—then as now—were more praised than sought by practical men generally. From this conviction, maintained along with an unrealised ideal of the knowledge that would solve all practical problems, springs the singular combination of qualities exhibited both by the teaching and the personality of this unique man, as they are presented to us with incomparable impressiveness in many dialogues of Plato. We seem to see self-sacrifice in the garb of self-regard; a lofty spirituality blended with a homely common sense; a fervid enthusiasm for excellence of character, and an unreserved devotion to the task of producing it in himself and others, half-veiled by a cool mocking irony; a subtle, intense, scepticism playing round a simple and resolute acceptance of customary duties, like a lambent flame that has somehow lost its corrosive qualities.

We are concerned here with the doctrine, not the man; but it is impossible to separate the two. For it is important, even for the history of ethical doctrine, to note that if the necessity for firmness of purpose,[1] as well as fulness of insight, was not adequately recognised in the Socratic doctrine, the former quality was all the more conspicuously manifested in his life. Indeed it was the very perfection in which he possessed this virtue that led him to the paradox of ignoring it. Of himself at least it was true, that whatever he believed to be "fair and good" he must necessarily do; when another acted apparently against knowledge, the easiest explanation seemed to him to be that true knowledge was not really there. He could give no account that satisfied him of good in the abstract; when pressed for one he evaded the questioners by saying that "he knew no good

[1] Xenophon, it is to be observed, describes Socrates as preaching "self-control" (ἐγκράτεια); but I see no difficulty in interpreting this consistently with the rest of his doctrine, by taking this "self-control" to consist in—or result inevitably from—knowledge of the small value of sensual indulgences in comparison with the harm they entail: so that the need of self-control in the ordinary sense, regarded as a quality different from knowledge, and required to supplement it, would still be unrecognised by him. And this was certainly the view taken of his teaching by the Aristotelian author of what now stands as Book VII. of the *Nicomachean Ethics*, who says (chap. ii.) that Socrates "argued on the theory that want of self-control (ἀκρασία) did not exist."

that was not good for something in particular"; but that good is consistent with itself, that the beautiful is also profitable, the virtuous also pleasant, he was always ready to prove in concrete cases. That "doing well" meant both virtuous action and prosperous life was to him—as to Plato and Aristotle after him—no mere verbal ambiguity, but the expression of a fundamental truth.[1] If he prized the wisdom that is virtue, the "good of the soul," above all other goods—if in his absorption in the pursuit and propagation of it he endured the hardest penury—he steadily maintained that such life was richer in enjoyment than a life of luxury; if he faced death rather than violate the laws of his country, he was prepared with a complete proof that it was probably his interest to die.

This many-sidedness in his view of good is strikingly illustrated by the curious blending of elevated and homely sentiment which his utterances about friendship show. If goodness of soul is the "finest of goods," a good friend must be the most valuable of external possessions; no effort is too great to keep or win such. At the same time, the good of friendship must be shown in its utility; a friend who can be of no service is valueless; and this "service" Socrates on occasion interpreted in the most commonplace sense. Still, he held, the highest of services that friend can render to friend is moral improvement.

I conceive, then, that while the Athenian community was not altogether wrong in the famous condemnation of Socrates as a "sophist who had undermined the morals of youth," the disciples of Socrates were altogether right in their indignant repudiation of the charge, so far as it affected either the personal morality of the master or his deepest

[1] See Xenophon, *Memorabilia*, III., ch. ix. 14, 15.

philosophic aims and convictions. On the one hand, when we compare Xenophon and Plato, we cannot but feel that the negative effect of Socratic reasoning must have been argumentatively stronger than the positive; so that on minds intellectually active and penetrating, but without moral earnestness, the former may easily have been the sole effect;—however uniformly, by his practical precepts and example alike, he encouraged obedience to "laws written and unwritten," an acute pupil would be liable to think that his reasons for this obedience lacked the cogency of his destructive arguments. On the other hand, it is really essential to the Socratic method that the perpetual particular scepticism it develops should be combined with a permanent general faith in the common sense of mankind. For while he is always attacking common opinion, and showing it, from its inconsistencies, not to be knowledge, still the premises of his arguments are always taken from the common thought which he shares with his interlocutors, and the knowledge which he seeks is implicitly assumed to be something that will harmonise and not overthrow these common beliefs. This is manifested in the essential place which dialogue holds in his pursuit of truth: it is only through discourse that he hopes to come to knowledge.

So far we have spoken of the knowledge sought by Socrates as knowledge of man's ultimate good; and this was in fact the chief and primary object of his dialectical research. But we are not to suppose that he regarded this as the only knowledge needful for the wise ordering of human life.[1] He is represented as continually inquiring

[1] This is the misinterpretation of the Socratic teaching into which the "one-sided Socratics"—especially the Cynics—appear to have more or less fallen.—Cf. *post*, pp. 33-35.

for definitions, not only of "Good," "Virtue," "Pleasure," but of all the notions that enter into our practical reasonings, whether they relate to public or to private affairs; and the attention bestowed by him on even the humbler arts that minister to human needs is one of his most noted characteristics. I have already said that he regarded all merely speculative inquiries into the nature of the physical universe as superfluous and futile; but he recognised that the adaptation of external things to the uses of man must always absorb a large share of human activity, and that a knowledge of these things and their qualities, so far as thus useful, was therefore necessary for completely rational conduct; it was indeed, in a certain sense, "knowledge of the good"—*i.e.* of what is relatively good as a means to the true end of life. Hence any rational and useful human labour had, in his eyes, an interest and value which contrasts strikingly with the contempt commonly felt by cultivated Greeks for base mechanic toil. Xenophon has recorded at length a dialogue with a corslet-maker, in which Socrates gradually draws out the *rationale* of corslet-making; and we find that his talk was ridiculed for its continual use of analogies drawn from vulgar trades—for his perpetual harping on shoemakers and carpenters and braziers and herdsmen. The truth was that—as Plato makes him say in his defence before his judges—the common artisans differed from politicians and professors in knowing their business: in the great work of transforming human life into a completely reasoned adaptation of means to definitely known ends, the vulgar arts had led the way, and were far in advance; they had learnt a great part of their lesson, while the "royal art" of life and government was still struggling with the rudiments.

These, then, seem the historically important characteristics of the great founder of moral philosophy, if we take (as we must) his teaching and character together:—(1) an ardent inquiry for knowledge nowhere to be found, but which, if found, would perfect human conduct—knowledge, primarily, of ultimate and essential good, but also secondarily of all things relatively good, all the means by which this ultimate end was to be realised by man; (2) a provisional adhesion to the commonly received view of good and evil, in all its incoherent complexity, and a perpetual readiness to maintain the harmony of its different elements, and demonstrate the superiority of virtue to vice by an appeal to the standard of self-interest; (3) personal firmness, as apparently easy as it was actually invincible, in carrying out consistently such practical convictions as he had attained. It is only when we keep all these points in view that we can understand how from the spring of Socratic conversation flowed the divergent streams of Greek ethical thought.

§ 4. The Socratic Schools.

Four distinct philosophical schools trace their immediate origin to the circle that gathered round Socrates—the Megarian, the Platonic, the Cynic, and the Cyrenaic. The impress of the master is manifest on all, in spite of the wide differences that divide them; they all agree in holding the most important possession of man to be wisdom or knowledge, and the most important knowledge to be knowledge of Good. Here, however, the agreement ends. The more philosophic part of the circle, forming a group in which Euclides of Megara seems at first to have taken the lead, regarded this good as the object of a still unfulfilled quest; and setting out afresh in search of it, with a profound sense of its mystery, were led to identify it with the hidden secret of the universe, and thus to pass from ethics to metaphysics. Others again, whose demand for knowledge was more easily satisfied, and who were more impressed with the positive and practical side of the master's teaching, made the quest a much simpler affair; in fact, they took the Good as already known, and held philosophy to consist in the steady application of this knowledge to conduct. Among these were Antisthenes the Cynic and Aristippus of Cyrene. It is by their unreserved recognition of the duty of living by consistent theory instead of mere impulse or custom, their sense of the new value given to life through this rationalisation, and their effort to maintain the easy, calm, unwavering firmness of the Socratic temper, that we recognise both Antisthenes and Aristippus as "Socratic men," in spite of the completeness with which they divided their master's positive doctrine into systems diametrically opposed. Of their contrasted principles we may perhaps say that, while Aristippus took the most obvious logical step for reducing the teaching of Socrates to clear dogmatic unity, Antisthenes certainly drew the most natural inference from the Socratic life.

Aristippus and the Cyrenaics.

Aristippus argued that, if all that is beautiful or admirable in conduct has this quality as being useful—*i.e.* productive of some further good; if virtuous action is essentially action done with insight, or rational apprehension of the act as a means to this good,—then surely this good can be but pleasure, which all living things with unperverted impulses seek, while they shun its opposite, pain. He further found a metaphysical basis for this conclusion in the doctrine to which the relativism of Protagoras led him, that we can know nothing of things without us except their impressions on ourselves. An immediate inference from this was that the "smooth motion" of sense which we call pleasure, from whatever source it comes, is the only cognisable good; no kind of pleasure being in itself better than any other, though some kinds are to be rejected for their painful consequences. Bodily pleasures and pains Aristippus held to be the most intense; though he does not seem to have maintained this on any materialistic theory, as he admitted the existence of purely mental pleasures, such as joy in the prosperity of one's native land. He fully recognised that his good was transient, and only capable of being realised in successive parts; giving even exaggerated emphasis to the rule of seeking the pleasure of the moment, and not troubling oneself about a dubious future. It was in the calm, resolute, skilful culling of such pleasures as circumstances afforded from moment to moment, undisturbed by passion, prejudices, or superstition, that he conceived the quality of wisdom to be exhibited; and tradition represents him as realising this ideal to an impressive degree. Among the prejudices from which the wise man was free he included all regard to customary morality beyond what was due to the actual penalties attached to its violation; though he held, with Socrates, that these penalties actually rendered conformity reasonable.

Antisthenes and the Cynics.

Far otherwise was the Socratic spirit understood by Antisthenes and the Cynics. They equally held that no speculative research was needed for the discovery and definition of Good and Virtue; but they maintained that the Socratic wisdom, on the exercise of which man's wellbeing depended, was exhibited, not in the skilful pursuit, but in the rational disregard of pleasure, from a clear apprehension of the intrinsic worthlessness of the objects of men's ordinary desires and aims. Pleasure, indeed, Antisthenes declared roundly to be an evil; "better madness than a surrender to pleasure," he is said to have exclaimed; and poverty, painful toil, and disrepute he regarded as positively useful as means of progress in spiritual freedom and virtue. He did not, indeed, overlook the need of supplementing merely intellectual insight by "Socratic force of soul"; but it seemed to him that, by insight and invincible self-mastery combined, an absolute spiritual independence might be attained which left nothing wanting for perfect wellbeing. The eccentricities [1] with which his disciple Diogenes flaunted his independence of imaginary and conventional needs have made him one of the most familiar figures of ancient social history, and one which in its very extravagance gives a vivid impression of that element in the Socratic pattern which it involuntarily caricatures.[2] The Cynic conviction that nothing but wisdom and virtue could have any value for the wise had, in its practical manifestation, two chief aspects: (1) resistance to one's own superfluous appetites and desires, as tending to cause labour and anxiety for what was worthless when obtained; and (2) indifference to the irrational prejudices and conventions of other men. It is in this latter aspect that the originality of the Cynic teaching, and its divergence from Socrates, is most marked. The Cynic sage could not submit to regulate his life by established laws and customs, merely because they were

[1] We are told that he slept on the bare ground, or in a tent; wore for his only garment a single loose mantle, doubling it in cold weather; ate meat raw to save fire, etc.

[2] It is to the deliberate disregard of customary notions of propriety shown by this school that the modern meaning of the term "cynical" is due. Indeed, the Greeks felt that the name of the school—derived originally from the gymnasium Cynosarges where Antisthenes taught—aptly suggested their affinity with the dog (κύων), a proverbial type of shamelessness.

established: the only laws he could recognise as binding on him were the laws dictated by wisdom, and so binding on all men as rational beings. Hence, if all were wise, the divisions of states and divergences of legal systems must disappear: there would be but one state governed by one law the same for all, for man and woman, for master and slave:—or rather there could be no slavery, for no one in this ideal state could *need* the commands of others to do what was rational, or could *obey* commands to do what was irrational. Thus it is to the Cynic school that we owe the conception of "cosmopolite," so profoundly important in the later and more influential Stoic system. Vainly, however, do we seek a definite positive import for the Cynic notion of wisdom or moral insight, besides the mere emancipation from irrational desires and prejudices. In emphasising this emancipation they seem to have left the freed reason with no definite aim but its own freedom. It is absurd, as Plato urged, to say that knowledge is the good, and then when asked "knowledge of what?" to have nothing positive to reply but "of the good"; but the Cynics do not seem to have made any serious effort to escape from this absurdity.

§ 5. Plato (427-347 B.C.)

The ultimate issues of these two one-sided Socraticisms we shall have to notice presently when we come to the post-Aristotelian schools. We must now proceed to the more complicated task of tracing the fuller development of the Socratic germ to its Platonic blossom and Aristotelian fruit. We can see that the influence of more than one of the earlier metaphysical schools combined with that of Socrates to produce the famous idealism which subsequent generations have learnt from Plato's dialogues; but the precise extent and manner in which each element co-operated is difficult even to conjecture.[1] Here, however, we may consider Plato's views merely in their relation to the teaching of Socrates, since to the latter is certainly due the ethical aspect of idealism with which we are at present concerned.

The ethics of Plato cannot properly be treated as a finished result, but rather as a continual movement from the position of Socrates towards the more complete and articulate system of Aristotle; except that there are ascetic and mystical suggestions in some parts of Plato's teaching which find no counterpart in Aristotle, and which, in fact, disappear from Greek philosophy soon after Plato's death until they are revived and fantastically developed in Neo-Pythagoreanism and Neo-Platonism. The first stage at which we can distinguish Plato's ethical view from that of Socrates is presented in the *Protagoras*, where he makes a serious, though clearly tentative, effort to define the object of that knowledge which he regards, with his master, as the essence of all virtue. Such knowledge, he here maintains, is really mensuration of pleasures and pains, whereby the wise man avoids those mistaken under-estimates of the value of future feelings in comparison with present which men commonly make when they are said to "yield to fear or desire." This hedonism has perplexed Plato's readers, and was probably never conceived by himself to be more than a partial expression of the truth. Still (as was said in speak-

[1] The difficulty arises thus: (1) Aristotle represents Platonism as having sprung from Socratic teaching combined with Heraclitus's doctrine of the flux of sensible things, and the Pythagorean theory that numbers were the ultimate realities; but (2) in the Megarian doctrine the non-Socratic element is clearly the one changeless being of Parmenides; while (3) the original connection of Plato and Euclides is equally evident.

ing of the similar view of the Cyrenaics) when a disciple sought to make clear and definite the essentially Socratic doctrine that the different current notions of good,—the beautiful, the pleasant, and the useful,—were to be somehow identified and interpreted by each other, hedonism presented itself as the most obvious conclusion. By Plato, however, this conclusion could only have been held before he had accomplished the movement of thought by which he carried the Socratic method beyond the range of human conduct, and developed it into an all-comprehensive metaphysical system.

This movement may be briefly expressed thus. "If we know," said Socrates, "what justice is, we can give a general account or definition of it"; true knowledge of justice must, therefore, be knowledge of such general facts or relations as are common to all the individual cases to which we apply our general notion of justice. But, further, this must be no less true of other objects of thought and discourse besides the objects of ethical knowledge: since the same relation of general notions to particular examples extends through the whole physical universe; we can only think and talk of it by means of such notions. True or scientific knowledge, then, of whatever can be known, must be general knowledge, relating not to individuals primarily, but to the general facts or qualities which individuals exemplify; in fact, our notion of an individual, when examined, is found to be an aggregate of such general characteristics. But, again, the object of true knowledge must be what really exists; hence the reality of the universe must lie in general facts or relations, and not in the individuals that exemplify them.

So far the steps are plain enough; but we do not yet see how this logical Realism (as it was afterwards called) comes to have the essentially ethical character that especially interests us in Platonism. For though Plato's philosophy is concerned with the whole universe of being, the ultimate object of his philosophic contemplation is still "the good" conceived as the ultimate ground of all being and knowledge. That is, the essence of the universe is identified with its end,—the "formal" with the "final" cause of things, to use the later Aristotelian phraseology. How comes this about?

Perhaps we may best explain this by recurring to the original application of the Socratic method to human affairs. Since all rational activity is for some end, the different arts or functions into which human industry is divided are naturally defined by a statement of their ends or uses; and similarly, in giving an account of the different artists and functionaries, we necessarily state their end, "what they are good for." It is only so far as they realise this end that they are what we call them. A painter who cannot paint is, as we say, "no painter"; or, to take a favourite Socratic illustration, a ruler is essentially one who realises the well-being of the ruled; if he fails to do this, he is not, properly speaking, a ruler at all. And in a society well-ordered on Socratic principles, every human being would be put to some use; the essence of his life would consist in doing what he was good for. But again, it is easy to extend this view throughout the whole region of organised life; an eye that does not attain its end by seeing is without the essence of an eye. In short, we may say of all organs and instruments that they are what we think them in proportion as they fulfil their function and attain their end: if, then, we conceive the whole universe organically, as a complex adaptation of means to ends, we shall understand how Plato

might hold that all things really *were*, or (as we say) "realised their idea," in proportion as they accomplished the
special end or good for which they were adapted. But this
special end, again, can only be really good so far as it is re
lated to the ultimate end or good of the whole, as one of the
means or particulars by or in which this is partially realised.
If, then, the essence or reality of each part of the organised
world is to be found in its particular end or good, the ultimate ground of all reality must be found in the ultimate end
or good of the universe. And if this is the ground of all
reality, the knowledge of it must also be the source of all
guidance for human life ; for man, as part and miniature of
the Cosmos, can have no good, as he can have no being,
which is not derived from the good and being of the universe.
Thus Plato, without definitely abandoning the Socratic limitation of philosophy to the study of human good, has deepened
the conception of human good until the quest of it takes
in the earlier inquiry into the essential nature of the external
world, from which Socrates turned away. Even Socrates,
in spite of his aversion to physics, was led by pious reflection to expound a teleological view of the physical universe,
as ordered in all its parts by Divine Wisdom for the realisation of some divine end ; what Plato did was to identify this
Divine End—conceived as the very Divine Being itself—with
the Good that Socrates sought, of which the knowledge would
solve all problems of human life. In this fusion of Socratic
ethics with Socratic theology, he was probably anticipated
by Euclides of Megara, who held that the one real being
is "that which we call by many names, Good, Wisdom,
Reason, or God" ; to which Plato, raising to a loftier significance the Socratic identification of the beautiful with the
useful, added the further name of Absolute Beauty ; explain-

difference between Plato and Socrates (handwritten margin note)

ing how man's love of the beautiful, elevated gradually from flesh to spirit, from the individual to the general, ultimately reveals itself as the yearning of the soul for the end and essence of all life and being.

Let us conceive, then, that Plato has taken this vast stride of thought, and identified the ultimate notions of ethics and ontology. We have now to see what attitude this will lead him to adopt towards the practical inquiries from which he started. What will now be his view of wisdom, virtue, pleasure, and their relation to human well-being?

The answer to this question is inevitably somewhat complicated. In the first place, we have to observe that philosophy has now passed from the market-place into the study or lecture-room. The quest of Socrates was for the true art of conduct for an ordinary member of the human society, a man living a practical life among his fellows. But if the objects of abstract thought constitute the real world, of which this world of individual things is but a shadow, it is plain that the highest, most real life must lie in the former region and not in the latter. It is in contemplating the abstract reality which concrete things obscurely exhibit, the type or ideal which they imperfectly imitate, that the true life of the Mind in man must consist: and, as man is most truly man in proportion as he is mind, that desire of one's own good, which Plato, following Socrates, held to be permanent and essential in every living thing, becomes in its highest form the philosophic yearning for knowledge. This yearning, he held, springs—like more sensual impulses—from a sense of want of something formerly possessed, of which there remains a latent memory in the soul, strong in proportion to its philosophic capacity;

hence it is that in learning any abstract truth by scientific demonstration we merely make explicit what we already implicitly know; we bring into clear consciousness hidden memories of a state in which the soul looked upon Reality and Good face to face, before the lapse that imprisoned her in an alien body and mingled her true nature with fleshly feelings and impulses. We thus reach the paradox that Plato enforced in more than one of his most impressive dialogues, that the true art of living is really an "art of dying" as far as possible to mere sense, in order more fully to exist in intimate union with absolute goodness and beauty. On the other hand, in so far as this philosophic abstraction from ordinary human interests can never be complete—since the philosopher must still live and act in the concrete sensible world—the Socratic identification of wisdom and virtue is fully maintained by Plato. Only he who apprehends good in its abstract reality can imitate it in such transient and imperfect good as admits of being realised in human life; and it is impossible, having this knowledge, that he should not act on it, whether in private or public affairs; true knowledge of Good necessarily carries with it a preference for the Best, whenever alternatives are presented for rational choice. Thus, in the true philosopher, we shall necessarily find the practically good man, he who being "likest of men to the gods is best loved by them"; and also the perfect statesman, if only the conditions of his society allow him a sphere for exercising his statesmanship.

§ 6. Plato's theory of Virtue.

The general characteristics of this practical goodness, in Plato's matured philosophy, are determined by the fundamental conceptions in his view of the universe. The soul of man, in its good or normal condition, must be ordered and harmonised under the government of Reason. The question then arises, "Wherein does this order or harmony precisely consist?" In explaining how Plato was led to answer this question, it will be well to notice that, while faithfully maintaining the Socratic doctrine that the highest virtue was inseparable from knowledge of the good, he had come, as his conception of this knowledge deepened and expanded, to recognise an inferior kind of virtue, possessed by men who were not philosophers. It is plain that if the good that is to be known is the ultimate ground of the whole of things, so that the knowledge of it includes all other knowledge, it is only attainable by a select and carefully trained few, and we can hardly restrict all virtue to these alone. What account, then, was to be given of ordinary "civic" bravery, temperance, and justice? It seemed clear that men who did their duty, resisting the seductions of fear and desire, must have right opinions, if not knowledge, as to the good and evil in human life; but whence comes this right "opinion"? Partly, Plato said, it comes by nature and "divine allotment"; but for its adequate development "custom and practice" are required. Hence the paramount importance of education and discipline, in which physical and æsthetic training must co-operate, for civic virtue of the best kind.[1] But such moral culture is not only required for those minds who cannot rise above

[1] Plato seems to have distinguished different kinds of unphilosophic virtue, having very different moral values, though he nowhere gives a systematic view of their differences; the lowest is that of the vulgar prudence which abstains from sensual vice, not from moral aversion, but from a calculation that abstinence will bring a balance of pleasure: the highest is that exhibited by an unphilosophic mind whose "spirited element" has been duly trained under the guidance of Philosophy. An interesting discussion of these differences will be found in Mr. Archer-Hind's edition of the *Phædo*, Appendix I.

this popular standard of virtue: it is equally or rather more indispensable for those who are ultimately to attain to philosophy—indeed Plato says sweepingly that "all virtues except wisdom are generated in the soul by habit and exercise." This does not seem to him inconsistent with the Socratic doctrine, which he still maintains, that knowledge of good must carry with it all the virtues; his point is that this knowledge cannot be implanted in a soul that has not gone through a course of preparation including much more than merely intellectual training.

How then exactly does this preparation operate? A distinct step in psychological analysis, beyond Socrates, was taken when Plato recognised that its effect was to produce the "harmony" above mentioned among different parts of the soul, by subordinating to reason those non-rational impulses which in ill-regulated souls continually become predominant, and "compel" to action contrary to rational judgment. These non-rational impulses he referred to two distinct elements of the soul—which we may call respectively "appetitive" and "spirited"[1]—the practical separateness of which, from each other and from reason, he held to be established by our inner experience of conflicting impulses; to the former of these he refers all those desires obviously due to bodily causes which we call in a special sense "appetites"; the latter he conceives as the common source of a group of emotions which modern psychology does not specially connect together, but which all have the

[1] (1) τὸ ἐπιθυμητικόν, and (2) τὸ θυμοειδές, or θυμός. I may observe that though the Greek word ἐπιθυμία is more commonly used in this special sense of bodily appetite, it is also used in a wider sense by Plato and other writers, just as the English word "appetite" is. "Spirited" seems to me the least objectionable of the various imperfect renderings of θυμοειδές that have been suggested.

same characteristic of prompting to energetic and combative action—anger, boldness or spirit, the love of honour, shame, and aversion to disgrace. The moral rank of these two elements is very different; the spirited element is the natural ally of reason in the conflicts of the soul, and under due training is capable of manifesting a special excellence of its own; the appetitive element is naturally baser, and capable of no virtue except submission to reason.

On this triple division of the soul Plato founds a systematic view of the four kinds of excellence chiefly recognised by the moral consciousness of Greece, and in later times known as the cardinal[1] virtues, (1) *φρόνησις*, or *σοφία*,[2] (2) *ἀνδρεία*, (3) *σωφροσύνη*, (4) *δικαιοσύνη*; notions which we may represent approximately by the English terms, (1) Wisdom, (2) Courage or Fortitude, (3) Temperance or Orderliness, (4) Justice or Uprightness. The two most important of these (as has already been indicated) are Wisdom—which in its highest and ideal form implies the full possession of the knowledge which the philosopher seeks—and that harmonious and regulated activity of all the elements of the soul, which Plato regards as the essential root of Uprightness in social relations, and which accordingly he names *δικαιοσύνη*. This peculiar interpretation of a term which in its ordinary use corresponds broadly to our "Justice," and certainly denotes a quality only manifested in social conduct, is perhaps partly due to the analogy which his analysis of the soul led him to draw between an

[1] The term "cardinalis" is Christian; it is first found in Ambrose (*In Luc.* § 62).

[2] These terms Aristotle distinguished, applying them to practical and speculative wisdom respectively; but in Plato's view of philosophy speculative and practical wisdom are inseparably combined; and—in the *Republic* at any rate—he appears to use the two terms as convertible.

individual man and a political society. For in a rightly ordered state, as he conceived it, there would be a governing class, the embodiment of Wisdom, and a combative class, specially characterised by Courage; which would both be kept distinct from the common herd of industrials, who—like appetites in the individual man—would have merely to provide for material needs, and whose relation to the State would simply be that of orderly obedience. In such a polity social and individual wellbeing alike would depend on that harmonious action of diverse elements, each performing its proper function, which in its social application is more naturally termed *δικαιοσύνη*. We see, moreover, how in Plato's view the two fundamental virtues, Wisdom and Justice, in their highest form, are mutually involved. A wise soul will necessarily be one in which all elements operate in harmonious activity; and this activity cannot be perfect unless the rational and governing element is truly wise. The two remaining virtues, again, are only different elements or aspects of this wisely regulated action of the complex soul: Courage or Fortitude being the special excellence of the spirited or combative element, when docile to reason, and trained to fear only what is truly fearful; while Temperance or Orderliness (*σωφροσύνη*) is related to Uprightness as the structure of an organism to its life—the former expresses the due submission of the non-rational elements to reason, whereas the latter denotes the harmonious functioning of the duly related elements.

In a later dialogue (*Politicus*) Plato treats Courage and Orderliness somewhat differently, considering them as contrasted original temperaments, which, if left unregulated, are liable to be exhibited in an extreme form by contrasted classes of citizens, but which a wise statesman will judiciously blend and combine. So again, in his latest ethical treatise (the *Laws*) the place of Courage—at least of the civic or popular sort—seems definitely lower as compared with Temperance; and the analysis of the soul into elements falls into the background and is somewhat modified, the distinction now taken among non-rational impulses being that between impulses caused by pain—such as anger and fear—and impulses due to pleasure. Still, on the whole, the fourfold division of Virtues—all four virtues in their highest forms being still conceived as mutually implicated and inseparable—is maintained by Plato without fundamental change.

We have further to observe that, Virtue being no longer simply identified with Wisdom, there must obviously be another source of bad conduct besides ignorance, viz. that internal disorder and conflict of the soul in which non-rational impulses prevail over Reason; and this is explicitly recognised in Plato's later ethical discussions.

If we ask for the particulars of outward conduct in which these virtues would be expressed, the answer takes us into the region of thought which we now—unlike Plato—separate from Ethics, under the name of Politics. For in Plato's view all branches of civic duty would be regulated in minute detail by a wise government, aiming at the promotion of moral excellence in its subjects as the main element of their wellbeing. Especially in the ideal state of his *Republic*, where the division of sentiment and life caused by *meum* and *tuum* would be excluded, and the relations of the sexes ordered with a single eye to perfection of breed and distribution of functions according to fitness, obedience to rules laid down by government would constitute the whole sphere of ordinary virtue; only philosophers would have, besides the functions of government and education, the still higher sphere of abstract contemplation. Even in the *Laws*,—where community of women and property is put aside as an ideal too high for practical politics,—education, marriage, and the whole daily life of the citizens from infancy to age, as well as all worship, are conceived as proper subjects of the most minute regulation, such as would supply the citizens generally with a sufficiently comprehensive and detailed moral guidance. Plato is careful, indeed, to point out that this regulation cannot be altogether secured by legal constraint; for a certain part of it the legislator should use precept and persuasion as well as judicial punishment—his ideal state, in short, has the functions of a modern church as well as those of a modern state. Still the amount of strictly legal control of the individual's life that he proposes to introduce is startling to a modern reader. His citizens would be prohibited by law from being handicraftsmen or retail traders, or practising forensic advocacy for gain. They would be compelled to learn music for three years and no more, to abstain from wine altogether until eighteen, and from the genial excess of the banquet until forty; only after this age would they be allowed to travel, and they would be fined for celibacy after thirty-five. It would be illegal for them either to deny the existence of gods, or to affirm that gods can be propitiated by sacrifices and gifts; their poetry and song would be subject to a severe censorship, and their banquets to strict sumptuary laws. And both laws and supplementary precepts alike would be unquestionably accepted by the mass of citizens on the authority of the legislators and guardians of the laws: the *rationale* of the legislation would be known only to a few philosophic minds.

§ 7. Plato's view of Pleasure; and its relation to Human Good.

Suppose now that the nature both of philosophy and of civic virtue has been adequately expounded, it remains to ask how far such an exposition gives a complete account of man's ultimate good. Here we must first observe—to avoid a fertile source of error and confusion—that neither Socrates nor Plato ever disputes that the ultimate good for any individual man is his own "welfare" or "wellbeing" (εὐδαιμονία):[1] both of them indeed frequently assume this in their arguments. In the view of both the practically important question, on which doubt and controversy existed, was not whether a man's ultimate good is his own welfare, but how far the particular objects recognised as good or desirable—Wisdom, Pleasure, Wealth, Reputation, etc.—constitute or conduce to his welfare; and both Socrates and Plato hold that to rightly answer this question—like other questions relating to "goods"—we require to know the real import of the general notion "good," the real nature of good in itself. But when Plato's idealism had definitely formed itself in his mind, and he had come to mean by "good in itself" the end and essence of the whole organised world, the investigation of the ultimate good for an individual man inevitably began to separate itself from the profound metaphysical research by which he sought to penetrate the secret of the universe. Grant that good in itself, or absolute good,

[1] There is no foundation for the belief, to which even writers of reputation in modern times have given countenance, that the notion of εὐδαιμονία ("welfare" or "wellbeing") as the end of human action was introduced by Aristotle in opposition to Plato. The error involved in this belief, however, would be less important if εὐδαιμονία were not currently rendered by the English word "happiness," and in consequence more or less definitely conceived as a whole of which the elements are pleasurable feelings: whereas both Plato and Aristotle —no less than Socrates—conceive "welldoing" to be the primary constituent of "wellbeing." See p. 56, *note* 2.

is the ultimate ground of things; still "the good" about which the Cynics and Cyrenaics disputed—and which Plato, in the *Philebus*, is ready to discuss with them—is admittedly something more concrete; something that belongs to the sphere of sensible existence within which the actual life of man is embraced. Is it a sufficient definition of this concrete human good to say that it consists in the exercise of Wisdom or Virtue? or is Pleasure an element of it? and if the latter, what is its importance?

On these points Plato's view seems to have gone through several oscillations. After apparently maintaining (*Protagoras*) that pleasure is *the* good, he passes first to the opposite extreme, and denies it (*Phædo*, *Gorgias*) to be a good at all. Not only is it, as concrete and transient, a mere "process" (γένεσις), obviously not the real essential good that the philosopher seeks; it is found further that the feelings most prominently recognised as pleasures are bound up with pain, as good can never be with evil; since they are the mere satisfaction of painful wants and cease with the removal of these; in so far, then, as common sense rightly recognises some pleasures as good, it can only be from their tendency to produce some further good. This view, however, was too violent a divergence from Socratism for Plato to remain in it. That pleasure is not the essential absolute good, was no ground for not including it in the good of concrete human life; and after all it was only coarse and vulgar pleasure that was indissolubly linked to the pains of want. Accordingly, in the *Republic* he has no objection to try the question of the intrinsic superiority of philosophic or virtuous[1] life

[1] It is highly characteristic of Platonism that the issue in this dialogue, as originally stated, is between virtue and vice; whereas, without any avowed change of ground, the issue ultimately discussed is between the philosophic life and the life of vulgar ambition or sensual enjoyment.

by the standard of pleasure; arguing that the philosophic (or good) man alone enjoys real pleasure, while the sensualist spends his life in oscillating between painful want and the merely neutral state of painlessness, which he mistakes for positive pleasure. Still more emphatically is it declared in the *Laws* that—when we are "discoursing to men not to gods"—we must show that the life which we praise as best and noblest is also that in which there is the greatest excess of pleasure over pain. But though Plato holds this inseparable connection of "best" and "pleasantest" to be true and important, it is only for the sake of the vulgar that he lays this stress on Pleasure. For in the more philosophic comparison in the *Philebus* between the claims of Pleasure and Wisdom, the former is altogether worsted; and though a place is allowed, in a complete statement of the elements of concrete human good, to the pure pleasures of colour, form, and sound, and of intellectual exercise, and even to the "necessary" satisfactions of appetite, it is only a subordinate place. At the same time, in his later view, Plato avoids the exaggeration of denying all positive quality of pleasure even to the coarser sensual gratifications; they are undoubtedly cases of that "replenishment" or "restoration" to its "natural state" of a bodily organ, in which he defines pleasure to consist:[1] he merely maintains that the common estimate of them is to a large extent illusory, as

[1] The latest and most developed form of Plato's physical theory of pleasure and pain is found in the *Timæus*, pp. 64, 65. Sensation is there explained as the result of molecular movement in parts of the body whose minute particles are in a mobile condition. If the movement is a violent and sudden disturbance of the part affected out of its natural state, the result is pain: while the restoration of the organ to its natural state produces pleasure. But either disturbance or restoration may be gradual and imperceptible, so that there may be pain without consequent pleasure, and pleasure without antecedent pain.

a false appearance of pleasure is produced by contrast with the antecedent or concomitant painful condition of the organ. It is not surprising that this somewhat complicated and delicately balanced view of the relations of "Good" and "Pleasure" was not long maintained within the Platonic school; and that under Speusippus, Plato's successor, the main body of Platonists took up a simply anti-hedonistic position, as we learn from the polemic of Aristotle.

§ 8. Plato and Aristotle.

When a student passes from Plato to Aristotle, he is so forcibly impressed by the contrast at once between the habits of mind and the literary manners of the two philosophers, that it is easy to understand how their systems have come to be popularly conceived as diametrically opposed to each other; and the uncompromising polemic which Aristotle, both in his ethical and in his metaphysical treatises, directs against Plato and the Platonists, has tended strongly to confirm this view. Yet when, more than two centuries after Plato's death, Antiochus of Ascalon—as president of the school commonly known as the "Academy,"[1] which looked to Plato as its founder—repudiated the scepticism which, during the greater part of the intervening period, had been accepted as the traditional Platonic doctrine, he confidently claimed Plato and Aristotle as consentient authorities for the ethical position that he took up; and a closer inspection shows that there were substantial grounds for his claim. For, though Aristotle's divergence from Plato is very conspicuous when we consider either his general conception of the relation of ethics to other studies, or the details of his

Aristotle (384-322 B.C.)

[1] The name was derived from the gymnasium called Ἀκαδήμεια, close to which was the garden in which Plato had taught, and which seems to have been bequeathed by him to his disciples, and handed down from president to president of the school.

system of virtues, still his agreement with his master is almost complete as regards the main outline of his theory of human good; the difference between the two practically vanishes when we view them in relation to the later controversy between Stoics and Epicureans. Even on the cardinal point on which Aristotle entered into direct controversy with Plato, the definite disagreement between the two is less than at first appears; the objections of the disciple chiefly hit that part of the master's system that was rather imagined than thought; the main positive result of Platonic speculation only gains in distinctness by the application of Aristotelian analysis.

Plato, we saw, held that there is one supreme science or wisdom, of which the ultimate object is absolute good; in the knowledge of this, the knowledge of all particular goods—that is, of all that we rationally desire to know—is implicitly contained; and also all practical virtue, as no one who truly knows what is good can fail to realise it. But in spite of the intense conviction with which he thus identified metaphysical speculation and practical wisdom, we find in his writings no serious attempt to deduce the particulars of human wellbeing from his knowledge of absolute good, still less to unfold from it the particular cognitions of the special arts and sciences. Hence when Aristotle urges that the science or art of human life—which he conceives as statesmanship, since human wellbeing must mainly depend upon political institutions—must define its own end, and that a knowledge of absolute good will be of no avail for this any more than it is for the more special arts and handicrafts, we find no definite Platonic argument that attempts to prove what he denies. Indeed—as I have already pointed out—the distinction which Aristotle explicitly draws between speculative science or wisdom, which is concerned with the eternal and immutable truths of being, and practical wisdom or statesmanship, which has for its object "human" or "practicable" good, is really indicated in Plato's later treatment of the subjects, although the express recognition of it is contrary to his principles. The discussion of good—*e.g.* in his *Philebus*, relates entirely to human good, and the respective claims of Thought and Pleasure to constitute this; he only refers in passing to the Divine Thought that is the good of the ordered world, as something clearly beyond the limits of the present discussion. So again, in his last great ethico-political treatise (the *Laws*) there is hardly a trace of his peculiar metaphysics. On the other hand, the relation between Human and Divine Good, as presented by Aristotle, is so close that we can hardly conceive Plato as having definitely thought it closer. The substantial Good of the universe, in Aristotle's view, is the pure activity of universal abstract thought, at once subject and object, which, itself changeless and eternal, is the final cause and first source of the whole process of change in the concrete world. And both he and Plato hold that a similar activity of pure speculative intellect is the highest and best mode of human existence, and that in which the philosopher will seek to exist as far as possible; though he must, being a man, concern himself with the affairs of ordinary human life, and in this region his highest good will be attained by realising perfect moral excellence. No doubt Aristotle's demonstration of the inappropriateness of attributing moral excellence to the Deity seems to contradict Plato's doctrine that the just man as such is "likest the gods"; but here again the discrepancy is reduced when we remember that the essence of Plato's "Justice" (δικαιοσύνη) is harmonious activity. No doubt, too, Aristotle's attribution of pleasure to the Divine Existence shows a profound metaphysical divergence from Plato; but it is a divergence which has no practical importance, and which only makes the analogy between Divine and Human good more definitely intelligible. Nor, again, is Aristotle's dissent from the Socratic principle that all "virtue is knowledge" substantially greater than Plato's, though it is more plainly expressed. Both hold that every one in deliberate action aims at what appears to him good, and that perfect virtue necessarily follows from perfect practical wisdom or moral insight if actual and operative. Both, however, recognise that this actuality of moral insight is not a function of the intellect only, but depends on the establishment of a right relation between the intellect and the non-rational, or semi-rational, elements of the soul; and that, accordingly, for education in virtue mere verbal instruction is less important than careful discipline applied to minds of good natural dispositions;—though this doctrine has no doubt a more definite and prominent place in Aristotle's system. The disciple certainly takes a step in advance by stating definitely, as an essential characteristic of virtuous action, that it is chosen for its own sake, for the beauty of virtue alone; but herein he merely formulates the conviction that his master more persuasively inspires. Nor, finally, does Aristotle's account of the relation of pleasure to human wellbeing differ very materially from the outcome of Plato's thought on this point, as the later dialogues present it to us; although he has to combat the extreme anti-hedonism to which the Platonic school under Speusippus had been led. Pleasure, in Aristotle's view, is not the primary constituent of wellbeing, but rather an inseparable accident of it; human wellbeing is essentially welldoing, excellent activity of some kind, whether its aim and end be abstract truth or noble conduct; and knowledge and virtue are objects of rational choice apart from the pleasure attending them; still all activities are attended and in a manner perfected by pleasure, which is better and more desirable in proportion to the excellence of the activity. He no doubt criticises Plato's account of the nature of pleasure, arguing that we cannot properly conceive pleasure either as a "process" or as "replenishment"—the last term, he truly says, denotes a material rather than a psychical fact. But this does not interfere with the general ethical agreement between the two thinkers; and the doctrine that vicious pleasures are not true or real pleasures is so characteristically Platonic that we are almost surprised to find it in Aristotle.

§ 9. Aristotle's view of Human Wellbeing.

In so far as there is any important difference between the Platonic and the Aristotelian views of human good, I conceive that the latter has substantially a closer correspondence to the positive element in the ethical teaching of Socrates, although it is presented in a far more technical and scholastic form, and involves a more distinct rejection of the fundamental Socratic paradox. The same result appears when we compare the methods of the three philosophers. Although the Socratic induction forms a striking feature of Plato's dialogues, his ideal method of ethics is purely deductive; he only admits common sense as supplying provisional steps and starting-points from which the mind is to ascend to knowledge of absolute good; through which knowledge alone, as he conceives, the lower notions of particular goods are to be truly conceived. Aristotle, discarding in Ethics the transcendentalism of Plato, retained from Plato's teaching the original Socratic method of induction[1] from and verification by common opinion. Indeed, the turns and windings of his exposition are best understood if we consider his literary manner as a kind of Socratic dialogue formalised and reduced to a monologue — transferred, we may say, from the market-place to the lecture-room. Thus it is by a genuinely Socratic induction that he leads us, in the outset of his treatise on Ethics, to the fundamental notion of ultimate end or good for man. All men, in acting, aim at some result, either for its own sake or as a means to some further end; but obviously everything cannot be sought merely as a means; there must therefore be some ultimate end (or ends), and the science or study that inquires into this must be "architectonic" in relation to all arts that aim at some special end or utility. We find, in fact, that men commonly recognise such an end, and agree to call it wellbeing[2] (εὐδαιμονία); but they take very different views of its nature. How, then, shall we find the true view? We observe that men are classified and named according to their functions; all kinds of man, and indeed all organs of man, have their special functions, and are judged as functionaries and organs to be in good or bad condition according as they perform their functions well or ill. May we not then infer that man, as man, has his proper function, and that the wellbeing or

[1] I use induction in a broad sense, to denote any process that starts from particular judgments to arrive at more general conclusions.

[2] This cardinal term is commonly translated "happiness"; and it must be allowed that this is the most natural term for what we (in English) agree to call "our being's end and aim." But the English word "happiness" so definitely signifies a state of feeling that it will not admit the interpretation that Aristotle (as well as Plato and the Stoics) expressly gives to εὐδαιμονία; hence, to avoid serious confusion, it seems to me necessary to render εὐδαιμονία by the more unfamiliar "wellbeing" or "welfare." See p. 48, *note*.

"doing well" that all seek, really lies in fulfilling well the proper function of man—that is, in living well, through the normal term of man's existence, that life of the rational soul which we recognise as man's distinctive attribute?

Again, this Socratic deference to common opinion is not merely shown in the way by which Aristotle reaches his fundamental conception; it equally appears in his treatment of the conception itself. In the first place, though in Aristotle's view the most perfect wellbeing consists in the exercise of man's "divinest part," pure speculative reason, he keeps far from the paradox of putting forward this and nothing else as human good; so far, indeed, that the greater part of his treatise is occupied with an exposition of the inferior good which is realised in practical life when the appetitive or impulsive (semi-rational) element of the soul operates under the due regulation of reason. Even when the notion of "good performance of function" was thus widened, and when it had further taken in the pleasure that is inseparably connected with such functioning, it did not yet correspond to the whole of what a Greek commonly regarded as indispensable to "human wellbeing." We may grant, indeed, that a moderate provision of material wealth is indirectly included, as an indispensable pre-requisite of a due performance of man's function as Aristotle conceives it,—his system admits of no beatitudes for the poor;—still, there remain other goods, such as beauty, good birth, welfare of progeny, etc., the presence or absence of which influenced the common view of a man's wellbeing, though they could hardly be shown to be even indirectly important to his "well acting." These Aristotle neither attempts to exclude from the philosophic conception of wellbeing nor to include in his formal definition of it. The deliberate looseness which is thus given to his fundamental doctrine characterises more or less his whole discussion of ethics. He plainly says that the subject does not admit of completely scientific treatment; his aim is to give not a perfectly definite theory of human good, but a practically adequate account of its most important constituents.

The most important element, then, of wellbeing or good life for ordinary men Aristotle holds to consist in welldoing, as determined by the notions of the different moral excellences. In expounding these he gives throughout the pure result of analytical observation of the common moral consciousness of his age. Ethical truth, in his view, is to be obtained by a careful comparison of particular moral opinions, as physical truth is to be obtained by induction from particular physical observations. Owing to the diversity and conflict of men's judgments of good and evil we cannot hope to obtain perfect clearness and certainty upon all ethical questions; still reflection will lead us to discard some of the conflicting views and find a reconciliation for others, and will furnish, on the whole, a practically sufficient residuum of moral truth. This adhesion to common sense, though it involves some sacrifice of both depth and completeness in Aristotle's account of the virtues, gives it at the same time a historical interest which renders it deserving of special attention, as an analysis of the current Greek ideal of "fair and good" life.[1]

[1] *καλοκἀγαθία*. I may observe that Aristotle follows Plato and Socrates in identifying the notions of *καλός* ("fair," "beautiful") and *ἀγαθός* ("good") in their application to conduct. We may observe, however, that while the latter term is used to denote the virtuous man, and (in the neuter) as equivalent to End generally, the former is rather chosen to express the quality of virtuous acts which in any particular case is the end of the virtuous agent. Aristotle no doubt faithfully

§ 10. Aristotle's theory of Virtue.

Let us begin with the generic definition of Moral Excellence or Virtue in the narrower sense. The term cannot denote a mere natural feeling or susceptibility to feeling, such as anger, fear, pity,—as these, considered merely as such, are not objects of praise or blame: it denotes a settled habit, formed by a course of actions under rule and discipline in which vicious excess and defect have been avoided, of experiencing the natural emotions just mentioned in a duly limited and regulated manner; so that the virtuous man, without internal conflict, wills actions that hit the happy mean in their effects. So far Virtue is like technical skill, which also is the result of practice, and is manifested in the successful avoidance of the contrasted errors of "too much" and "too little"; but Virtue differs from skill in involving a deliberate choice of virtuous acts for the sake of their intrinsic moral beauty, and not for any end external to the act. The "happy mean" or due degree in feeling and outward act in which virtue is realised, is not a mere arithmetical mean between the possible alternative extremes: it is determined in each case relatively to the agent, and to the circumstances of the action; indeed, it is often markedly nearer to one of the two vicious extremes—courage, *e.g.* is much nearer to rashness than to cowardice. The precise determination, however, of the right mean must be given by the reasoning and judgment of men of practical wisdom.

So much for the general conception, in which Aristotle is mainly formulating the results to which Plato's development and correction of the Socratic notion of Virtue had

represents the common sense of Greece in considering that, in so far as virtue is in itself good to the virtuous agent, it belongs to that species of good which we distinguish as beautiful. In later Greek philosophy the term καλόν seems to have become still more technical in the signification of "morally good."

gradually led. His list of particular virtues is also partly framed on the basis of Plato's; it is Plato's list enlarged by a number of notions introduced from common discourse, and defined with that close adhesion to common sense of which I have before spoken. But the two thinkers differ strikingly in their treatment of the cardinal virtues; for Plato, impressed by the essential unity of virtue and the mutual implication of the virtues commonly recognised, tends in his account of each particular virtue to enlarge the notion until it might fairly stand for Virtue in general, whereas Aristotle's analytical intellect and inductive method leads him rather to define too narrowly the terms that he takes from common discourse. Reserving for separate treatment the conceptions of Wisdom and Justice or Uprightness (δικαιοσύνη), he begins with Courage and Temperance, considering them, after Plato, as excellences of the "irrational element" of the soul. Courage he analyses with special care and subtlety, corresponding to the importance attached to it in the current distribution of praise and blame. In the strict and proper use of the word its sphere is nearly restricted to war. It is manifested in the fearless facing of the chances that bring death, where death is noble, and such occasions are chiefly met in war;—*e.g.* in a storm at sea the courageous man will indeed be fearless, but he cannot exhibit courage,[1] properly speaking, since there is nothing noble in the threatened death. Further, Courage proper—in the sense in which it is a virtue and involves a choice of

[1] I have not thought it right to deviate in the text from the traditional rendering of ἀνδρεία. But I may observe that "valour" rather than "courage" appears to me the most appropriate equivalent of the term as defined by Aristotle, since we find in its current usage just that degree of restriction to war which Aristotle finds in the current usage of ἀνδρεία.

the courageous act for its intrinsic goodness or nobleness—is to be distinguished from the "civic courage" of which the motive is the fear of disgrace or pain, from the confidence due to experience, or to a sanguine disposition, or to ignorance, and from mere physical courage or high spirit; this last, however, is, as it were, a raw material, which may be developed into Virtue by implanting the higher motive.

As Courage is restricted to war, Temperance is similarly, in accordance with usage, taken as solely concerned with the pleasures of hunger, thirst, and sex. The temperate man abhors the vicious indulgence of these appetites, and does not take excessive delight even in a lawful satisfaction of them; nor does he unduly long for such pleasures or feel pain at their absence. It is noteworthy that error on the side of deficiency, in the case of this virtue—undue insensibility to the pleasures of appetite—is, according to Aristotle, hardly to be found in human beings. It is to be observed, further, that the important distinction between Virtue in the strict sense, which implies the performance of right actions without internal conflict, and "Self-restraint" (ἐγκράτεια), which involves a struggle with misdirected impulses, is treated by Aristotle [1] as specially belonging to the sphere of Temperance,—chiefly, it would seem, because in ordinary Greek usage the terms denoting Self-restraint and its opposite (ἀκρασία) were in strictness applicable only to

[1] I do not regard Book VII. of the *Nicomachean Ethics*, in which this topic is discussed, or Books V. and VI., as being Aristotle's work in the same sense in which the rest of the treatise is. But I conceive that they were intended by the disciple who composed them to convey pure Aristotelian doctrine; and that therefore they sufficiently justify the brief and general statement of Aristotle's view given in the paragraph to which this note is appended; and also what is said later on of Justice, Intellectual Excellences, and Practical Reasoning.

the case of bodily appetites, their application to anger or other non-rational impulses being regarded as secondary and metaphorical.

After Courage and Temperance, which are concerned with the regulation of the primitive or animal aversions and appetites, Aristotle gives two pairs of virtues which are occupied respectively with the two chief objects of man's more refined and civilised desire and pursuit—Wealth and Honour; distinguishing in each case the kind of excellence which is possible only to a select few from that which is more widely attainable. Thus, in the case of wealth, persons of moderate means may exercise Liberality—a virtue chiefly shown in giving or spending ungrudgingly but without lavishness on proper objects, though it also involves abstinence from all disgraceful sources of gain; but the more brilliant quality of Magnificence is only attainable by persons of large estate and high social position, to whom it is becoming to make grand offerings to the gods, or give splendid banquets, or equip choruses or ships of war in imposing style. The performance of these expensive functions was a kind of extra taxation imposed on wealthy citizens, by law or custom, at Athens and elsewhere; but it is plain that they were often eagerly seized as occasions of display, and that the excess which the magnificent man is required to avoid, the vulgar extravagance of "entertaining one's club with a wedding-feast, and dressing one's comic chorus in purple," was a type illustrated in actual life.

Similarly the due pursuit of Honour or Reputation, by men generally, is regarded by Aristotle as the province of a special virtue; for which, however, he finds no name in the current moral vocabulary—both "Ambitious" and its opposite "Unambitious" being sometimes used for censure and sometimes for eulogy. But he is specially interested in delineating the attitude of mind in respect of this "greatest of external goods," exhibited by the "High-minded man," who, possessing a rare degree of merit, values himself as he deserves. Such High-mindedness is a kind of crown of accomplished virtue, since it at once presupposes other virtues—for any marked vice would be incompatible with the rare degree of merit which it implies—and enhances them. Having this perfection of virtue the high-minded man will be only moderately pleased even by great honour from men of repute, as this is no more than his due; while as he rightly despises the common herd he will be altogether indifferent to the honour they pay him. The traits by which Aristotle characterises in detail this flower of noble life are all the more interesting from their discrepancy with the Christian ideal. The high-minded man is likely to be rich and well-born; he loves to confer favours, but feels shame at receiving them, and does not like to be reminded of any that he may have received; he shuns all subordinate positions, and is inert and dilatory except when there is something great to do; he is open in his enmities and his friendships—for he fears no one—and generally candid, except that he affects irony with the common herd; he is free from malice, no gossip, careless of the little needs and concerns of life, not given to wonder or praise; his walk is slow, his accents grave, his speech deliberate.

After the virtues relating to Honour comes Gentleness, the moral excellence manifested in duly limited resentment; and the list is concluded by the excellences of social intercourse, Friendliness (as a mean between obsequiousness and surliness), Truthfulness, and Decorous Wit.

There is enough just and close analytical observation

contained in this famous account of virtues and vices to give it a permanent interest over and above its historical value; but it does not seem to be based on any serious attempt to consider human conduct exhaustively, and exhibit the patterns of goodness appropriate to the different parts, functions, and relations of life; and the restriction of the sphere of courage to dangers in war, and of that of temperance to certain bodily pleasures, as well as the want of distinction between selfish and benevolent expenditure in describing liberality, illustrate the fragmentariness and superficiality of treatment to which mere analysis of the common usage of ethical terms is always liable to lead. Nor is Aristotle's general formula for virtue,—that it is a mean or middle state, always to be found somewhere between the vices which stand to it in the relation of excess and defect,—of much avail in rendering his treatment really systematic. It was important, no doubt, to express the need of limitation and regulation, of observing due measure and proportion, in order to attain good results in human life no less than in artistic products;[1] but Aristotle's quantitative statement of the relation of virtue to vice is misleading, even where it is not obviously inappropriate, and sometimes leads him to such eccentricities as that of making simple veracity a mean between boastfulness and mock-modesty.

§ 11. Aristotle's account of Justice, Friendship, and Practical Wisdom.

The cardinal virtue of Justice or Uprightness (δικαιοσύνη), omitted from the list above given, was reserved by Aristotle for separate treatment; partly because he finds the term, as commonly used, to have two distinct meanings, blended in Plato's conception of the virtue: in the wider meaning—which I have tried to suggest by "Uprightness"—it is

[1] It may be observed that Plato's teaching had already driven this point home.

opposed to all law-breaking (ἀδικία or ἀνομία), and thus may be taken to stand for the whole of virtue, considered in its social aspect: in the narrower meaning, more nearly represented by our "justice," it is specially opposed to grasping or unfair treatment. Of Justice in this narrower sense he distinguishes primarily two species; (1) Distributive Justice, exhibited in the distribution in proportion to Desert[1] of any public fund or stock of wealth, honours, or whatever else may have to be divided among the members of a community; and (2) Reparative Justice, realised in the exaction from a wrongdoer, for the benefit of the person wronged, of damages just equivalent to the loss suffered by the latter. He further explains that in the exchanges of commodities which bind society together Justice is attained when the amounts of any two commodities exchanged are in "reciprocal proportion" to their relative values—the superiority in quality on one side being balanced by superiority in quantity on the other. The distinctions are instructive: though they do not guide us in determining what are fair shares, fair damages, fair bargains, in particular cases. Further, taking up the question —much discussed at the outset of moral reflection in Greece—whether Justice is "natural" or "conventional," Aristotle decides that there is properly a mixture of both elements in "civic justice," as realised in the maintenance of the rights legally allotted to the citizens of a constitutional state; since for the complete definition of such rights many details have to be settled which natural justice leaves indeterminate. But he does not attempt to separate clearly the two elements, or to lay down precise principles of

[1] "Desert" must not be understood to mean "moral worth"; it will, in fact, vary according to circumstances; thus when public money has to be distributed, the Desert of each citizen will depend on the amount of his contribution to the public treasury.

Natural Justice from which the natural rights of the members of a justly ordered state may be deduced. He notes, however, the need of "equity" as a kind of justice superior to that which is realised by strict adhesion to the letter of law, and rightly overruling it, where the literal application of the prescriptions of the law to special unforeseen cases would fail to realise its intention.

One defect in Aristotle's account of Virtue which strikes a modern reader is that Benevolence is not recognised, except obscurely in the imperfect form of Liberality. This deficiency, however, is to some extent supplied by a separate discussion on the relations of kind affection which bind men together. This mutual kindness, if not strictly a virtue, is an indispensable element of human wellbeing: as a bond of union among members of a state, it is "more the concern of the legislator even than justice": in the narrower and intenser form which we specially call Friendship, it is needful to complete the happiness even of the philosopher. The proper basis of Friendship is the mutual recognition of goodness: there are indeed relations known by this name that are based merely on "utility" or "pleasure"; but these lack the characteristic, essential to true friendship, of "wishing good to another for that other's sake." True friendship, therefore, can only exist between the good, whose happiness it completes by enlarging through sympathy that consciousness of life which is itself a good: especially it gives them, in fuller measure than their own virtue, the delight of contemplating excellent achievements as something belonging to them. Aristotle, however, supplements this ideal treatment of the basis of friendship by a more empirical discussion of the natural conditions of human affection: recognising, for instance, that in the parental relation it is produced by a sense of quasi-physical unity: the parent's love for the child is a sort of extended self-love.

From moral excellences Aristotle passed to analyse the intellectual. Here his most important point is the determination of the relation between the two kinds of wisdom which Plato blended in one conception—Speculative Wisdom (σοφία) and Practical Wisdom (φρόνησις). He holds, as we saw, that Speculative Wisdom does not guide us in determining moral questions: still, it is in a sense practical, in so far as its exercises are the highest forms of human activity: it does not define human good, but it pre-eminently constitutes it. Practical Wisdom, on the other hand, is really involved in moral excellence as already defined, if we suppose this perfect; for it is required to determine in any particular case that due limitation of feeling and action in which perfect virtue consists; and it cannot be conceived as existing apart from moral excellence—we do not count a man practically wise for such mere intellectual cleverness as a vicious man may exhibit. The man we count wise must be not merely skilful in the selection of means to any ends: his ends must also be rightly chosen. It is, however, difficult to form a distinct general idea of the practical syllogism by which Aristotle conceived right action to be ordinarily determined. And, indeed, it would not have been easy for him to make this point plain, without bringing into prominence a profound discrepancy between his own view of rational action and the common opinion and practice of mankind. The kind of reasoning which his view of virtuous conduct requires is one in which the ultimate major premise states a distinctive characteristic of some virtue, and one or more minor premises show that such characteristic belongs to a certain mode of conduct under given circumstances;

since he holds it essential to good conduct that it should contain its end in itself, and be chosen for its own sake. But he has not failed to observe that practical reasonings are not commonly of this kind, but are rather concerned with actions as means to ulterior ends; indeed, he lays stress on this as a characteristic of the practical or "political" life, when he wishes to prove its inferiority to the life of pure speculation. Though common sense will admit that virtues are the best of goods, it still undoubtedly conceives practical wisdom as chiefly exercised in providing those inferior goods which Aristotle, after recognising the need or use of them for the realisation of human wellbeing, has dropped out of sight; and the result is that, in trying to make clear his conception of practical wisdom, we find ourselves fluctuating continually between the common notion, which he does not distinctly reject, and the notion required as the keystone of his ethical system.

§ 12. Plato and Aristotle on The Voluntary. There is another respect in which Aristotle's view of the relation of intellect to moral action is apt to be found confusing by the modern reader: in its bearing, namely, on the question of Free Will. On this point it may be said both of Plato and Aristotle that their psychology compels them to teach by implication the opposite doctrine to that which they expressly maintain and desire to enforce. They have every wish to resist and explode the Determinism which presents itself to them as providing a dangerous excuse for vice: but their psychological system has no place for that deliberate choice of evil recognised as such, which, for the Christian moral consciousness, is the primary and prominent type of bad volition; and hence they inevitably fail in their attempts to fix on the wrongdoer the full and final responsibility for his acts. The only states of mind which they recognise as immediate antecedents of bad acts are (1) predominance of irrational impulse overpowering rational judgment or prompting to action without deliberation, and (2) mistaken choice of evil under the appearance of good. In either case the action would seem, according to the account given of it by both these thinkers, to be "necessitated"—as Plato expressly says—by causes antecedent in time to the bad volition. It is true that Plato gives himself much pains to eliminate this necessitation from the ultimate causation of vice; in semi-fanciful or semi-popular expressions of his view—as in the fable at the close of the *Republic* and in the *Laws*—he affirms emphatically that each individual soul has full responsibility for its vicious conduct: but in his more scientific analysis of human action it is always presented as due either to Reason determined by the prospect of good, or to Passion or Appetite in blind or disorderly opposition to Reason; the inadequate control of reason in the latter case being completely explained by the original composition of the disordered soul and the external influences that have moulded its development.[1] Similarly the "voluntariness" which Aristotle attributes to the acts of a vicious man does not exclude complete determination of them, from moment to moment, by formed character and present external influences; and hence does not really amount to "free agency"

[1] It ought to be added that the inconsistency which I find in Plato's doctrine of the origin of bad volition belongs only to the ethical side of the doctrine and not to its theological side. There is no similar difficulty in accepting the view that the pure being of eternal universal Thought, which Plato—and Aristotle after him—identifies with Divine Being, can neither contain evil nor cause it; and that, therefore, evil originates wholly in the inevitable conditions of concrete sensible existence. What I contend is merely that Plato cannot consistently regard evil as originating in any individual soul.

in the modern philosophical sense. At any given time Aristotle's vicious man, so far as he acts from deliberate purpose, must aim at what then appears to him good; and however misleading this appearance may be, he has no control over it. We may admit, as Aristotle urges, that it is his previous bad conduct which has caused evil to seem good to him: but this argument only seems strong until we fix our attention on that previous bad conduct and investigate its causation. For this conduct, on Aristotle's view, must (if purposed) have been equally directed towards an end apparently though not really good: and this appearance must again be attributed to still earlier wrongdoing: so that the freedom of will recedes like a mirage as we trace back the chain of purposed actions to its beginnings, and cannot be made to rest anywhere. If it be said, as Aristotle probably would say, that in its beginnings vice is merely impulsive, and that it only gradually becomes deliberate as bad habits are formed, it is still more easy to show that Aristotle's psychology provides no philosophical justification for fixing finally on the agent the responsibility for impulsive bad acts: for when he comes to analyse the state of mind in which such acts are done in spite of the knowledge that they are bad, his explanation is that the knowledge at such moments is not really actualised in the mind; it is reduced by appetite or passion to a condition of latency.

§ 13. Transition to Stoicism.

On the whole, there is probably no treatise so masterly as Aristotle's *Ethics*, and containing so much close and valid thought, that yet leaves on the reader's mind so strong an impression of dispersive and incomplete work. I note this that we may better understand the small amount of influence that his system exercised during the five centuries after his death, in which the schools sprung from Socrates were still predominant in Greco-Roman culture, as compared with the effect which it has had, directly or indirectly, in shaping the thought of modern Europe. Partly, no doubt, the limited influence of the "Peripatetics"[1] (as Aristotle's disciples were called) is to be attributed to that exaltation of the purely speculative life which distinguished the Aristotelian ethics from other later systems; since this was too alien from the common moral consciousness to find much acceptance in an age in which the ethical aims of philosophy had again become paramount. Partly, again, the analytical distinctness of Aristotle's manner brings into special prominence the difficulties that attend the Socratic effort to reconcile the moral aspirations of men, and the principles on which they agree to distribute mutual praise and blame, with the principles on which their practical reasonings are commonly conducted. The conflict between these two elements of Common Sense was too profound to be compromised; and the moral consciousness of mankind demanded a more trenchant partisanship than Aristotle's. Its demands were met by a school which separated the moral from the worldly view of life, with an absoluteness and definiteness that caught the imagination; which regarded practical goodness as the highest result and manifestation of its ideal of wisdom; and which bound the common notions of duty into an apparently complete and coherent system, by a formula that comprehended the whole of human life, and exhibited its relation to the ordered process of the universe. This school was always known as

[1] The term is derived from περιπατεῖν, "to walk about," and was applied to the disciples of Aristotle in consequence of the master's custom of giving instruction while walking to and fro in the shady avenues of the gymnasium where he lectured.

Zeno (prob. 342-270 B.C.)

the "Stoic," from the Porch or portico (στοά) in which its original founder[1] Zeno used to teach. The intellectual descent of its ethical doctrines is principally to be traced to Socrates through the Cynics, though an important element in them must be referred to the influence of the Academic school. Both Stoic and Cynic maintained, in its sharpest form, the fundamental tenet that the practical knowledge which they identify with virtue is or involves[2] a condition of soul that is alone sufficient for complete human wellbeing. It is true that the Cynics were more concerned to emphasise the negative side of the sage's wellbeing, its independence of bodily health and strength, beauty, pleasure, wealth, good birth, good fame; while the Stoics brought into more prominence its positive side, the magnanimous confidence, the tranquillity undisturbed by grief, the joy and good cheer of the spirit, which inseparably attended the possession of wisdom. This difference, however, did not amount to disagreement. The Stoics, in fact, seem generally to have regarded the Cynic practice of rigidly reducing the provision for physical needs to a minimum, without regard to conventional proprieties, as an emphatic manner of expressing the essential antithesis between philosophic aims and vulgar desires; a manner which, though not necessary or even normal, might yet be advantageously adopted by the sage under certain circumstances.[3]

[1] I use the term "original founder" because the part taken by Chrysippus (about 280-206 B.C.) in the development of the Stoic system was so important that some regarded it as no less essential than Zeno's. "Had not Chrysippus been, no Porch had been," says a poet quoted by Diogenes Laertius, vii. 183.

[2] See p. 83.

[3] It has been suggestively said that Cynicism was to Stoicism what monasticism was to early Christianity. The analogy, however, must

§ 14. Stoicism. The passionless Sage.

Wherein, then, does this knowledge or wisdom that makes free and perfect consist? Both Cynics and Stoics agreed that its most important function, that which constitutes the fundamental distinction between the wise and the unwise, consists in recognising that the sole good of man lies in this knowledge or wisdom itself. It must be understood that they did not, any more than Socrates, conceive true knowledge of good to be possible apart from its realisation in a good life;—though they held that the duration of such a life was a matter of indifference, and that the perfection of human wellbeing would be attained by any individual in whom perfect wisdom was realised even for a moment. This return of the Stoics to the Socratic position, after the divergence from it which we have seen gradually taking place in Platonic-Aristotelian thought, is very noteworthy; it is to be attributed to the stress that their psychology laid on the essential unity of the rational self that is the source of conscious human action, which prevented them from accepting Plato's analysis of the springs of such action into a regulative element and elements needing regulation. They held that what we call passion is a morbid and disorderly condition of the rational soul, involving erroneous judgment as to what is to be sought or shunned. From such passionate errors the truly wise man will, of course, be free. He will, indeed, be conscious of the solicitations of physical appetite; but he will not be misled into supposing that its object is really a good; he cannot, therefore, strictly speaking, hope for the attainment of this object or fear to miss it,

not be pressed too far, since orthodox Stoics do not ever seem to have regarded Cynicism as the more perfect way. They held, however, that it was a "short road to virtue," and that a Cynic who became a sage should abide in his Cynicism: and we find that Epictetus gives the name of Cynic to Socrates and other moral heroes.

as these emotions involve the conception of it as a good. Similarly, though he will be subject like other men to bodily pain, this will not cause him mental grief or disquiet, as his worst agonies will not disturb his clear conviction that it is really indifferent to his true reasonable self. And so of all other objects that commonly excite men's hope, fear, joy, or grief: they cannot produce these states in the sage, because he cannot judge them to be really good or bad. We are not therefore to regard the sage as an altogether emotionless being; there is a reasonable elation over the attainment of what is truly good, movements of inclination or aversion to what reason judges preferable[1] or the reverse, which the wisest man may experience; but the passions that sway ordinary human minds cannot affect him. That this impassive sage was a being hardly to be found among living men the later Stoics at least were fully aware. They faintly suggested that one or two moral heroes of old time might have realised the ideal; but they admitted that, except these, even all other philosophers were merely in a state of progress towards it. This admission, however, did not in the least diminish the rigour of their demand for absolute loyalty to the exclusive claims of wisdom. The assurance of its own unique value that such wisdom involved they held to be an abiding possession for those who had attained it;[2] and without this assurance no act could be truly wise or virtuous. Whatever was not of knowledge was of sin; and the distinction between right and wrong being absolute and not admitting of degrees, all sins were equally sinful; whoever broke the

[1] For the distinction between the "Preferred" or "Preferable" and the "Good," see pp. 79, 80.

[2] The Stoics were not quite agreed as to the immutability of virtue, when once possessed; but they were agreed that it could only be lost through the loss of reason itself.

least commandment was guilty of the whole law. Similarly, all wisdom was somehow involved in any one of the manifestations of wisdom, commonly distinguished as particular virtues;—in classifying which the Stoics seem generally to have adopted Plato's fourfold division as at least the basis of their own scheme;[1] though whether these virtues were specifically distinct, or only the same knowledge in different relations, was a subtle question on which they do not seem to have been agreed.

Was, then, this rare and priceless knowledge something which it was possible for man to attain, or were human shortcomings really involuntary? There is an obvious danger to moral responsibility involved in the doctrine that vice is involuntary; which yet seems a natural inference from the Socratic identification of knowledge with virtue. Hence, as we have seen, Aristotle had already been led to attempt a refutation of this doctrine; but his attempt had only shown the profound difficulty of attacking the paradox, so long as it was admitted that no one could of deliberate purpose act contrary to what seemed to him best. Now, Aristotle's divergence from Socrates had not led him so far as to deny this; while for the Stoics who had receded to the original Socratic position, the difficulty was still more patent. In fact, a philosopher who maintains that virtue is essentially knowledge has to choose between alternative paradoxes: he must either allow vice to be involuntary, or affirm ignorance to be voluntary. The latter horn of the dilemma is at any rate the less dangerous to morality, and

Stoic Freedom and Determinism.

[1] The Stoic definitions of the four virtues appear to have varied a good deal. Zeno, according to Plutarch, defined Justice, Temperance, and Fortitude, as Wisdom in "things to be distributed," "things to be chosen," and "things to be endured"; and this statement may be taken as expressing briefly the general view of the school.

as such the Stoics chose it. But they were not yet at the end of their perplexities; for while they were thus driven on one line of thought to an extreme extension of the range of human volition, their view of the physical universe involved an equally thorough-going determinism. How could the vicious man be responsible if his vice were strictly predetermined? The Stoics answered that the error which was the essence of vice was so far voluntary that it could be avoided if men chose to exercise their reason; no doubt it depended on the innate force and firmness[1] of a man's soul whether his reason was thus effectually exercised; but moral responsibility was thought to be saved if the vicious act proceeded from the man himself and not from any external cause.

§ 15. Stoic Wisdom and Nature.

With all this we have got little way towards ascertaining the positive practical content of Stoic wisdom. How are we to emerge from the barren circle of affirming (1) that wisdom is the sole good and unwisdom the sole evil, and (2) that wisdom is the knowledge of good and evil? how are we to find a method for determining the particulars of good conduct? Both Cynicism and Stoicism stood in need of such a method to complete their doctrine; since neither school was prepared to maintain that what the sage resolves to do is indifferent—no less than what befalls him—provided only he does it with a full conviction of its indifference. The Cynics, however, seem to have made no philosophical provision for this need; they were content to mean by virtue what any plain man meant by it, except in so far as their

[1] Hence some members of the school, without rejecting the definition of virtue=knowledge, also defined it as "strength and force." This force the Stoics conceived materialistically, as a certain tension of the subtle æther or spirit that, in their view, was the substance of the soul. See note 1, p. 78.

sense of independence led them to reject certain received precepts and prejudices. The Stoics, on the other hand, not only worked out a detailed system of duties—or, as they termed them, "things meet and fit" (καθήκοντα)[1]—for all occasions of life; they were further especially concerned to comprehend them under a general formula. They found this by bringing out the positive significance of the notion of Nature, which the Cynic had used chiefly in a negative way, as an antithesis to the "conventions" (νόμος), from which his knowledge had made him free. Even in this negative use of the notion, it is implied that whatever active tendencies in man are found to be "natural"—that is independent of and uncorrupted by social customs and conventions—will properly take effect in outward acts; but the adoption of "conformity to nature," as a general positive rule for outward conduct, seems to have been due to the influence on Zeno of Academic teaching. Whence, however, can this authority belong to the Natural, unless Nature, the ordered creation of which man is a part, be itself somehow reasonable, an expression or embodiment of divine law and wisdom? The conception of the world, as organised and fitted by divine thought, was common, in some form, to all the philosophies that looked back to Socrates as their founder; and an important section of these philosophies had been led to the view that this divine thought was the one real Being of the universe. This pantheistic doctrine harmonised thoroughly with the Stoic view of human good; but being unable to conceive substance idealistically, they (with con-

[1] The word "duty" in the modern sense is perhaps misleading as a translation of καθῆκον; because an act so termed is not a "right act" (κατόρθωμα), unless performed from a right motive, *i.e.* in a purely reasonable or wise state of mind; otherwise it has merely an external fitness or suitability.

siderable aid from the earlier system of Heraclitus) supplied a materialistic side to their pantheism,—conceiving divine thought as a function of the primary and most pure material substance, a subtle fiery æther. They held the physical world to have been developed out of Zeus, so conceived; to be, in fact, a modification of his eternal substance into which it would ultimately be sublimated and re-absorbed;[1] meanwhile it was throughout permeated with the fashioning force of his divine spirit, and perfectly ordered by his prescient law. The world, being thus essentially divine, they held to be perfect, regarded as a whole; whatever defects may appear in its parts must be conceived to become evanescent in the sight of that Supreme Reason which "knows how to even the odd and to order the disorderly, and to whom the unlovely is dear."[2] This theological view of the physical universe had a double effect on the ethics of the Stoic. In the first place, it gave to his cardinal conviction of the all-sufficiency of wisdom for human wellbeing a root of cosmical fact, and an atmosphere of religious and social emotion. The exercise of wisdom was now viewed as the pure life of that particle of divine substance which was in very truth the "god within him"; the reason whose

[1] This primary substance—in its material aspect—was conceived as originally a highly elastic body; which was supposed by successive condensations to become differentiated into portions of unequal density and tension,—the four elements. Other differences in the qualities of matter, as empirically known to us, were explained to be due to the presence in earth and water of currents of æther varying in tension (or, in some cases of fire and air, the rarer and more elastic pair of elements). And, by what appears to us a most bizarre confusion of ideas, these æther-currents were conceived to be the forces that held together—or, adopting Aristotelian language, the very "forms" that constituted—the different kinds of matter, *quâ* different.

[2] The quotation is from the hymn attributed to Cleanthes, who presided over the Stoic school between Zeno and Chrysippus.

supremacy he maintained was the reason of Zeus, and of all gods and reasonable men, no less than his own; its realisation in any one individual was thus the common good of all rational beings as such; "the sage could not stretch out a finger rightly without thereby benefiting all other sages,"—nay, it might even be said that he was "as useful to Zeus as Zeus to him." It is, I conceive, in view of this union in reason of rational beings that friends are allowed to be "external goods" to the sage, and that the possession of good children is also counted a good. But again, the same conception served to harmonize the higher and the lower elements of human life. For even in the physical or non-rational man, as originally constituted, we may see clear indications of the divine design, which it belongs to his rational will to carry into conscious execution; indeed, in the first stage of human life, before reason is fully developed, uncorrupted natural impulse effects what is afterwards the work of reason. Thus the formula of "living according to nature," in its application to man as the "rational animal, may be understood both as directing that reason is to govern, and as indicating how that government is to be practically exercised. In man, as in every other animal, from the moment of birth natural impulse prompts to self-preservation, and to the maintenance of his physical frame in its original integrity; then, when reason has been developed and has recognised itself as its own sole good, these "primary ends of nature," and whatever promotes these, still constitute the outward objects at which reason is to aim; there is a certain value (ἀξία) in them, in proportion to which they are "preferred" (προηγμένα) and their opposites "rejected" (ἀποπροηγμένα); indeed, it is only in the due and consistent exercise of such preference and rejection that wisdom can find its practical manifestation. In this way all or most of the things commonly judged to be "goods"—health, strength, wealth, fame,[1] etc.—are brought within the sphere of the sage's choice, though his real good still lies solely in the wisdom of the choice, and not in the thing chosen; just as an archer aims at the bull's-eye, his end being not the mark itself, but the manifestation of his skill in hitting it.[2]

We may illustrate the distinction just explained by referring to a point in the practical teaching of the Stoics which modern readers sometimes find perplexing,—their encouragement of suicide. This at first sight seems to us inconsistent, at once with the virtuous fortitude which they commend and with their belief in the providential ordering of the world. Men are commonly driven to suicide by the miseries of life; but how, we ask, can the sage, to whom pain is no evil, be thus moved to quit the post which Divine Reason has assigned to him? The answer is, that if pain be not an evil, it is yet an alternative to be rejected, if painlessness is properly obtainable; and on the other hand, life is not a good in the view of wisdom, and though its preservation is generally to be preferred, cases may arise in which the sage receives unmistakable natural indications that death is preferable to life. Such indications, the Stoics held,

[1] The Stoics seem to have varied in their view of "good repute," εὐδοξία; at first, when the school was more under the influence of Cynicism, they professed an outward as well as an inward indifference to it; ultimately they conceded the point to common sense, and included it among "preferred" things.

[2] This comparison appears to have been variously applied by different Stoics; but it appears to me well adapted to illustrate the important doctrine with which I have connected it; and we may infer from Cicero (*De Finibus*, Book III.) that it was so used at least by some members of the school.

were given by mutilations, incurable diseases, and other disasters, — even by extreme pain; and when they were clearly given, wisdom and strength were as much manifested in following these leadings of nature or Providence as they were manifested at other times in resisting the seductions of pleasure and pain.

So far we have considered the "nature" of the individual man apart from his social relations; but it is obvious that the sphere of virtue, as commonly conceived, lies chiefly in such relations. And this was fully recognised in the Stoic account of duties (καθήκοντα); indeed, their exposition of the "natural" basis of justice, the evidences in man's mental and physical constitution that he was born not for himself but for mankind, is the most important part of their work in the region of practical morality. Here, however, we especially notice the double significance of "natural," as applied to (1) what actually exists everywhere or for the most part, (2) what would exist if the original plan of man's life were fully carried out; and we find that the Stoics have not clearly harmonised the two elements of the notion. That man was "naturally" a political animal Aristotle had already taught: in the ideal view of nature which the Stoics framed, he was, we may say, *cosmopolitical;* for it was an immediate inference from the Stoic conception of the universe as a whole that all rational beings, in the unity of the reason that is common to all, form naturally one community with a common law. That the members of this "city of Zeus" should observe their contracts, abstain from mutual harm, combine to protect each other from injury, were obvious points of natural law; while, again, it was clearly necessary to the preservation of human society that its members should form sexual unions, produce children, and bestow care on their rearing and training. But beyond this nature did not seem to go in determining the relations of the sexes; accordingly, we find that community of wives was a feature of Zeno's ideal commonwealth, just as it was of Plato's; and other Stoics are represented as maintaining, and illustrating with rather offensive paradoxes, the conventionality and relativity of the received code of sexual morality. Again, the strict theory of the school recognised no government or laws as true or binding except those of the sage; he alone is the true ruler, the true king. So far, the Stoic "nature" seems in danger of being as revolutionary as Rousseau's. Practically, however, this revolutionary aspect of the notion was kept for the most part in the background; the rational law of an ideal community remained peacefully undistinguished from the positive ordinances and customs of actual society; and the "natural" ties that actually bound each man to family, kinsmen, fatherland, and to unwise humanity generally, supplied the outline on which the external manifestation of justice was delineated.[1] So, again, in the view taken by the Stoics of the duties of social decorum, and in their attitude to the popular religion, we find a fluctuating compromise between the tendency to repudiate what is artificial and conventional, and the tendency to revere what is actual and established; each tendency expressing in its own way an adhesion to the principle of "conforming to nature."

§ 16. Stoics and Hedonists.

Among the primary ends of nature, in which wisdom recognised a certain preferability, the Stoics included free-

[1] It seems to have been a generally accepted maxim that the Stoic sage would take part in public life, unless some special obstacle prevented him; the critics of the school, however, observed that in practice such obstacles were usually found by the Stoic philosophers.

dom from bodily pain; but they refused, even in this outer court of wisdom, to find a place for pleasure. They held that the latter was not an object of uncorrupted natural impulse, but an "aftergrowth" (ἐπιγέννημα), a mere consequence of natural impulses attaining their ends. They thus endeavoured to resist Epicureanism even on the ground where the latter seems *primâ facie* strongest—in its appeal, namely, to the natural pleasure-seeking of all living things. Nor did they merely mean by pleasure (ἡδονή) the gratification of bodily appetite; *e.g.* we find Chrysippus urging, as a decisive argument against Aristotle, that pure speculation was "a kind of amusement, that is, pleasure." Even the "joy and gladness" (χαρά, εὐφροσύνη) that accompany the exercise of virtue seem to have been regarded by them as merely an inseparable accident, not the essential constituent of wellbeing. Thus it is only by a later modification of Stoicism[1] that cheerfulness or peace of mind is taken as the real ultimate end, to which the exercise of virtue is merely a means; in Zeno's system it is good volition, and not the feeling that attends it, which constitutes the essence of good life. At the same time, since pleasant feeling of some kind must always have been a prominent element in the popular conception of "wellbeing" or "welfare" (εὐδαιμονία), it is probable that the serene joys of virtue, and the grieflessness which the sage was conceived to maintain amid the worst tortures, formed the main attractions of Stoicism for most minds. In this sense, then, it may be fairly said that Stoics and Epicureans made rival offers to mankind of the same kind of happiness; the philosophical peculiarities of either system may

[1] This modification—so far as I am aware—is not definitely to be found earlier than Cicero. Cf. *post*, p. 95, note 2.

be equally traced to the desire of maintaining that independence of the changes and chances of life which seemed essential to a settled serenity of soul. The Stoic claims on this head were the loftiest; as the wellbeing of their model sage was independent, not only of external things and bodily conditions, but of time itself; it was fully realised in a single exercise of wisdom and could not be increased by duration. This paradox is violent, but it is quite in harmony with the spirit of Stoicism; and we are more startled to find that the Epicurean sage, no less than the Stoic, is to be happy even on the rack; that his happiness, too, depends almost entirely upon insight and right calculation, fortune having very little to do with it, and is unimpaired by being restricted in duration, when his mind has apprehended the natural limits of life; that, in short, Epicurus makes hardly less strenuous efforts than Zeno to eliminate imperfection from the conditions of human existence. This characteristic is the key to the chief differences between Epicureanism and the more naïve hedonism of Aristippus. The latter system gave the simplest and most obvious answer to the inquiry after ultimate good for man; but besides being liable, when developed consistently and unreservedly, to offend the common moral consciousness, it admittedly failed to provide the "completeness" and "security" which, as Aristotle says, "one divines to belong to man's true Good."[1] Philosophy, in the Greek view, should be the art as well as the science of good life; and hedonistic philosophy would seem to be a bungling and

[1] It was admitted by the Cyrenaics that even the sage could not count on a life of uninterrupted pleasure; and Theodorus, the frankest of the school, is said to have expressly taught that the sage would, under certain circumstances, commit theft, adultery, and sacrilege.

uncertain art of pleasure, as pleasure is ordinarily conceived. Nay, it would even be found that the habit of philosophical reflection often operated adversely to the attainment of this end; by developing the thinker's self-consciousness, so as to disturb that normal relation to external objects on which the zest of ordinary enjoyment depends. Hence we find that later thinkers of the Cyrenaic school felt themselves compelled to change their fundamental notion; thus Theodorus defined the good as "gladness" (χαρά) depending on wisdom, as distinct from mere pleasure; while Hegesias proclaimed that happiness was unattainable, and that the chief function of wisdom was to render life painless by producing indifference to all things that give pleasure. But by such changes the system lost the support that it had had in the pleasure-seeking tendencies of ordinary men; indeed, with Hegesias the pursuit of pleasure has turned into its opposite, and one is not surprised to learn that this hedonist's lectures were forbidden as stimulating to suicide. It was clear that if philosophic hedonism was to be established on a broad and firm basis, it must somehow combine in its notion of good what the plain man naturally sought with what philosophy could plausibly offer. Such a combination was effected, with some little violence, by Epicurus; whose system, with all its defects, showed a remarkable power of standing the test of time, as it attracted the unqualified adhesion of generation after generation of disciples for a period of some six centuries.

§ 17. Epicurus (341-270 B.C.)

Epicurus maintains, on the one hand, as emphatically as Aristippus, that pleasure is the sole ultimate good, and pain the sole evil; that no pleasure is to be rejected except for its painful consequences, and no pain to be chosen except as a means to greater pleasure; that the stringency of all laws and customs depends solely on the penalties attached to their violation; that, in short, all virtuous conduct and all speculative activity are empty and useless, except as contributing to the pleasantness of the agent's life. And he assures us that he means by pleasure what plain men mean by it; and that if the gratifications of appetite and sense are discarded, the notion is emptied of its significance. So far the system would seem to suit the inclinations of the most thorough-going voluptuary. But its aspect changes when we learn that the highest point of pleasure, whether in body or mind, is to be attained by the mere removal of pain or disturbance, after which pleasure admits of variation only and not of augmentation; that therefore the utmost gratification of which the body is capable may be provided by the simplest means, and that "natural wealth" is no more than any man can earn. This doctrine has a curious affinity to the depreciatory view of sensual pleasure expounded in Plato's *Republic;* but it must be carefully distinguished from it. Plato's point is, that mere removal of the pain of want is mistaken by the sensualist for a pleasure, from the illusion produced through contrast; what Epicurus maintains is that the satisfaction of want restores the tranquil agreeable feeling which accompanies the mere sense of normal life, unruffled by pain or anxiety; and that this "pleasure of stable condition" (καταστηματικὴ ἡδονή) has in the highest degree the quality of positive pleasure. A second and no less decided divergence from vulgar sensualism, and from the Cyrenaic system, is found in the Epicurean doctrine that, though the body is the original source and root of all pleasure, still the pleasures and pains of the mind are actually far more important than those of the body, owing to the accumulation of feeling caused by memory and anticipation. If these two positions be granted, Epicurus is confident of providing for his sage that secure continuity of happiness which obviously cannot be realised by the pursuit of pleasure as ordinarily understood. He could not promise his disciples that bodily pain should never preponderate over bodily pleasure, though he endeavoured to comfort them by the consideration that all organic pains are *either* short in duration *or* slight in intensity; but though for a transient period the flesh may yield an overplus of pain even to the sage, it will always be possible for him to redress the balance by mental pleasures and bring out a net result of present good, if only his mind be kept duly free from the disturbance of idle fears for the future.

To provide this undisturbedness, then, is the important, the indispensable function of philosophy; for men's most serious alarms for the future arise from their dread of death and their dread of the displeasure of the gods; and these sources of dread can only be removed by a true theory of the physical universe and man's position in it; the deliverance that Ethics shows to be needed must be sought from Physics. Epicurus found this deliverance in the atomism of Democritus,[1] which explained the whole constitution of the

[1] The only important modification introduced by Epicurus in the fundamental principles of Democritean physics was to attribute to the falling atoms—which he, like Democritus, assumed as the original elements of things—a spontaneous tendency to deviate infinitesimally from the perpendicular. This supposition seemed necessary to explain the collisions of atoms which resulted in the formation of worlds; it was also used as a physical basis for the doctrine of Free Will in man, which Epicurus thought it ethically important to maintain—in contrast to the Stoic submission to the decrees of destiny. I have already mentioned that Epicurus's ethical position was also partially anticipated by Democritus; his system may be regarded as generated by a combination of Democritean and Cyrenaic elements.

physical universe in a purely mechanical manner, without the intervention of an ordering intelligence. Gods, on this theory, become superfluous from a cosmological point of view; but Epicurus is no atheist; he accepts as well founded the common belief that these blessed and immortal beings exist, and even holds that phantasms of them are from time to time presented to men in dreams and waking visions; but there is, he holds, no reason to be afraid of their wrath and vengeance. "The blessed and incorruptible has no troubles of its own, and causes none to others; it is not subject to either anger or favour."

The dread of something after death being thus removed, there remains the dread of death itself. But this, Epicurus argues, is due to a mere illusion of thought; death appears to us formidable because we confusedly conceive ourselves as meeting it; but in fact no such meeting can occur, because "when we are, death is absent from us; when death is come, we are no more." Thus death is really nothing to us; the sage will dismiss the thought of it, and will live in the fruition of "deathless goods"—the delights of serene unperturbed existence, of which the limitations are *unfelt* just because they are so thoroughly *known*.

Temperance and Fortitude of a sort will manifestly belong to a philosophic life consistently framed on the basis of this wisdom; but it is not so clear that the Epicurean sage will be always just. He will of course not regard Justice as a good in itself; "natural justice," says Epicurus, "is merely a compact of expediency to prevent mutual harm"; still the sage will doubtless enter into this compact to escape harm from his fellow-men; but why should he observe it if he finds secret injustice possible and convenient? Epicurus frankly admits that his only motive will be to avoid the painful anxieties that the perpetual dread of discovery would entail; but he maintains that this motive is adequate, and that Justice is inseparable from a life of true pleasure. A similar sincere but imperfectly successful effort to free his egoistic hedonism from anti-social inferences may be found in his exuberant exaltation of the value of friendship; it is based, he conceives, solely on mutual utility; yet he tells us that the sage will on occasion die for a friend, and his only objection to complete "community of goods among friends" is that the suggestion implies an absence of the perfect mutual trust that belongs to friendship. Such utterances are all the more striking because in other respects the model sage of Epicurus exhibits a coldly prudent detachment from human ties: he will not fall in love, nor become the father of a family, nor—unless under exceptional circumstances—enter into political life. And in fact we find that this paradox of devoted friendship based on pure self-interest was one of the few points in the master's teaching that caused perplexity and division of opinion among Epicureans; who appear, however, to have accepted the doctrine unreservedly, though they offered different explanations of it. We may believe that on this point the example of Epicurus, who was a man of eager and affectionate temperament, and peculiarly unexclusive sympathies,[1] supplied what was lacking in the argumentative cogency of his teaching. The genial fellowship of the philosophic community that he collected in his garden remained a striking feature in the traditions of his school; and certainly the ideal which Stoics and Epicureans equally

[1] It is noted of him that he did not disdain the co-operation either of women or of slaves in his philosophical labours.

cherished, of a brotherhood of sages united in harmonious smooth-flowing existence, was most easily realised on the Epicurean plan of withdrawing from political and dialectical conflict to simple living and serene leisure,—in imitation of the eternal leisure of the gods, apart from the fortuitous concourse of atoms that we call a world.

§ 18. Later Greek Philosophy. The two systems which have just been described were those that most prominently attracted the attention of the ancient world, so far as it was directed to ethics, from their almost simultaneous origin to the end of the 2nd century A.D., when Stoicism almost vanishes from our view. But side by side with them the schools of Plato and Aristotle still maintained a continuity of tradition, and a more or less vigorous life; and philosophy, as a recognised element of Greco-Roman culture, was understood to be divided among these four branches. The internal history, however, of the four schools was very different. We find no development worthy of notice in Aristotelian ethics;—the philosophic energy of Aristotle's disciples seems to have been somewhat weighed down by the inheritance of the master's vast work, and distracted by the example of his many-sided activity. The Epicureans, again, from their unquestioning acceptance of the "dogmas"[1] of their founder, almost deserve to be called a sect rather than a school. On the other hand, the outward coherence of tradition in Plato's school was strained by changes of great magnitude, so that the historians of philosophy reckon not one but several "Academies." We have already had occasion to note the two most important characteristics of the ethical doctrine of the "Old Academy" that immediately succeeded the master—

[1] The last charge of Epicurus to his disciples is said to have been, Τῶν δογμάτων μεμνῆσθαι.

viz. that at least its main body,[1] under Speusippus, denied that pleasure was a constituent of human wellbeing, and that it adopted "conformity to nature" as a fundamental practical maxim. Both these points appear to bring the older Academics into close affinity with Stoicism: indeed the most definite difference between the two doctrines was that what the Stoics only allowed to be "preferred" the Academics admitted as "good." The latter thus attained the old threefold division of good into (1) good of the soul, *i.e.* virtue, (2) good of the body, *i.e.* health and high fitness of organs for their respective functions, and (3) external goods, such as wealth, power, reputation; and they accordingly regarded virtue as the chief but not the sole constituent of wellbeing.[2] A view not very different from this, but allowing more importance to outward circumstances, was held by the Peripatetics; on whom, when the energies of Plato's school were absorbed in Scepticism (about 275–100 B.C.), it chiefly devolved to maintain what may be called the moderate[3] orthodox view of the relation of morality to wellbeing,—in opposition to the

[1] We learn, however, from Aristotle that Eudoxus, who seems to have been at any rate for some time a member of the school, adopted, in opposition to the main body, a purely hedonistic interpretation of Ultimate Good: and the extreme anti-hedonism of Speusippus seems to have been transient in the school, since we are told that Krantor admitted pleasure in his scale of goods, placing it after health and before wealth.

[2] It should be noted that the Academic school seem soon to have substantially admitted that separation of Ethics from Theology which Aristotle advocated against Plato; for if, as we are told (Clem. Alex. II. v. 24), Xenocrates distinguished two kinds of Wisdom (φρόνησις), one of which is practical, while the other, also called σοφία, is speculative and concerned with "first causes and intelligible being," it is merely a verbal adhesion to Plato which prevents his assertion from being altogether Aristotelian.

[3] There were different degrees of this moderation, but in no case was it very moderate, if we may judge from the extent to which Aristotle's

Stoic paradoxes, which insisted on attributing to their sage's condition all desirable qualities without reserve or limitation.

Academic Scepticism and Eclecticism.

It was under the leadership of Arcesilaus (*b.* 315, *d.* 240 B.C.) that the remarkable turn of Plato's school in the direction of philosophical scepticism took place. The Academics were not, it is to be observed, the first sceptics of the post-Aristotelian era; before them Pyrrho of Elis—a contemporary of Zeno and Epicurus—had taught that a settled abstinence from dogmatic affirmation was the best way of attaining that passionless tranquillity of soul which Stoics and Epicureans agreed in extolling. The degree of affinity between Pyrrho and Arcesilaus is difficult exactly to ascertain; since, apart from any influence of Pyrrhonism, we can easily understand how, when the tradition of Plato's personal teaching had faded away, the negative aspect of the Socratic method, so powerfully presented in many of the Platonic dialogues, should give to those who learnt the master's doctrine from books an irresistible impulse towards scepticism. Even in so constructive a dialogue as the *Republic* Plato represents the concrete sensible world in which the philosopher has to act as not, strictly speaking, a subject of knowledge, but of opinion; hence Arcesilaus might well regard himself as following Plato in denying the dogmatic certainty which the Stoics attributed to the "apprehensive impressions" of the senses, and in teaching that "probability" (τὸ εὔλογον) must be men's guide to well-being.[1] Of the particulars of the ethical teaching of

successor Theophrastus was attacked for his weakness in conceding that there was a degree of torture which would prevent a good man from being happy.—Cf. Cic. *Tusc.* V. viii. 24.

[1] I follow Zeller in this view of the moral teaching of Arcesilaus: it is based on a passage of Sextus Empiricus (*Math.* vii. 158). I ought, however, to say that other authorities treat the scepticism of Arcesilaus as nearly indistinguishable from Pyrrho's.

Arcesilaus we know little or nothing; but his more brilliant successor, Carneades (*b.* 213, *d.* 128 B.C.), appears to have applied his scepticism in a morally dangerous manner: we are told that, on the occasion of a famous embassy of philosophers to Rome (155 B.C.)—when he produced quite a *furore* among the Roman youth—after arguing on the side of justice one day he triumphantly refuted his own arguments on the second day. Perhaps it was partly the desire for a greater practical certainty than scepticism could yield which led the Academy back from its sceptical position to a kind of eclecticism, in which something like Stoic doctrine with the most extravagant elements eliminated was taught as identical with the moral teaching of Plato and Aristotle. The completion of this change is represented by Antiochus of Ascalon,[1] whose lectures, as President of the Academy, were attended by Cicero in 91 B.C. A similar disposition to compromise had already been manifested in the Stoic school, especially by Panætius, who presided over the school at Athens for some time in the latter half of the 2nd century B.C.;[2] it had also appeared among the Peripatetics. The broad result of these movements seems to have been a widespread acceptance, among Stoics, Academics, and Peripatetics alike, of a moral doctrine of which the main content was really of Stoic origin; the chief contro-

[1] Philo, the predecessor and master of Antiochus, is said to have occupied an intermediate position between Carneades and the latter, and is accordingly regarded by some as the founder of a Fourth Academy, that of Antiochus being ranked as Fifth. It is to be noted that Antiochus, while rejecting some of the Stoic paradoxes—as that all sins were equally sinful, and that virtue was sufficient for perfect wellbeing—still admitted others that were very startling to common sense. We learn from Cicero that he held with the Stoics that the sage alone can be truly wealthy, beautiful, royal, free.

[2] Probably about 130-110 B.C.

versy between the Stoics and the other two schools turning not on the determination of the particulars of Virtue and Duty, but on the question of the degree in which Virtue was sufficient for Wellbeing.[1] In both cases this tendency to Eclecticism was favoured by the spread of Greek philosophy in cultivated circles at Rome; since the practical Roman mind could not easily be brought to a genuine and earnest acceptance either of scepticism or of the more paradoxical positions of the Stoics.

§ 19. Philosophy in Rome.

In the history of Greco-Roman civilisation the introduction of Hellenic philosophy into Rome—along with other elements of Hellenism—is a change of great moment; but in the development of ethical theory its importance is of a secondary kind, as the Romans never emerged from the state of discipleship to Greek teachers—at least as regards fundamental points of philosophical doctrine. Indeed a certain indisposition in the Roman intellect to philosophy appears in the efforts made at first to exclude the new thought. In 161 B.C. a decree of the Senate forbade "philosophers and rhetoricians" to reside in Rome; and Plutarch (*Cato Major*, chap. xxii.) has described the aversion produced in the mind of the elder Cato by the philosophic embassy six years later—to which I before referred. But the invasion was found irresistible; first Epicureanism gained hearers and followers among Romans open to new ideas; not long after, Stoicism was represented in Rome by Panætius, who remained there for several years and was admitted to the intimacy of Scipio and Lælius;

[1] The orthodox opponents of Stoicism—Academics or Peripatetics—do not seem to have ever disputed the absolute preferability of Virtue to all competing objects of desire, nor even its sufficiency for Wellbeing in some degree; but only its sufficiency for *perfect* Wellbeing.

early in the 1st century we find Philo there, teaching a semi-sceptical phase of Academic doctrine; nor were Peripatetics wanting. One of the greatest works of Roman literature—the poem of Lucretius—gives evidence of the genuine and intense enthusiasm with which Epicureanism was welcomed by a certain class of minds in Rome; it does not, however, seem to have been the hedonistic view of ultimate good which attracted Lucretius, but rather the efficacy of the atomistic explanation of the physical world to give tranquillity of soul by banishing superstitious fears. The Academy, in its sceptical or its eclectic phase,[1] had a still more famous Roman advocate in Cicero; whose work, if we were studying the history of ethical *literature*, would claim a large share of our attention,—since there is probably no ancient treatise which has done more than his *De officiis* to communicate a knowledge of ancient morality to mediæval and modern Europe. But in the development of ethical *doctrine* the importance of Cicero is comparatively small, since he scarcely exhibits any real independence of philosophic thought; indeed his own claim—and he is not usually over-modest—is that he has presented his fellow-countrymen with Greek philosophy in a Roman dress. He declares himself a disciple of the sceptical Academy; but the chief significance of this adhesion—in Ethics at least—seems to have been that he felt relieved from the necessity of making up his mind finally on the controversy between the limited and the unlimited advocacy of the claims of Virtue to constitute or confer happiness.[2] At any rate the chief part of

Cicero (106-43 B.C.)

[1] Cicero declares himself to belong to the Academy regarded as maintaining Scepticism; but his adhesion to the sceptical position seems to have been of a broad and unphilosophical kind: and in ethics, with which we are here concerned, he is certainly rather eclectic than sceptical.

[2] I say "constitute or confer happiness," because it seems to me

the contents of the above-mentioned treatise on (external) duties, is simply taken from the Stoic Panætius, and may be regarded as a specimen of the practical teaching of Stoicism in its eclectic phase. We may note certain leading features of this doctrine, the framework of which is supplied by the old scheme of four cardinal virtues. (1) In defining the sphere of Wisdom something is conceded to the Aristotelian advocacy of the pursuit of knowledge for its own sake, though speculation is still subordinated to action. (2) Along with, but distinct from, the strict Justice that bids men mutually abstain from unprovoked harm, respect property, and fulfil contracts, is placed Beneficence or Liberality, manifested in rendering to all men such services as can be given without sacrifice, and aiding more largely those bound to us by closer ties—fellow-citizens, kinsmen in various degrees, friends, benefactors, and especially the Fatherland, which has the strongest claim of all. (3) Under the head of Fortitude or Greatness of Soul two different qualities are distinguished as praiseworthy,—the philosopher's contempt of external things and events, and the spirit that impels the man of action to difficult and dangerous enterprises. Finally (4), the fourth virtue, Temperance, is conceived as the realisation in a special sphere of "propriety" or "becomingness," which, in a wider sense, is an aspect or accompaniment of all virtue. It is further noteworthy that, in a popular treatment of ethics, Stoicism, as represented by Panætius, did not disdain to discuss the "expediency" (*utile*)—in a vulgar sense—of

clear that Cicero—unlike (at least) the earlier Stoics—understands *εὐδαιμονία* or *beata vita* to be a result produced by virtuous action, not something of which virtuous action is the sole or main element. See *De Finibus*, V. viii. 23.

conduct, as distinct from its moral goodness (*honestum*);[1] and especially to enforce the duties of mutual kindness by an exposition of the resulting worldly advantages to those who fulfil them. It seems even to have allowed that there were cases of apparent conflict between expediency and virtue, deserving of careful consideration: it was held, of course, that virtue was always truly expedient, but it was an open question how far the realisation of virtue involved the sacrifice of the agent's worldly interests to social duty—*e.g.* it was disputed how far a trader in bargaining was bound to disclose circumstances materially affecting the value of his wares.

It is, however, in jurisprudence rather than philosophy that the independent contribution of Rome to the development of human thought is mainly to be found; accordingly, the most interesting manifestation of the Stoic influence on Cicero is given when he comes to treat of morality in its jural aspect. We have already noted, as a prominent feature of Stoicism, the conception of a law binding upon a man as a rational being and a member of the great cosmic commonwealth of all rational beings,—a law divine and eternal, and so superior in dignity and validity to the laws of particular political societies. In giving prominence to this conception, Stoicism furnished the transition from the old Greek view of ethics, in which the notions of Good and Virtue were taken as fundamental, to the modern view in which ethics is conceived as primarily a study of the "moral code"; and in this transition the part taken by Cicero is of great historical importance. For this idea of an immutable law emanating

[1] In this rendering of καλόν the old generic meaning of "beautiful" is dropped and the more distinctly ethical signification "noble" or "honourable" alone expressed.

from God, Reason, or Nature, was apprehended by Cicero with more real assimilation than most of the philosophical notions which he endeavoured to transfer from Greek to Roman thought; the most ethically impressive passages in his writings are those in which he speaks of this law,—conceived sometimes objectively as a code, valid for all at all times and places, superior in authority to any positive legislation that may conflict with it; sometimes subjectively as Supreme Reason, implanted in the mind of each man at birth, and, when duly developed, commanding him unmistakably what he is to do or forbear. Through Cicero primarily, aided by later writers more avowedly Stoical, this conception of Natural Law obtained currency among Roman jurists; and, blending with the already established notion of a law common to all nations, which the Roman genius for law-making had gradually developed to meet the actually felt needs of commercial intercourse with foreigners, it became the recognised source of what jurists call the "Equity" of Rome. Then, many centuries afterwards, when the study of Roman jurisprudence had revived in the later period of the Middle Ages, this conception received a fresh importance, and became, as we shall see, the leading or cardinal conception of modern ethical speculation in its first stage.

§ 20. Roman Stoicism.

Stocism then, among all the products of Greek speculation, was that with which the moral consciousness of Rome had most real affinity; and accordingly it is in this school that we seem to trace most distinctly a reaction of the Roman mind on the doctrine it received from Greece;[1] the

[1] I ought not here to overlook the one avowedly independent school of ethical thought which presents itself in Rome as of native origin—the school of the Sextii; the founder of which, Quintus Sextius, was born about 70 B.C. It does not, however, appear to have had sufficient philosophic independence or importance to deserve more than a passing

effect of which, however, is difficult to distinguish precisely from the natural inner development of the Stoic system. It was natural that the earlier Stoics should be chiefly occupied with delineating the inner and outer characteristics of ideal wisdom and virtue, and that the gap between the ideal sage and the actual philosopher, though never ignored, should yet be somewhat overlooked. But when the question "What is man's good?" had been answered by an elaborate exposition of perfect wisdom, the other question, "How may a man emerge from the misery and folly of the world, and get on the way towards wisdom?" would naturally attract attention; while the preponderance of moral over scientific interest, which was characteristic of the Roman mind, would also tend to give this question the prominence that it has in those writings of the Imperial period which afford us the most direct means of studying Stoic doctrine. In Seneca, for instance, this aspect of later Stoicism is strongly marked; he does not claim to be a sage, but only in progress towards Wisdom: and though the way to virtue is easy to find, the life of one who treads it is a continual struggle with lusts and faults, a campaign in which there is no repose; in preparation for which a man needs such ascetic practice as is given by days of meagre diet and rough raiment deliberately chosen. Similarly Epictetus lays stress on the impossibility of finding the Stoic sage in actual experience: rare, indeed, are those who like himself are even in earnest progress towards Wisdom, who duly take to heart the momentous words "Endure" and "Refrain." Thus philosophy, in the

Seneca (*d.* 65 A.D.)

Epictetus

glance in so summary a survey as the present. It seems to have been, in the main, a variation on Stoicism, with a certain infusion of Pythagorean elements; but to have manifested its Roman origin in a fresh vigour of moral zeal and a contempt for dialectical hairsplitting.

view of Seneca and Epictetus, comes to present itself as the healer whom men seek from a sense of their weakness and disease,—whose business is "with the sick, not with the whole"; the wisdom by which she heals is a quality that needs not long dissertations or dialectical subtleties, but rather continual practice, self-discipline, self-examination. The same sense of the gap between theory and fact gives to the religious side of Stoicism a new force and meaning in these later utterances of the school: the soul, conscious of its weakness, leans more on the thought of its kinship with God, whose prophet and messenger the Stoic feels himself to be; and in his ideal attitude towards external events self-poised indifference is now less prominent than pious resignation. The old self-reliance of the reason, looking down on man's natural life as a mere field for its exercise, seems to have shrunk and dwindled, making room for a positive aversion to the flesh as an alien element imprisoning and hampering the spirit; the body has come to be a "corpse which the soul sustains,"[1] and life a "sojourn in a strange land"[2] or a voyage on a stormy sea, where the only haven is death.[3]

Marcus Aurelius (120-180 A.D.)

The intensified religiousness of later Stoicism takes on a peculiar warmth of emotion in the meditations of the Stoic emperor, Marcus Aurelius Antoninus. "Everything," he exclaims, in one of the most touching expressions of the characteristic sentiment of his school which has been handed down to us—"Everything is harmonious to me that is harmonious to thee, O Universe; nothing is too early or too late for me that is in due time for thee. Everything is fruit to me that thy seasons bring, O Nature: from thee are all things, in thee are all things, to

[1] Epictetus. [2] Marcus Aurelius. [3] Seneca.

thee all things return. 'Beloved City of Cecrops,' says the poet: shall I not say, 'O beloved City of God'?" To remember man's kinship with deity, and cherish the bond which unites the "god or dæmon" that properly rules in each human breast with the universal soul of which it is a portion, to live with the gods, to do nothing except what God will approve and take cheerfully whatever He may give, to call on the gods on all occasions, to pass from one social act to another thinking of God,—such precepts as these perpetually recur in his self-exhortations. "Reverence the gods and help men" is his summary formula for good life; and its two parts are inseparable, for injustice—refusal of the aid that nature fashioned us to give to other rational animals—is itself impiety. And his philanthropy has a strain of tenderness and sympathy with weakness that does not belong to the somewhat severe and abstract cosmopolitanism of the earlier Stoics; his aim is not merely to perform his duty as a member of the cosmic system of rational and social beings, but to "love men from the heart," to "love even those who do wrong," reflecting that they are kinsmen who err through ignorance.

At the same time, other passages in these unaffected and impressive utterances bring home to us forcibly the difficulty of combining (1) philosophic reverence for the world as a whole, as the perfect product of supreme reason, and for man as the crown of this divine creation, with (2) philosophic indifference to all the objects of worldly aims and desires, and the consequent inevitable sense of alienation from most of the actual human beings with whom the philosopher is brought into contact. On the one hand Marcus Aurelius bids himself contemplate the wise order in which all things are bound together by holy bonds, the inferior things made for the sake of the superior and the superior fitted to one another; but equally he bids himself reflect how contemptible and perishable all sensible things are, how the whole course of mundane events is a stream of familiar, ephemeral, and worthless change, "quarrels and sports of children, labourings of ants and runnings about of puppets pulled by strings,"—or a furious torrent in the midst of which the wise man has to stand like a "promontory against which the waves continually break,"—or, worse still, sordid and disgusting, "such as bathing appears, oil, sweat, dirt, filthy water, so is every part of life and everything." He tells himself that death is to be respected and prepared for as an operation of nature; but what most truly reconciles him to death is the consideration of the things and the characters from which death will remove him. Nor can this gap between the actual and the ideal be filled by the thought of a better and brighter world to which he is to be removed. For, though the Stoic school traditionally maintained the prolongation of the individual life after death—until the great conflagration that was destined to close each mundane period and transmute all things again to the original fiery and divine substance from which they were derived—they were not accustomed to lay any stress on this belief in their ethical teaching; and, in this age of Stoicism at least, the belief seems to have been very dubiously held, where it was not altogether dropped.[1] Marcus Aurelius seems usually to leave it an open question whether death is mere change or extinction, transition to another life or to a state without

[1] It is a matter of difficulty to trace the variations and changes in Stoic doctrine on the question of the life after death. Of the older teachers we are told that according to Cleanthes all souls survived bodily death—according to Chrysippus only the souls of the wise; and it is noted as a peculiarity of Panætius that he denied the survival alto-

sensation; sometimes, however, he tends decidedly to the negative view. "In a little while," he tells himself, "thou wilt be nobody and nowhere, like Hadrianus and Augustus." He even wonders, in a striking passage, "how it can be that the gods, having ordered all things rightly and benevolently towards man," have yet allowed most virtuous men, who have communed most with the divinity, to be utterly extinguished after death; and can only console himself with the reflection, "were it just that they should survive, it would also be possible; were it according to nature, nature would have had it so." This last sentence gives the characteristic note of Stoicism: to take the world as it is and resolutely find it now perfect, not to postulate a better future in which present imperfections will be removed. Indeed we may say that the fundamental ethical doctrine of Stoicism rests on the inversion of a leading argument of modern moral theology. "It is not possible," says Aurelius, "that the nature of the universe has made so great a mistake, either through want of power or want of skill, as that good and evil should happen indiscriminately to the good and the bad";—so far the Stoic and the Christian philosopher agree; but while the Christian inference is that a future life must be assumed in which what is inequitable in the present indiscriminate distribution of good and evil will be repaired, the Stoic inference is that the things now so indiscriminately distributed—"death and life, honour and dishonour, pain and pleasure"—are neither good nor evil.

There was, however, one among the four leading post-

gether. Epictetus had clearly discarded the belief; on the other hand, Seneca in some passages expatiates on the bliss of the soul released from its bodily prison, in a manner almost Platonic: in other passages, however, he seems to balance between extinction and change much as Aurelius does.

§ 21. Later Platonism and Neo-Platonism.

Aristotelian schools—the Platonic—in whose founder's teaching the doctrine of the immortality of the individual soul had occupied a prominent place;[1] and it was to be expected that the ascetic tendencies which we have noticed in Stoicism—the alienation from the actual world of trivial and sordid corporeal change—would manifest themselves still more impressively in the later history of this school; where, indeed, they appear as the natural development of one element of the master's teaching. Thus it is not surprising that when we come to Plutarch we find that the old Academic conception of a moral harmony between the higher and lower elements of human life is no longer the recognised Platonic doctrine; the side of Plato's teaching that deals with the inevitable imperfections of the world of concrete experience has again become prominent. For example, we find Plutarch adopting and amplifying the suggestion in Plato's *Laws* that this imperfection is due to a bad world-soul that strives against the good,—a suggestion which appears to have lain unnoticed during most of the intervening period. We observe, again, the value that Plutarch attaches, not merely to the sustainment and consolation of rational religion, but to the supernatural communications vouchsafed by the divinity to certain human beings in certain states,—as in dreams, through oracles, or by special warnings, like those of the genius of Socrates. For these flashes of intuition, he holds, the soul should be prepared by tranquil repose, and the subjugation of sensuality through abstinence. The same estrangement between mind

Plutarch (*circ.* 48-120 A.D.)

[1] I am not myself prepared to maintain that Plato really held this doctrine at the latest stage of his system; but I believe that ancient readers of his dialogues attributed it to him without qualification or reserve—chiefly on the strength of the argument in the *Phædo*, in which it is certainly maintained.

and matter, the same ascetic effort to attain by aloofness from the body a pure receptivity for divine or semi-divine influences, is exhibited in the revived Pythagoreanism of the 1st and 2nd centuries A.D.; indeed the view of Plutarch and others whom he represents is due to a combination of these Neo-Pythagorean influences with Platonic doctrine. But the general tendency that we are noting did not find its full expression in a reasoned philosophical system until we come to the latest-born of the great thinkers of antiquity—the Egyptian Plotinus.

Plotinus (205-270 A.D.)

The system of Plotinus is a striking development of that element of Platonism which has had most fascination for the mediæval and even for the modern mind, but which had almost vanished out of sight in the controversies of the post-Aristotelian schools. At the same time the differences between the original Platonism and this Neo-Platonism are all the more noteworthy from the reverent adhesion to the former which the latter always maintains. Plato, we saw, identified good with the real essence of things; and this, again, with that in them which is definitely conceivable and knowable. It belongs to this view to regard the imperfection or badness of things as somewhat devoid of real being, and so incapable of being definitely thought or known; accordingly, we find that Plato has no technical term for that in the concrete sensible world which hinders it from perfectly expressing the abstract ideal world, and which in Aristotle's system is distinguished as absolutely formless matter (ὕλη). And so, when we pass from the ontology to the ethics of Platonism, we find that, though the highest life is only to be realised by turning away from concrete human affairs and their material environment, still the sensible world is not yet an object of positive moral aversion; it is rather something which the philosopher is seriously concerned to make as harmonious, good, and beautiful as possible. But in Neo-Platonism the inferiority of the condition in which the embodied human soul finds itself is more intensely and painfully felt; hence an express recognition of formless matter (ὕλη) as the "first evil," from which is derived the "second evil," body (σῶμα), to whose influence all the evil in the soul's existence is due. Accordingly the ethics of Plotinus represent, we may say, the moral idealism of the Stoics cut loose from nature. The only good of man is the pure intellectual existence of the soul, which in itself, apart from the contagion of the body, would be perfectly free from error or defect; if it can only be restored to the untrammelled activity of its original being, nothing external, nothing bodily, can positively impair its perfect welfare. It is only the lowest form of virtue—the "civic" virtue delineated in Plato's *Republic*—that is employed in limiting and regulating those animal impulses whose presence in the soul is due to its mixture with the body; higher or philosophic wisdom, temperance, courage, and justice are essentially purifications from this contagion; until, finally, the highest mode of goodness is reached, in which the soul has no community with the body, and is entirely turned towards reason, and restored to the likeness of God. It should be observed that Plotinus himself is still too Platonic to hold that the absolute mortification of natural bodily appetites is required for purifying the soul; but this ascetic inference was drawn to the fullest extent by his disciple Porphyry.

There is, however, a yet higher point to be reached in the upward ascent of the Neo-Platonist from matter; and here the divergence of Plotinus from Platonic idealism is none the less striking, because it is a *bonâ fide* result of reverent reflection on Plato's teaching. The cardinal assumption of Plato's metaphysic is, that the real is definitely thinkable and knowable in proportion as it is real; so that the further the mind advances in abstraction from sensible particulars and apprehension of real being, the more definite and clear its thought becomes. Plotinus, however, urges that, as all thought involves difference or duality of some kind, it cannot be the primary fact in the universe, what we call God. He must be an essential unity prior to this duality, a Being wholly without difference or determination; and, accordingly, the highest mode of human existence, in which the soul apprehends this absolute, must be one in which all definite thought is transcended, and all consciousness of self lost in the absorbing ecstasy. Porphyry tells us that his master Plotinus attained this highest state four times during the six years which he spent with him.

Neo-Platonism is originally Alexandrine, and more than a century of its existence has elapsed before we find it flourishing on the old Athenian soil. Hence it is often regarded as Hellenistic rather than Hellenic, a product of the mingling of Greek with Oriental civilisation. But, however Oriental may have been the cast of mind that eagerly embraced the theosophic and ascetic views that have just been described, the forms of thought by which these views were philosophically reached are essentially Greek; and it is by a thoroughly intelligible process of natural development, in which the intensification of the moral consciousness represented by Stoicism plays an important part, that the Hellenic pursuit of knowledge culminates in a preparation for ecstasy, and the Hellenic idealisation of man's natural life ends in a settled antipathy to the body and its works. At the same time we ought not to overlook the affinities between the doctrine of Plotinus and that remarkable combination of Greek and Hebrew thought which Philo-Judæus had expounded two centuries before; nor the fact that Neo-Platonism was developed in conscious antagonism to the new religion which had spread from Judea, and which when Plotinus wrote was already threatening the conquest of the Greco-Roman world; nor, finally, that it furnished the chief theoretical support in the last desperate struggle that was made under Julian to retain the old polytheistic worship. To the new world of thought, that after the failure of this struggle was definitely established upon the ruins of the old, we have now to turn.

CHAPTER III

CHRISTIANITY AND MEDIÆVAL ETHICS

§ 1. The characteristics of Christian morality to be distinguished.

IN the present work we are not concerned with the origin of the Christian religion, nor with its outward history; the causes of its resistless development during the first three centuries; its final triumph over Greco-Roman paganism; its failure to check the decay of the Hellenistic civilisation that centred in Constantinople, or to withstand in the east and south the force of the new religious movement that burst from Arabia in the 7th century; its success in dominating the social chaos to which the barbarian invasions reduced the Western empire; the important part it took in producing out of this chaos the new civilised order to which we belong; the complex and varying relations in which it has since stood to the political organisations, the social life, the progressive science, the literary and artistic culture of our modern world. Nor have we to consider the special doctrines that have formed the bond of union of the Christian communities in any other than their ethical aspect, their bearing on the systematisation of human aims and activities. This aspect, however, must necessarily be prominent in discussing Christianity, which cannot be adequately treated if considered merely as a system of theological beliefs divinely revealed, and special observances divinely sanctioned; as it essentially claims to rule the whole man, and leave no part of his life out of the range of its regulating and transforming influences. It was not till the 4th century A.D. that the first attempt was made to offer anything like a systematic exposition of Christian morality; and nine centuries more had passed away before a genuinely philosophic intellect, trained by a full study of the greatest Greek thinker, undertook to give complete scientific form to the ethical doctrine of the Catholic Church. Before, however, we take a brief survey of the development of ethical thought that culminated in Thomas Aquinas, it may be well to examine the chief features of the new moral consciousness that had spread through Greco-Roman civilisation, and was awaiting philosophic synthesis. In making this examination it will be convenient to consider first the new *form* or universal characteristics of Christian morality, and afterwards to note the chief points in the *matter* or particulars of duty and virtue which received an important development or emphasis from the new religion.

§ 2. Christian and Jewish "law of God"

The first point to be noticed as novel is the conception of morality as the positive law of a theocratic community, possessing a written code imposed by divine revelation, and sanctioned by express divine promises and threatenings It is true that we find in ancient thought, from Socrates downwards, the notion of a law of God, eternal and immutable, partly expressed and partly obscured by the various and shifting codes and customs of actual human societies. But the sanctions of this law were vaguely and, for the most part, feebly imagined; its principles were essentially unwritten and unpromulgated, and thus not referred to the external will of an Almighty Being who claimed unquestioning submission, but rather to the reason that gods and men shared, by the exercise of which alone this eternal law could be adequately known and defined. Hence, even if the notion of law had been more prominent than it was in ancient ethical thought, it could never have led to a juridical, as distinct from a philosophical, treatment of morality. In Christianity, on the other hand, we early find that the method of moralists determining right conduct is to a great extent analogous to that of jurists interpreting a code. It is assumed that divine commands have been implicitly given for all occasions of life, and that they are to be ascertained in particular cases by application of the general rules obtained from texts of Scripture, and by analogical inference from scriptural examples. This juridical method descended naturally from the Jewish theocracy, which was universalised in Christendom. Moral insight, in the view of the most thoughtful Jews of the age immediately preceding Christianity, was conceived as knowledge of a divine code, emanating from an authority external to human reason, which latter had only the function of interpreting its rules and applying them to difficult cases. The normal motives to obey this law were trust in the promises and fear of the judgments of the Divine Lawgiver, who had made a special covenant to protect the Jewish people, on condition that they rendered Him due obedience; and the sources from which knowledge of the law was actually gained had the complexity often exhibited by the jurisprudence of an advanced community. The original nucleus of the code, it was believed, had been written and promulgated by Moses, other precepts had been revealed in the fervid utterances of the later prophets, others had been handed down through oral tradition from immemorial antiquity; and the body of prescriptions and prohibitions thus composed had, before Judaism gave birth to Christianity, received an extensive development through the commentaries and supplementary maxims of several generations of students. Christianity inherited the notion of a written divine code acknowledged as such by the "true Israel"—now potentially including the whole of mankind, or at least the chosen of all nations,—on the sincere acceptance of which the Christian's share of the divine promises to Israel depended. And though the ceremonial part of the old Hebrew code was altogether rejected, and with it all the supplementary jurisprudence resting on tradition and erudite commentary, still God's law was believed to be contained in the sacred books of the Jews, supplemented by the records of Christ's teaching and the writings of His apostles. By the recognition of this law the Church was constituted as an ordered community, essentially distinct from the State; the distinction between the two being sharpened and hardened by the withdrawal of the early Christians from civic life, to avoid the performance of idolatrous ceremonies imposed as official expressions of loyalty; and by the persecutions which they had to endure, when the spread of an association apparently so hostile to the framework of ancient society had at length caused serious alarm to the imperial government. Nor was the distinction obliterated by the recognition of Christianity as the state religion under Constantine. The law of God and its interpreters still remained quite separate from the secular law and jurists of the Roman empire; though the former was of course binding on all mankind, the Church was none the less a community of persons who regarded themselves as both specially pledged and specially enabled to obey it,—a community, too, that could not be entered except by a solemn ceremony typifying a spiritual new birth.

Thus the fundamental difference between morality and (human) legality only came out more clearly in consequence of the jural form in which the former was conceived. The ultimate sanctions of the moral code were the infinite rewards and punishments awaiting the immortal soul hereafter; but the Decian persecutions, while they manifested in the unalterable constancy of martyrs and confessors the strength of the spreading faith, also pressed forcibly on the Church the problem of dealing with apostate members; and it was felt to be necessary to withdraw the privileges of membership from such persons, and only allow them to be regained by a protracted process of prayer, fasting, and ceremonies expressive of contrite humiliation, in which the sincerity of the repentant apostates might be tested and manifested. This formal and regulated "penitence" was extended from apostacy to other grave—or, as they subsequently came to be called, "deadly"—sins; while for slighter offences the members of the Church generally were called upon to express contrition by abstinence from pleasures ordinarily permitted, as well as verbally in public and private devotions. "Excommunication" and "penance" thus came to be temporal ecclesiastical sanctions of the moral law; as the graduation of these sanctions naturally became more careful and minute, a correspondingly detailed classification of offences was rendered necessary; the regulations for observing the ordinary fasts and festivals of the Church grew similarly elaborate; and thus a system of ecclesiastical jurisprudence, prohibitive and ceremonial, was gradually produced, somewhat analogous to that of the rejected Judaism. At the same time this tendency to develop and make prominent a scheme of external duties has always been balanced and counteracted in Christianity by the ineffaceable remembrance of the founder's opposition to Jewish legalism. Indeed the influence of this opposition, as fantastically understood and exaggerated by some of the Gnostic sects of the 2nd and 3rd centuries A.D., led to a dangerous depreciation of rules of external duty;—sometimes even (if the charges of orthodox opponents are not entirely to be discredited) to gross immorality of conduct: and a similar tendency has shown itself at other periods of Church history. And though such "antinomianism" has always been sternly repudiated by the moral consciousness of Christendom in general, it has never been forgotten that "inwardness," rightness of heart or spirit, is the special and pre-eminent characteristic of Christian goodness. It must not, indeed, be supposed that the need of something more than mere fulfilment of external duty was ignored even by the later Judaism. Rabbinic erudition could not forget the repression of vicious desires in the tenth commandment, the stress laid in Deuteronomy on the necessity of heartfelt and loving service to God, or the inculcations by later prophets of humility and faith. "The real and only Pharisee," says the Talmud, "is he who does the will of his Father because he loves Him." But it remains true that the contrast with the "righteousness of the scribes and Pharisees" has always served to mark the requirement of "inwardness" as a distinctive feature of the Christian code,—an inwardness not merely negative, tending to the repression of vicious desires as well as vicious acts, but also involving a positive rectitude of the inner state of the soul.

§ 3. Christian and Pagan inwardness.

In this aspect Christianity invites comparison with Stoicism, and indeed with pagan ethical philosophy generally, if we except the hedonistic schools. Rightness of purpose, preference of virtue for its own sake, suppression of vicious desires, were made essential points by the Aristotelians, who attached the most importance to outward circumstances in their view of virtue, no less than by the Stoics, to whom all external things were indifferent. The fundamental differences between pagan and Christian ethics do not depend on any difference in the value set on rightness of heart or purpose, but on different views of the essential form or conditions of this inward rightness. In neither case is it presented purely and simply as moral rectitude. By the pagan philosophers it was always conceived under the form of Knowledge or Wisdom,—it being inconceivable to all the schools sprung from Socrates that a man could truly know his own good and yet deliberately choose anything else. This knowledge, as Aristotle held, might be permanently precluded by vicious habits, or temporarily obliterated by passion, but if present in the mind it must produce rightness of purpose. Or even if it were held with some of the Stoics that true wisdom was out of the reach of the best men actually living, it none the less remained the ideal condition of perfect human life; though all actual men were astray in folly and misery, knowledge was none the less the goal towards which the philosopher progressed, the realisation of his true nature. By Christian evangelists and teachers, on the other hand, the inner springs of good conduct were generally conceived as Faith and Love. Of these notions the former has a **Faith.** somewhat complex ethical import; it seems to blend several elements differently prominent in different minds. Its simplest and commonest meaning is that emphasised in the contrast of "faith" with "sight," where it signifies belief in the invisible divine order represented by the Church, in the actuality of the law, the threats, the promises of God, in spite of all the influences in man's natural life that tend to obscure this belief. Out of this contrast there ultimately grew an essentially different opposition between faith and knowledge or reason, according to which the theological basis of ethics was contrasted with the philosophical; the theologians maintaining sometimes that the divine law is essentially arbitrary, the expression of will, not of reason; more frequently that its reasonableness is inscrutable, and that actual human reason should confine itself to examining the credentials of God's messengers, and not the message itself. But in early Christianity this latter antithesis is as yet undeveloped; faith means simply force in clinging to moral and religious conviction, whatever their precise rational grounds may be; this force, in the Christian consciousness, being inseparably bound up with personal loyalty and trust towards Christ, the leader in the battle with evil that is being fought, the ruler of the kingdom to be realised. So far, however, there is no ethical difference between Christian faith and that of Judaism, or its later imitation, Mahometanism; except that the personal affection of loyal trust is peculiarly stirred by the blending of human and divine natures in Christ, and the rule of duty impressively taught by the manifestation of His perfect life. A more distinctively Christian, and a more deeply moral, significance is given to the notion in the antithesis of "faith" and "works." Here faith means more than loyal acceptance of the divine law and reverent trust in the lawgiver; it implies a consciousness, at once continually present and continually transcended, of the radical imperfection of all merely human obedience to the law, and at the same time of the irremissible condemnation which this imperfection entails. The Stoic doctrine of the worthlessness of ordinary human virtue, and the stern paradox that offenders are equally, in so far as all are absolutely, guilty, find their counterparts in Christianity; but the latter, while maintaining this ideal severity in the moral standard, with an emotional consciousness of what is involved in it quite unlike that of the Stoic, at the same time overcomes its practical exclusiveness through faith. This "saving" faith, again, may be conceived in two modes, essentially distinct though usually combined. In one view it gives the believer strength to attain, by God's supernatural aid or "grace," a goodness of which he is naturally incapable; in another view it gives him an assurance that, though he knows himself a sinner deserving of utter condemnation, a perfectly just God still regards him with favour on account of the perfect services and suffering of Christ. Of these views the former is the more catholic, more universally present in the Christian consciousness at all periods of its history; the latter claims to penetrate more deeply the mystery of Christ's atonement, as expounded in the Pauline epistles.

Love.

But faith, however understood, is rather an indispensable pre-requisite than the essential motive principle of Christian good conduct. This is supplied by the other central notion, love. On love depends the "fulfilling of the law," and the whole moral value of Christian duty,—that is, on love of God, in the first place, which in its fullest development must spring from Christian faith; and, secondly, love of all men, as the objects of divine love and sharers in the humanity ennobled by the incarnation. This derivative philanthropy, whether conceived as mingling with and intensifying natural human affection, or as absorbing and transforming it, characterises the spirit in which all Christian performance of social duty is to be done;

loving devotion to God being the fundamental attitude of mind that is to be maintained throughout the whole of the Christian's life. But further, as regards abstinence from unlawful acts and desires prompting to them, we have to notice another form in which the inwardness of Christian morality manifests itself, which, though less distinctive, should yet receive attention in any comparison of Christian ethics with the view of Greco-Roman philosophy. The profound horror with which the Christian's conception of a suffering as well as an avenging divinity tended to make him regard all condemnable acts was tinged with a sentiment which we may perhaps describe as a ceremonial aversion moralised,—the aversion, that is, to foulness or impurity. In Judaism, as in other—especially Oriental—religions, the dislike of material defilement was elevated into a religious sentiment, and made to support a complicated system of quasi-sanitary abstinences and ceremonial purifications; then, as the ethical element predominated in the Jewish religion, a moral symbolism was felt to reside in the ceremonial code, and thus aversion to impurity came to be a common form of the ethico-religious sentiment. Then, when Christianity threw off the Mosaic ritual, this religious sense of purity was left with no other sphere besides morality; while, from its highly idealised character, it was peculiarly well adapted for that repression of vicious desires which Christianity claimed as its special function.[1]

Purity.

§ 4. Distinctive particulars of Christian Morality.

When we examine the details of Christian morality, we find that most of its distinctive features are naturally connected with the more general characteristics just stated; though many of them may also be referred directly to the

[1] I here understand "purity of heart" in its wider sense:—as opposed to vice in general, not merely to sexual vice.

example and precepts of Christ, and in several cases they are clearly due to both causes inseparably combined. We may notice, in the first place, that the conception of morality as a code which, if not in itself arbitrary, is yet to be accepted by men with unquestioning submission, tends naturally to bring into prominence the virtue of obedience to authority; just as the philosophic view of goodness as the realisation of reason gives a special value to self-determination and independence—at least in the philosopher—(as we see more clearly in the post-Aristotelian schools where ethics is distinctly separated from politics). Again, the opposition between the natural world and the spiritual order into which the Christian had been born anew led—in the early and mediæval Church—not merely to a contempt equal to that of the Stoic for wealth, fame, power, and other objects of worldly pursuit, but also to a comparative depreciation of the domestic and civic relations of the natural man. This tendency was exhibited most simply and generally in the earliest period of the Church's history. In the view of primitive Christians, ordinary human society was a world temporarily surrendered to Satanic rule, over which a swift and sudden destruction was impending; in such a world the little band who were gathered in the ark of the Church could have no part or lot; the only attitude they could maintain towards it was that of passive alienation. On the other hand, it was difficult practically to realise disengagement of the spirit from worldly life with the completeness which the highest Christian consciousness required; and a keen sense of this difficulty induced the same hostility to the body as a clog and hindrance, that we find to some extent in Plato, but more fully developed in Neo-Platonism, Neo-Pythagoreanism, and other products of the mingling of

Obedience.

Alienation from the World

and the Flesh.

Greek with Oriental thought. This feeling is exhibited in the value set on fasting[1] in the Christian Church from the earliest times, and afterwards in an extreme form in the self-torments of monasticism; while both tendencies, anti-worldliness and anti-sensualism, seem to have combined in causing the preference of celibacy to marriage which is common to most early Christian writers.[2] In consequence of this opposition between the Church and the World, patriotism and the sense of civic duty, the most elevated and splendid of all social sentiments in the pre-Christian civilisation of the Greco-Roman world, tended, under the influence of Christianity, either to expand into universal philanthropy, or to be concentrated on the ecclesiastical community. "We recognise one commonwealth, the world," says Tertullian; "we know," says Origen, "that we have a fatherland founded by the word of God." We might further derive from the general spirit of Christian unworldliness that repudiation of the secular modes of conflict, even in a righteous cause, which substituted a passive patience and endurance for the old pagan virtue of courage, in which the active element was prominent. Here, however, we clearly trace the influence of Christ's express prohibition of violent resistance to violence, and his inculcation, by example and precept, of a love that was to conquer even natural resentment. An extreme result of this influence is shown in Tertullian's view, that no Christian could properly hold the office of a secular magistrate in which he would have to doom to death, chains, imprisonment; in the declaration of Lactan-

Patience.

[1] Fasting, in some form or other, is a very widespread religious observance; but it is still noteworthy that it was retained—and gradually made regular and elaborate—by Christianity, while Christianity was yet keenly conscious of its independence of Jewish legalism.

[2] *E.g.*, Justin Martyr, Origen, Tertullian, Cyprian.

tius, that a Christian must not accuse any one of a capital crime, since slaying by word is as bad as slaying by deed; in the doctrine of even so sober a writer as Ambrose, that Christian long-suffering precludes the shedding of blood even in self-defence against a murderous assault. The common sense of Christendom gradually shook off these extravagances; though the reluctance to shed blood lingered long, and was hardly extinguished even by the growing horror of heresy.[1] Similarly, the reluctance of primitive Christians to take oaths even for judicial purposes, though supported by the most obvious interpretation of their Master's words, gave way to considerations of public need, when the Church in the 4th century entered into formal union with the secular organisation of society.

Beneficence.

It is, however, in the impulse given to practical beneficence in all its forms, by the exaltation of love as the root of all virtues, that the most important influence of Christianity on the particulars of civilised morality is to be found; although the exact amount of this influence is here somewhat difficult to ascertain, since it merely carries further a development distinctly traceable in the history of pagan morality considered by itself. This development clearly appears when we compare the different post-Socratic systems of ethics. In Plato's exposition of the different virtues there is no mention whatever of benevolence, although his writings show a keen sense of the importance of friendship as an element of philosophic life, especially of the intense personal affection naturally arising between master and disciple. Aristotle goes somewhat further in

[1] We have a curious relic of this in the later times of ecclesiastical persecution, when the heretic was doomed to the stake that he might be punished without bloodshed.

recognising the moral value of friendship (φιλία); and though he considers that in its highest form it can only be realised by the fellowship of the wise and good, he yet extends the notion so as to include the domestic affections, and takes notice of the importance of mutual kindness in binding together all human societies. Still in his formal statement of particular virtues, positive beneficence is only discernible under the notion of "liberality"; in which form its excellence is hardly distinguished from that of graceful profusion in self-regarding expenditure. Cicero, on the other hand, in his treatise on external duties (*officia*), ranks the rendering of positive services to other men as an important department of social duty; while in later Stoicism the recognition of the universal fellowship and natural mutual claims of human beings as such is sometimes expressed with so much warmth of feeling as to be hardly distinguishable from Christian philanthropy. Nor was this regard for humanity merely a doctrine of the school. Partly through the influence of Stoic and other Greek philosophy, partly from the general expansion of human sympathies, the legislation of the Roman empire, during the first three centuries, shows a steady development in the direction of natural justice and humanity; and some similar progress may be traced in the tone of common moral opinion. Still the utmost point that this development reached fell considerably short of the standard of Christian charity. Without dwelling on the immense impetus given to the practice of social duty generally by the religion that made beneficence a form of divine service, and identified "piety" with "pity," we have to put down as definite changes introduced by Christianity into the current moral view—(1) the severe condemnation and final suppression of the practice of exposing infants; (2)

effective abhorrence of the barbarism of gladiatorial combats; (3) immediate moral mitigation of slavery, and a strong encouragement of emancipation; (4) great extension of the eleemosynary provision made for the sick and the poor.

Christianity and Wealth.

On this fourth point, however, it has to be observed that the free communication of wealth to the needy was not merely a manifestation of the brotherly love enjoined on all Christians—though its importance in this aspect has caused it to usurp, in several modern European languages, the general name of "charity"—it was partly due to a special apprehension of the spiritual dangers attaching to the possession of wealth, signalised by Christ's emphatic utterances. From both these causes the communism attempted in the apostolic age was cherished in the traditions of the early and mediæval Church as the ideal form of Christian society; and though the common sense of Christendom resisted the suggestions that were from time to time made for its practical revival, it was widely recognised that the mere ownership of wealth as such gave a Christian no moral right to its enjoyment. This right could only be given by real need; and though, when the Church had reconciled itself with the World, "need" for ordinary Christians was generally allowed to be determined by the customs of the social class or profession to which they belonged, a stricter obedience to the evangelical counsel, "sell all thou hast and give to the poor," was no less generally approved.[1] It

[1] The attitude of primitive, and even, to some extent, of mediæval Christianity towards private property and towards slavery, is, I think, best understood by trying to look at the two institutions as much as possible in the same light. Both were regarded as encroachments on the original rights of all members of the human family—since men were naturally free, and the fruits of the earth naturally common; both would disappear in the future, when Christ's kingdom came to be realised;

should be noted, too, that in laying stress on almsgiving Christianity merely universalised a duty which has always been inculcated and maintained in conspicuous fulness by Judaism, within the limits of the chosen people. The same may be said of the prohibition of usury, which the Church maintained with certain reserves and accommodations down to quite modern times.

Purity (in special sense).

So again, the strictness with which Christianity prohibited illicit intercourse of the sexes was inherited from Judaism. The younger religion, however, went further in maintaining the permanence of the marriage-bond, and laid more stress on "purity of heart" as contrasted with merely outward chastity. Even the peculiarly Christian virtue of humility, which presents so striking a contrast to the Greek "highmindedness," was to some extent anticipated in the Rabbinic teaching. Its far greater prominence under the new dispensation may be partly referred to the express teaching and example of Christ; partly, in so far as the virtue is manifested in the renunciation of external rank and dignity, or of the glory of merely secular gifts and acquirements, it is one aspect of the unworldliness which we have already noticed; while the deeper humility that represses the claim of personal merit even in the saint belongs to the strict self-examination, the continual sense of imperfection, the utter reliance on strength not his own, which characterise the inner moral life of the Christian. Humility in this latter sense, "before God," is an essential condition of all truly Christian goodness.

Humility.

both, however, were to be accepted as parts of the actually established order of secular society; but the harshness of both kinds of inequality could even now be removed, and ought to be removed, by brotherly treatment of bondsmen and of the poor.

Religious Duty.

Obedience, patience, benevolence, purity, humility, alienation from the "world" and the "flesh," are the chief novel or striking features which the Christian ideal of conduct suggests, so far as it can be placed side by side with that commonly accepted in Greco-Roman society. But we have yet to notice the enlargement of the sphere of ethics due to its new connection with Revelational Theology; for while this added religious force and sanction to ordinary moral obligations, it equally tended to impart a more definitely moral aspect to religious belief and worship. "Duty to God"—as distinct from duty to man—had not, indeed, been unrecognised by pagan moralists; not only Pythagoras and Plato and the Neo-Pythagorean and Neo-Platonic schools, but also Stoicism—in a different manner—had laid much stress upon it: but the generally mixed and dubious relations in which philosophic theism stood to the established polytheism tended to prevent the offices of piety from occupying, in any philosophic system, the definite and prominent place allotted to them in Christian teaching. Again,—just as the Stoics held wisdom to be indispensable to real rectitude of conduct, while at the same time they included under the notion of wisdom a grasp of physical as well as ethical truth,—so the similar emphasis laid on inwardness in Christian ethics caused orthodoxy or correctness of religious belief to be regarded as essential to goodness, and heresy as the most fatal of vices, corrupting as it did the very springs of Christian life. To the philosophers, however, convinced as they were that the multitude must necessarily miss true wellbeing through their folly and ignorance, it did not usually [1] occur to guard against these

[1] Plato is an important exception to this generalisation, as in his *Laws* he makes elaborate provision not only for the regulation of public

evils by any other method than that of providing philosophic instruction for the few; whereas the Christian clergy, whose function it was to offer truth and eternal life to all mankind, naturally regarded theological misbelief as insidious preventible contagion. Indeed, their sense of its deadliness was so keen that, when they were at length able to control the secular government, they overcame their aversion to bloodshed, and initiated that long series of religious persecutions to which we find no parallel[1] in the pre-Christian civilisation of Europe. It was not that Christian writers did not feel the difficulty of attributing criminality to sincere ignorance or error. But the difficulty is not really peculiar to theology; and the theologians usually got over it (as some philosophers had surmounted a similar perplexity in the region of ethics proper) by supposing some latent or antecedent voluntary sin, of which the apparently involuntary heresy was the fearful fruit.

Christianity and Free Will.

Lastly, we must observe that in proportion as the legal conception of morality, as a code of which the violation deserves supernatural punishment, predominated over the philosophic view of ethics as the method for attaining natural felicity, the question of man's freedom of will to obey the law necessarily became prominent. At the same time it cannot be broadly said that Christianity took a decisive side in the metaphysical controversy on free will and necessity; since, just as in Greek philosophy the need of maintaining freedom as the ground of responsibility clashes

worship, but for the severe punishment of unauthorised rites and opinions opposed to (Platonic) orthodoxy.

[1] The imperial persecutions of Christianity itself, externally viewed, might seem to furnish a parallel; but, from the point of view here taken, they are not analogous, since they were in no degree due to the conception of theological error as essentially criminal.

with the conviction that no one deliberately chooses his own harm, so in Christian ethics it clashes with the attribution of all true human virtue to supernatural grace, as well as with the belief in divine foreknowledge. All we can say is that in the development of Christian thought the conflict of conceptions was more profoundly felt, and more serious efforts were made to evade or transcend it.

§ 5. Development of opinion in early Christianity.

In the preceding account of Christian morality it has been already indicated that the characteristics delineated did not all exhibit themselves simultaneously to the same extent, or with perfect uniformity, throughout the Church. Partly the changes in the external condition of Christianity, and the different degrees of civilisation in the societies of which it was the dominant religion, partly the natural process of internal development, continually brought different features into prominence. Again, the important antagonisms of opinion, that from time to time expressed themselves in sharp controversies within Christendom, sometimes involved ethical issues;—even in the Eastern Church, until in the 4th century it began to be absorbed in the labour of dogmatic construction. Thus, *e.g.*, the anti-secular tendencies of the new creed, to which Tertullian (160-220) gave violent and rigid expression, were exaggerated in the Montanist heresy which he ultimately joined; on the other hand, Clemens of Alexandria, in opposition to the general tone of his age, maintained the value of pagan philosophy for the development of Christian faith into true knowledge (Gnosis), and the value of the natural development of man through marriage for the normal perfecting of the Christian life. Then we have to observe that when the Church, through Constantine, entered into organic relation with civil society, the tendency of its more enthusiastic members to advocate an ascetic breach with man's natural life took a new direction. Total renunciation of the world and mortification of the flesh were no longer held to be prescribed to all Christians as the sole way of salvation, but were rather regarded as recommended by evangelical "counsels of perfection," which individual Christians were free to follow or pass by. A double morality was thus gradually developed out of the original simplicity of Christian teaching: a distinction was established between ordinary Christian virtue and monastic virtue which has a certain analogy to the old pagan antithesis between "philosophic" and "civic" excellence,—an analogy which was emphasised in Eastern monasticism by the assumption of such terms as "sacred" or "divine philosophy" to denote the anachoretic way of life. By strict seclusion and celibacy, severe simplicity of food and raiment, by fasting, prayer, and perpetual self-examination, by rigid regulation of all hours of work and leisure—sometimes by the wild extravagances of self-mortification, of which Simeon Stylites is the popular example—the Eastern monk sought to strip off the soiled and clinging garment of carnal desires and worldly cares, and to fit himself for a purer and closer walk with God than the life of the world would allow. At first the tendency to seek the complete isolation of the desert predominated: afterwards it became the accepted view that most of those who aspired after this more perfect way needed the support and control of an ordered community of persons with similar aspirations: thus when in the 4th century monasticism began to spread in Western Christendom, the ideal of life which it generally commended was the life of the cloister. This, in the West, became more practical and less contemplative than in the East; under the direction of Benedict (about 480-543) it came to include useful labour

Monastic Morality.

as a regular element—at first manual labour only, but afterwards, by an enlargement of view important in the history of Western civilisation, the study of secular letters was admitted. It was in the intense and concentrated struggle with human weakness—the "Olympian contest with sin"—of which the cloister was the arena, that the list of principal sins was first framed, which afterwards held an established place in mediæval expositions of morality. These "deadly sins" were at first commonly reckoned as eight; but a preference for mystical numbers characteristic of mediæval theologians finally reduced the received list to seven. The statement of them is somewhat differently given by different writers:—Pride, Avarice, Anger, Gluttony, Unchastity, are found in all the lists; the remaining two (or three) are variously selected from among Envy, Vain-glory, and the rather singular sins Gloominess (Tristitia) and Languid Indifference (Acidia or Acedia, from Greek ἀκηδία). These latter notions show plainly, what indeed might be inferred from a study of the list as a whole, that it especially represents the moral experience of the monastic life; in particular, the state of moral lassitude and collapse denoted by "Acedia" is easily recognisable as a spiritual disease, which—in this age of the world at least—would be peculiarly incident to the cloister.

§ 6. Development of ethical doctrine.

While the newly-imported monasticism was spreading and gaining strength in the West, a development in Christian morality of a different kind took place through the more precise conception of the relation between human and divine agency in Christian good conduct which resulted from the Pelagian controversy; and, more generally, through the impressive ethical influence of Augustine. By Justin and other apologists the need of redemption, faith, grace, is indeed recognised, but the theological system depending on these notions is not sufficiently developed[1] to come into even apparent antagonism with the freedom of the will. Christian teaching is for the most part conceived as essentially a proclamation through the Divine Word, to immortal beings gifted with free choice—and therefore justly punishable for wrong choice—of the true code of conduct sanctioned by eternal rewards and punishments.[2] It is plain, however, that on this external legalistic view of duty it was difficult to maintain a difference in kind between Christian and pagan morality; the philosopher's conformity to the rules of chastity and beneficence, so far as it went, seemed indistinguishable from the saint's. If, however, a faculty of fulfilling such duty as he is capable of recognising be granted even to the natural man, the new light of revelation given to the Christian would seem to carry with it at least a possibility of completely avoiding sin. But this inference, as developed in the teaching of Pelagius, seemed inconsistent with that absolute dependence on Divine Grace to which the Christian consciousness resolutely clung; and it was accordingly repudiated as heretical by the Church, under the leadership

[1] To show the crudity of the notion of redemption in early Christianity, it is sufficient to mention that more than one leading writer represents Christ's ransom as having been paid to the devil; sometimes adding that by the concealment of Christ's divinity under the veil of humanity a certain deceit was (fairly) practised on the great deceiver.

[2] It may be observed that the contrast between this view and the efforts of pagan philosophy to exhibit virtue as its own reward, is triumphantly pointed out by more than one early Christian writer. Lactantius (*circ.* 300 A.D.), for example, roundly declares that Plato and Aristotle, referring everything to this earthly life, "made virtue mere folly"; though himself maintaining, with pardonable inconsistency, that man's highest good did not consist in mere pleasure, but in the consciousness of the filial relation of the soul to God.

of Augustine; by whom the doctrine of man's incapacity to obey God's law by his unaided moral energy was pressed to a point at which it was difficult to reconcile it with the freedom of the will. Augustine is fully aware of the theoretical importance of maintaining Free Will, from its logical connection with human responsibility and divine justice; but he considers that these latter points are sufficiently secured if actual freedom[1] of choice between good and evil is allowed in the single case of our progenitor Adam. For since the "seminal nature" from which all men were to arise already existed in Adam, in his voluntary preference of self to God humanity chose evil once for all; for which ante-natal guilt all men are justly condemned to perpetual absolute sinfulness and consequent punishment, unless they are elected by God's unmerited grace to share the benefits of Christ's redemption. Without this grace it is impossible for man to obey the "first greatest commandment" of love to God; and, this unfulfilled, he is guilty of the whole law, and is only free to choose between degrees of sin; his apparent external virtues have no moral value, since inner rightness of intention is wanting. "All that is not of faith is of sin"; and faith and love are mutually involved and inseparable; faith springs from the divinely imparted germ of love, which in its turn is developed by faith to its full strength, while from both united springs hope, joyful yearning towards ultimate perfect fruition of the object of love. These three Augustine (after St. Paul) regards as the three essential elements of Christian virtue; along with these, indeed, he recognises the old fourfold division of virtue into prudence, temperance, courage, and justice, according

Augustine (354-430 A.D.)

[1] It is to be observed that Augustine prefers to use the term "freedom," not for the power of willing either good or evil, but the power of willing good. The highest freedom, in his view, excludes the possibility of willing evil.

to their traditional interpretation; but he explains these virtues to be in their deepest and truest natures only the same love to God in different aspects or exercises. "Temperance is love keeping itself uncontaminated for its object, Fortitude is love readily enduring all for the beloved's sake, Justice is love serving only the beloved and therefore rightly governing, Prudence is love sagaciously choosing the things that help her and rejecting the things that hinder." This love of God—in which the self-love of the human soul finds its true development, and of which love of one's neighbour is an outgrowth—is the sole source of enjoyment to the redeemed soul: the world is not to be enjoyed but only to be used: contemplation of God, the last stage reached in the upward progress of the soul, is alone Wisdom, alone happiness. The uncompromising mysticism of this view may be at once compared and contrasted with the philosophical severity of Stoicism. Love of God in the former holds the same absolute and unique position as the sole element of moral worth in human action, which, as we have seen, was occupied by knowledge of Good in the latter; and we may carry the parallel further by observing that in neither case is severity in the abstract estimate of goodness necessarily connected with extreme rigidity in practical precepts. Indeed, an important part of Augustine's work as a moralist lies in the reconciliation which he laboured to effect between the anti-worldly spirit of Christianity and the necessities of secular civilisation. For example, we find him arguing for the legitimacy of judicial punishments and military service against an over-literal interpretation of the Sermon on the Mount: and he took an important part in giving currency to the distinction before-mentioned between evangelical "counsels" and "commands," and so defending the life of marriage and temperate enjoyment of natural good against the attacks of the more extravagant advocates of celibacy and self-abnegation; although he fully admitted the superiority of the latter method of avoiding the contamination of sin.

The attempt to Christianise the old Platonic list of virtues, which we have noticed in Augustine's system, was perhaps due to the influence of his master Ambrose; in whose treatise *De officiis ministrorum* we find for the first time an exposition of Christian duty systematised on a plan borrowed from a pre-Christian moralist. It is interesting to compare Ambrose's account of what through him came to be known as the "four cardinal virtues" with the corresponding delineations in Cicero's *De officiis* which has served the bishop as a model. Christian Wisdom, so far as speculative, is of course primarily theological; it has God, as the highest truth, for its chief object, and is therefore necessarily grounded on faith. Christian Fortitude is essentially firmness in withstanding the seductions of good and evil fortune, resoluteness in the conflict perpetually waged against wickedness without carnal weapons—though Ambrose, with the Old Testament in his hand, will not quite relinquish the ordinary martial application of the virtue. "Temperantia" retains the meaning of "observance of due measure" in all conduct, which it had in Cicero's treatise; but its notion is partly modified by being blended with the newer virtue of humility. Finally in the exposition of Christian Justice the Stoic doctrine of the natural union of all human interests is elevated to the full height of evangelical philanthropy; the brethren are reminded that the earth was made by God a common possession of all, and are bidden to administer their means for the common

Ambrose (*circ.* 340-397 A.D.)

benefit, and give from the heart with joy; wealth, indeed, should not be lavished,—still, no one should be ashamed if he becomes poor through giving. Ambrose, we should observe, lays stress on the inseparability of these different virtues in Christian morality, though he does not, like Augustine, resolve them all into the one central affection of love to God.

§ 7. Ecclesiastical morality in the "Dark Ages."

Under the influence of Ambrose and Augustine, the four cardinal virtues furnished a generally accepted scheme for the treatment of systematic ethics by subsequent ecclesiastical writers. Often the triad of Christian graces—Faith, Hope, and Love—was placed by their side, after Augustine's example: the seven gifts of the Spirit, enumerated by Isaiah (ch. xi. 2), are also introduced; while on the other side of the great moral battle the forces of vice are arrayed under the heads of the seven (or eight) deadly sins. The list of these sins, as I have already said, was transplanted from the special experience of the monk into the conception of morality applicable to Christians generally; but, on the whole, the separation between monastic and common Christian duty, as higher and lower forms of religious obedience, remained distinct and established in the mediæval Church. It was complicated by a separation, of different origin and significance, between the clerical and the lay rule of life; but the moral codes applied by the common opinion of Christendom to clergy and ascetics respectively had a tendency to approximate, even before clerical celibacy was made universally obligatory in the 11th century. The distinction, however, between "deadly" and "venial" sins was applied to laity as well as clergy: it had, as we have seen, a technical reference to the quasi-jural administration of ecclesiastical discipline, which grew gradually more organised as the spiritual power of the Church established itself amid the disorder that followed the overthrow of the Western Empire, and developed into the theocracy that partially dominated mediæval Europe. "Deadly" sins were those for which a specially prescribed penance was held to be necessary, in order to save the sinner from eternal damnation; for "venial" sins he might obtain forgiveness through prayer, almsgiving, and the observance of the regular fasts. We find that "penitential books" for the use of the confessional, founded partly on traditional practice and partly on the express decrees of synods, come into general use—spreading from Ireland and Britain into France and Germany—in the 7th and 8th centuries. At first they are little more than mere inventories of sins, with their appropriate ecclesiastical punishments;[1] gradually cases of conscience come to be discussed and decided, and the basis is laid for that system of casuistry which reached its full development in the 14th and 15th centuries. This elaboration of ecclesiastical jurisprudence—intended to be kept in vigorous exercise by episcopal visitations—was probably indispensable to the accomplishment of the Church's great task of maintaining moral order in the earlier semi-anarchical period of the Middle Ages; but it

[1] It may be instructive to note some of those punishments. For gluttony and drunkenness a penitential fast of from three to forty days is imposed; for sexual sins the days of penitence grow to years, and even in an extreme case may extend to the end of life; for homicide the penalty varies from a month to ten years, according to motives and circumstances. Monks and clergy have severer penances; on the other hand, double penance is exacted from one who kills a clergyman. Superstitious practices—such as burning the grass in places where a man has died—can only be expiated by year-long penances (cf. Gass, *Christliche Ethik*, IV. ch. i. § 92). The fact that the Church itself was partially barbarised during this period made the need of organised discipline all the more urgent.

had a dangerous tendency to encourage an unduly external and legal view of morality. Still a certain counterpoise to this tendency was continually maintained by the influence of the fervid inwardness of Augustine, transmitted, in a subdued and attenuated form, through the *Moralia* of Gregory the Great (*d.* 604), the *Sententiæ* of Isidore of Seville (*d.* 636), the works of Alcuin (*d.* 804), Hrabanus Maurus (*d.* 856), and other writers of the philosophically barren period that intervened between the destruction of the Western Empire and the rise of Scholasticism.

§ 8. Scholastic Ethics.

Scholastic ethics, like scholastic philosophy generally, attained its most complete and characteristic result in the teaching of Thomas of Aquino. But before giving a brief account of the ethical system of this great teacher, it will be well to notice the chief steps in the process of thought and discussion which led up to it. We must begin with Johannes Scotus Erigena, the earliest noteworthy philosopher of the Middle Ages, though it is only in a wide sense of the term that he can be called a scholastic; since he is separated by a considerable interval of time from the main body of scholastics, and—while he aims at philosophising in harmony with the Christian faith—he does not show either the unqualified respect for authority in his method of reasoning or the unqualified orthodoxy in his conclusions, which are characteristic of scholasticism, strictly taken. The philosophy of Erigena is to be traced in the main to the influence of Plato and Plotinus, transmitted through an unknown author of the 5th century, who assumed the name of Dionysius the Areopagite: accordingly the ethical side of his doctrine has the same negative and ascetic character that we have observed in Neo-Platonism. He teaches that God alone truly is: that everything else exists only in so far as God manifests

Johannes Erigena (*circ.* 810-877).

Himself in it; that evil is essentially unreal and incognisable by God, only existing in the world of illusory appearance into which man has fallen; that the true aim of man's life is to return to perfect union with God out of this illusory material existence. This doctrine found little acceptance among Erigena's contemporaries, and was certainly unorthodox enough to justify the condemnation which it subsequently received from Pope Honorius III.; but its influence, together with that of the Pseudo-Dionysius, had a share in developing the more emotional orthodox mysticism of the 12th and 13th centuries; and Neo-Platonism, or Platonism received through a Neo-Platonic tradition, remained a distinct element in mediæval thought, though obscured, in the period of mature Scholasticism, by the predominant influence of Aristotle.

Anselm (1033-1109).

Scholastic philosophy, in the stricter sense, may be taken to begin with Anselm's comprehensive and profound attempt to render the dogmatic system of orthodox Christianity, so far as possible, intelligible to reason. In ethics, however, Anselm's work is only noteworthy on the question of Free-will. We observe that the Augustinian doctrine of original sin and man's absolute need of unmerited grace is retained in his theory of salvation; he also follows Augustine in defining freedom as the "power not to sin";—but in saying that Adam fell "spontaneously" and "by his free choice," though not "through his freedom," he has implicitly made the distinction that Peter the Lombard afterwards expressly draws between the freedom that is opposed to necessity and freedom from the slavery to sin. Anselm further softens the statement of Augustinian predestinationism by explaining that the freedom to will what is right is not strictly lost even by fallen man; it is inherent in a rational nature, though since Adam's sin it only exists potentially in humanity,—like the faculty of sight in a dark place, —except where it is made actual by grace.

Abelard (1079-1142).

In a more modern way Abelard tries to establish the connection between man's ill desert and his free choice by a more precise conception of sin. He distinguishes sin, strictly taken, both from the mere propensity to bad conduct which fallen man inherits and from the externally bad action in which it takes effect. The bad propensity, so far as involuntary, is not sin; its existence indeed, as he points out, is presupposed in our conception of human virtue, which essentially consists in fighting successfully against wrongly directed desires. Nor, again, can sin lie in the outward effects of our action; it is evident that these may occur without moral culpability on our part, through ignorance or compulsion. It must therefore lie in the contempt of God and His commands, which is manifested in conscious consent to vicious inclination: accordingly it is upon this inward consent to evil that repentance must be directed, and not upon any outward effects of the act; the essence of true repentance is aversion to the sin itself, not to its consequences. He does not shrink from drawing the inference that, since rightness of conduct depends solely on intention, all outward acts as such are indifferent; but he avoids the dangerous consequences of this paradox, with some loss of consistency, by explaining that "good intention" must be understood to mean intention to do what really is right, not merely what seems so to the agent. In the same spirit, under the reviving influence of ancient philosophy—with which, however, he is very imperfectly acquainted, and the relation of which to Christianity he extravagantly misunderstands[1]—he argues

[1] He endeavours to prove that the ancient philosophers had at least a partial knowledge of the doctrine of the Trinity.

that the old Greek moralists, as inculcating disinterested love of good, were really nearer to Christianity than Judaic legalism was; and he boldly contends that they set an example of control of irrational desires, contempt of worldly things and devotion to the things of the soul, which might well put to shame most monks of his age. He carries his demand for disinterestedness so far as to require that the Christian "love to God" should only be regarded as pure if purged from the self-regarding desire of the happiness which God gives. The general tendency of Abelard's thought was suspiciously regarded by contemporary orthodoxy;[1] and the over-subtlety of the last-mentioned distinction provoked vehement replies from more than one of the orthodox mystics of the age. Thus Hugo of St. Victor (1077-1141) argues that all love is necessarily so far "interested" that it involves a desire for union with the beloved; and since eternal happiness consists in this union, it cannot truly be desired apart from God; while Bernard of Clairvaux (1091-1153) more elaborately distinguishes four stages by which the soul is gradually led from (1) merely self-regarding desire for God's aid in distress, to (2) love Him for His loving-kindness to it, then also (3) for His absolute goodness, until (4) in rare moments this love for Himself alone becomes the sole all-absorbing affection.

The conflict of Abelard with Bernard and Hugo of St. Victor illustrates the antagonism, sometimes latent, sometimes open, which we find in mediæval thought between the *dialectical* effort to obtain satisfaction for the reason under the conditions fixed by the traditional dogmas of orthodox faith, and the *mystical* effort to find in the same dogmas an adequate support or framework for the emotional

[1] He was condemned by two synods in 1121 and 1140.

and intuitive religious consciousness. These diverse tendencies appear in conflict both before and after the culmination of scholastic philosophy in the 13th century; but the prevailing aim of scholasticism in its best period is to find a harmonious reconciliation of this and other antagonisms. We find this eclectic or harmonistic character in the *Libri Sententiarum* of Peter the Lombard, which was for a long time the most widely accepted manual of theological teaching in Western Europe, but of which the historical interest now lies mainly in its method and plan of construction. It aims at presenting a compendious but comprehensive exposition of Christian Theology as developed by the Catholic Church, giving with each important proposition the chief arguments *pro* and *con* drawn from Scripture and the Fathers, and endeavouring to reconcile the apparently conflicting authorities by subtle distinctions of meaning in the terms used. This famous scholastic art of distinctions was always somewhat open to the attacks which Bacon and others made on its later developments; but something like it was indispensable if a systematic and coherent body of doctrine was to be built up from materials so diverse in their sources; and it became still more inevitable when the complexity of authorities was increased in the following century, by the acceptance of Aristotle as "The Philosopher" whose dictum was almost indisputable on all matters falling properly within the domain of human reason. The revival of the study of Aristotle was due to the work and influence of Arabian and Jewish commentators; but the remarkable union of Aristotelian and Christian thought achieved in the 13th century—which determined for a long period the orthodox philosophy of the Catholic Church—was initiated by Albert the Great and completed by Thomas of Aquino.

Scholastic Method.

Peter the Lombard (*d.* 1164).

§ 9. Thomas Aquinas (1225-1274).

The moral philosophy of Thomas Aquinas is, in the main, Aristotelianism with a Neo-Platonic tinge, interpreted and supplemented by a view of Christian doctrine derived chiefly from Augustine. He holds that all action or movement, of all things irrational as well as rational, is directed towards some end or good; which in the case of rational creatures is represented in Thought, fixed by Intention, and aimed at by Will under the influence of Practical Reason. There are many ends actually sought—riches, honour, power, pleasure—but none of these satisfies and gives happiness; this can only be given by God Himself, the ground and first cause of all being, and unmoved principle of all movement. It is, then, towards God that all things are really though unconsciously striving in their pursuit of Good; but this universal striving after God, since he is essentially intelligible, exhibits itself in its highest form in rational beings as a desire for knowledge of Him; such knowledge, however, is beyond all ordinary exercise of reason, and may only be partially revealed to man here below. Thus the *summum bonum* for man is objectively God, subjectively the happiness to be derived from loving vision of His perfections; although there is a lower kind of happiness to be realised here below in a normal human existence of virtue and friendship, with mind and body sound and whole and properly trained for the needs of earthly life. The higher happiness is given to man by free grace of God; but it is only given to those whose heart is right, and who have merited it by a number of virtuous actions. Passing to consider what actions are virtuous, we first observe generally that the morality of an act is in part, but only in part, determined by its particular end or motive; it partly depends on its external object and circumstances, which render it either objectively in harmony with the "order of reason" or the reverse,—except in the case of acts externally indifferent, of which the goodness or badness is determined entirely by the motive. In the classification of particular virtues and vices, we can distinguish very clearly the elements supplied by the different teachings which Thomas has imbibed. In his treatment of the virtues which belong to the nature of man as a rational creature, and can be acquired (though not perfectly) as a mere natural result of training and practice, he is in the main Aristotelian. He follows Aristotle closely in dividing those "natural" virtues into intellectual and moral, and the intellectual virtues, again, into "speculative" and "practical"; in distinguishing within the speculative class the "intellect" that is conversant with principles, the science that deduces conclusions, and the "wisdom" to which belongs the whole process of knowing the sublimest objects of knowledge; and in treating practical wisdom or prudence as inseparably connected with moral virtues, and therefore in a sense moral.[1] When, again, among moral virtues he distinguishes Justice, manifested in actions by which others receive their due, from the virtues that primarily relate to the passions of the agent himself, he is giving his interpretation of Aristotle's doctrine; and his list of the latter virtues, to the number of ten, is taken *en bloc* from the *Nicomachean Ethics*. On the other hand, his classification of passions depends on a division of the non-rational element of the soul into "concupiscible" and "irascible," which is rather Platonic than Aristotelian;[2] to the "concupiscible" element he refers

[1] His justification, however, for classing "prudentia" both among intellectual and moral virtues—that it is intellectual *secundum essentiam* and moral *secundum materiam*—is rather scholastic than Aristotelian.

[2] The distinction is adopted by Aristotle in several passages, but as a popular rather than a scientific division.

the passions that are stirred by the simple apprehension of sensible good or evil—love, hate, desire, aversion, joy, sorrow; while to the "irascible" element he attributes the passions excited by some difficulty or obstacle in the way of the attainment of the desired object—viz. hope, despair, fear, boldness, anger. And in arranging his list of the virtues that control these passions he defers to the established doctrine of the four cardinal virtues, derived originally from Plato and the Stoics through Cicero; accordingly, the Aristotelian ten have to stand under the higher genera of (1) the Prudence which gives reasoned rules of conduct, (2) the Temperance which resists misleading desire, and (3) the Fortitude that resists misleading fear of dangers or toils. The relation, however, of the cardinal virtues to the different elements of the soul is conceived in a manner which is not either Platonic, Aristotelian, or Stoic; since, along with the Rational, Concupiscible, and Irascible elements—which have Prudence, Temperance, and Fortitude respectively as their special virtues—Thomas's system recognises, as a fourth distinct element, Will (*Voluntas*), to which Justice, whose sphere is outward action, specially belongs. Still, as regards these partly "natural" and partly "acquired" virtues the authority of "the Philosopher" is predominant: along with these, however, and before them in rank, Thomas places the Pauline triad of "theologic" virtues, Faith, Love, and Hope, which are supernaturally "instilled" by God, and directly relate to Him as their object. By faith we obtain that part of our knowledge of God which is beyond the range of mere natural wisdom or philosophy;—naturally, *e.g.*, we can know God's existence, but not His Trinity in Unity, though philosophy is useful to defend this and other revealed verities:—and it is essential for the attainment of the soul's welfare that all articles of the Christian creed, however little they can be known by natural reason, should be apprehended through faith; the Christian who rejects a single article loses hold altogether of faith and of God. Faith, then, is the substantial basis of all Christian morality, but without love —the essential form of all the Christian virtues—it is "formless" (*informis*). Christian love is conceived (after Augustine) as primarily love to God (beyond the natural yearning of the creature after its ultimate good), which expands into love towards all God's creatures as created by Him, and so ultimately includes even self-love. But creatures are only to be loved in their purity as created by God; all that is bad in them must be an object of hatred till it is destroyed. In the classification of sins the Christian element predominates; still we find the Aristotelian vices of excess and defect, along with the modern divisions into "sins against God, neighbour, and self," "mortal and venial sins," sins of "omission and commission," of "heart, speech, and act," etc.

From the notion of sin—treated in its jural aspect—Thomas passes naturally to the discussion of Law. The exposition of this latter conception presents, to a great extent, the same matter that was dealt with by the exposition of moral virtues, but in a new form; the prominence of which, in Thomas's treatise, may perhaps be attributed to the growing influence of the study of Roman jurisprudence, which attained in the 12th century so rapid and brilliant a revival in Italy. This side of Thomas's system has a special historical interest; since, as we shall presently see, it is just this blending of theological conceptions with the abstract theory of the later Roman law that gave the starting-point for independent ethical thought in the modern world. Under the general idea of law, defined as an "ordinance of reason for the common good, promulgated by him who has charge of the community," Thomas distinguishes (1) the eternal law or regulative reason of God, which embraces all his creatures, rational and irrational; (2) "natural law," being that part of the eternal law that relates to rational creatures as such; (3) human law, which properly consists of natural law particularised and adapted to the varying circumstances of actual communities; (4) divine law specially revealed to man. As regards natural law, he teaches that God has firmly implanted in the human mind a knowledge of its immutable general principles; and not only knowledge, but a disposition, to which Thomas applies the peculiar scholastic term "synderesis,"[1] that unerringly prompts to the realisation of these principles in conduct, and protests against their violation. All acts of natural virtue are implicitly included within the scope of this law of nature; but in the operation of applying its principles to the particular circumstances of human life—to which the term "conscience" should be restricted[2]—man's judgment is liable to err; so that duty is imperfectly known, the light of nature being obscured and perverted by bad education and custom. Human law is required, not merely to determine the details for which man's apprehension of natural law gives no intuitive guidance, but also to supply the force necessary for practically securing, among imperfect men, abstinence from acts that are both bad and disturbing to others. The rules of this law must be either

[1] The term is derived from συντήρησις, used in this sense in a passage of Jerome (*Com. in Ezek.*, i. 4-10).

[2] "Conscientia," as he recognises, is also used to include what he terms "synderesis."

deductions from principles of natural law, or determinations of particulars which it leaves indeterminate; a rule contrary to natural law could not be valid as law at all. Human law, however, can only deal with outward conduct, and even here cannot attempt to repress all evil, without causing worse mischief than it prevents; while natural law, as we saw, is liable to be obscure and uncertain in its particular applications; and neither natural nor human law take into their view that supernatural happiness which is man's highest end. Hence they needed to be supplemented by a special revelation of divine law. This revelation, again, is distinguished into the law of the old covenant and the law of the Gospel; the latter of these is productive as well as imperative, since it carries with it the divine grace that makes its fulfilment possible. We have, however, to distinguish in the case of the Gospel between (1) absolute commands, and (2) counsels, which recommend, without positively ordering, the monastic life of poverty, celibacy, and obedience, as the best method of effectively turning the will from earthly to heavenly things.

But how far is man able to attain either natural or Christian perfection? This is the part of Thomas's system in which the cohesion of the different elements composing it seems weakest. He is scarcely aware that his Aristotelianised Christianity inevitably combines two different difficulties in dealing with this question: first, the old pagan difficulty of reconciling the proposition, that will or purpose is a rational desire always directed towards apparent good, with the freedom of choice between good and evil that the jural view of morality seems to require; and, secondly, the Christian difficulty of harmonising this latter notion with the absolute dependence on divine grace which the religious consciousness affirms. The latter difficulty Thomas, like many of his predecessors, avoids by supposing a "co-operation" of free will and grace, but the former he does not fully meet. It is against this part of his doctrine that the most important criticism, in ethics, of his rival Duns Scotus (1266-1308) was directed. He urged that will could not be really free if it were bound to reason, as Thomas (after Aristotle) conceives it; a really free choice must be perfectly indeterminate between reason and unreason. Scotus consistently maintained that the divine will is similarly independent of reason, and that the divine ordering of the world is to be conceived as absolutely arbitrary. On this point he was followed by the acute intellect of William of Occam (*d.* 1347); though the doctrine is obviously dangerous to all reasoned morality that rests for support on the moral government of the world. In a more general way, the Nominalism of Occam and his followers is indirectly important in the history of scholastic ethics: since the denial of the reality of Universals shattered the bridge which the earlier scholasticism had sought to construct between the particulars of sensible experience and God conceived as the ultimate ground and end of all existence. In this way what was most certain for faith came to be regarded as least cognisable by human intellect; which had to content itself with establishing the reasonableness of believing, not the reasonableness of what was believed. The result did not at first seem unfavourable to orthodoxy; theology retained the services of philosophy while relieved from its rivalry; but the change none the less involved the decay of scholasticism; for though the dialectical faculty might still find ample occupation, the task marked out for it could no longer claim the devotion of a philosophic intellect

Duns Scotus.

Occam.

of high order. Thus the work of Thomas remained indubitably the crowning result of the great constructive effort of mediæval philosophy. The effort was, indeed, foredoomed to failure, since it attempted the impossible task of framing a coherent system out of the heterogeneous data furnished by Scripture, the Fathers, the Church, and "the Philosopher"; and whatever philosophic quality is to be found in the work of Thomas belongs to it in spite of, not in consequence of, its method. Still its influence has been great and long-enduring,—in the Catholic Church primarily, but indirectly among Protestants; especially in England, since the famous first book of Hooker's *Ecclesiastical Polity* is largely indebted to the *Summa Theologiæ* of Aquinas.

§ 10. Mediæval Mysticism.

Alongside of scholasticism, and partly in conscious antithesis to the erudite labours and dialectical conflicts of the schoolmen, though in close affinity to their central ethico-theological doctrine, we have to note the development of mysticism in the Christian Church—meaning by "mysticism" the tendency to subordinate all moral effort and intellectual exercise to the attainment of a state of intuitive, or even ecstatic, vision of God. This manner of thought is partly to be traced to Platonic and Neo-Platonic influence transmitted through various channels; but its development in strict connection with Christian orthodoxy begins in the first half of the 12th century, with Bernard of Clairvaux and Hugo of St. Victor. According to Bernard, the Christian who seeks divine truth must ascend to the higher life of the spirit through love and humility—of which there are many grades to be surmounted; then through discursive "consideration" of divine truth he must press forward to intuitive contemplation, in which state moments of ecstatic absorption in the object contemplated will be granted him—transient anticipations of the perfect self-forgetfulness that the glorified soul will attain hereafter. Similarly, in the more systematic and completely developed theology of Hugo of St. Victor, it is through divine grace intensifying man's love for God to the point at which he only loves himself and his neighbour for God's sake, that the "eye of the soul" is opened by which God is seen in His true nature; the perception of matter by the outer eye of the soul, and the intuition of self introspectively, being only valuable as steps to attain the intuition of divine truth and goodness. The process of preparation is more elaborately and imposingly conceived by Bonaventura, whose description of it I select as a specimen of orthodox mysticism as found in harmonious combination with scholasticism.[1] In Bonaventura's view the mind must ascend to the final vision through six stages. First, it must contemplate the evidence of the power, wisdom, and goodness of God in the external world of things distinguished and ordered by weight, number, and measure; in the course of this world's history, as directed by Infinite Wisdom, from its creation by Infinite Power, to its final judgment by Absolute Righteousness; in the scale of created things rising from mere Being through Life to Intelligence. Secondly, it must contemplate the relation of the world to man, the "microcosm"; noting how external things enter the mind through the gates of sense by their similitudes, delight it by the various modes of harmony between sense and its objects, and awaken the activity of the intellect; it will thus find adumbrated the eternally generated similitude of the Son to the Father, and be directed upwards to the

Bonaventura (1221-1274).

[1] What follows is abstracted—with the assistance of Stöckl—from the *Itinerarium Mentis ad Deum*.

source of all beauty and delight, and all apprehension of truth. Thirdly, withdrawing from the outer world and concentrating attention on its own nature and faculties, it must see how memory, uniting past, present, and future, and indelibly retaining the impress of immutable universal truths, affords an image of the Eternal; how intellect is governed in its operation by the indispensable conception of a most perfect, changeless, and necessary being, and how the operation of rational choice equally involves the conception of a supreme Good; and then, observing how in itself memory generates intelligence, and from both proceed love, it will see as through a mirror the Triune being of God. So far the natural powers of the soul might carry it: but for the fourth stage, it needs to be clothed by Divine Grace with the supernatural virtues of Faith, Hope, and Charity, through which it develops an immediate spiritual sense of the Divine nature, disposing it to ecstasies of devotion, admiration, and joy; thus purged, illuminated, and transformed, it can contemplate in itself an image of the angelic hierarchy, with God dwelling in and operating through all. Then in the first stage the soul's pure intelligence apprehends God no longer through itself as a mirror, or in itself as an image, but above itself in His true essence,—Pure Being without negation, the original source of all conceivable reality. But there is a higher stage still, in which that "synderesis," that clinging of the soul to good which exists in some degree in every man, being the undying and unerring element of what we vaguely speak of as conscience, receives its full development; by this faculty God is contemplated not as Absolute Being but as Absolute Goodness, whose essence it is to communicate itself in its fulness; at this stage, therefore, the mystery of the Trinity is directly apprehended, for the essence of this mystery is the communication of Divine Goodness through the Son and the Holy Spirit. Then after these six stages of mental activity comes the Sabbath of perfect ecstasy, in which all intellectual operations are suspended and the soul is wholly passive in its ineffable union with God.

Bonaventura represents mediæval Platonism or Neo-Platonism, as Thomas represents mediæval Aristotelianism, in docile subordination to dogmatic orthodoxy; and the same subordination is maintained more than a century later by Gerson, whose mysticism carries on the tradition of the "Victorines"[1] and Bonaventura. But before Gerson there had been developed in Germany the more original and daring mysticism of Eckhart and his followers, which is free from the trammels not only of scholasticism but of ecclesiastical orthodoxy. In Eckhart's teaching that alienation from the world and finite things, which characterises mysticism generally, is intensified into a fervid yearning to get rid altogether of the self-hood that separates the individual soul from the divine reality of its Being—to know nothing, will nothing, think nothing but God. In this abolition of creatureship Eckhart conceives all morality to be contained; though he is at pains to guard against the quietistic and immoral consequences that might be drawn from this fundamental doctrine, and to represent good works as the natural outflow of the transcendent union of the soul's inmost essence with God.

Eckhart.

§ 11. Casuistry.

In the brief account before given of the general ethical view of Thomas Aquinas no mention has been made of the detailed discussion of particular duties included in the

[1] This is the name often used to denote together Hugo of St. Victor and Richard, a later mystical writer of the same monastery.

Summa Theologiæ;[1] the tone of which—allowance being made for the heterogeneity of the materials put together from very diverse sources—shows, on the whole, moral elevation and sobriety of judgment combined; though on certain points the scholastic pedantry of precise and exhaustive consideration is unfavourable to due delicacy of treatment. It was to this practical side of ethics that the acumen and industry of ecclesiastical writers was largely directed in the 14th and 15th centuries, as the speculative interest of scholasticism decayed; and we have to note, as one result of this, a marked development and systematisation of casuistry. The solution of doubtful cases of conscience had always, as a matter of course, formed part of the work of ecclesiastical moralists; from the earlier period of the Church a number of questions and answers relating to various departments of morality had been handed down under the names of Justin Martyr, Athanasius, Augustine; and the growth of ecclesiastical jurisprudence, the penitential books, the systematic morality of the schoolmen, furnished a continually increasing amount of casuistical discussion. A need, however, began to be felt of arranging the results attained in a form convenient for the conduct of auricular confession; and to meet this need various manuals of casuistry (*Summæ Casuum Conscientiæ*) were compiled in the 14th and 15th centuries. Of these the oldest, called *Astesana*, from Asti in Piedmont, is arranged as a kind of text-book of morality on a scholastic basis; later manuals (*e.g.* the *Summa Rosella*, Venet. 1495) are reduced to mere alphabetical collections of casuistical questions and answers. It was inevitable that the quasi-legal treatment of morality involved in this development of casuistry,—aiming as it did

[1] Occupying the portion of the treatise called *Secunda Secundæ*.

at a precise determination of the limits between the prohibited and the allowable, with doubtful points closely scrutinised and illustrated by fictitious cases,—would have a tendency to weaken the moral sensibilities of ordinary minds; while, again, the more industry and ingenuity were spent in deducing conclusions from the diverse authorities accepted in the Church, the greater necessarily became the number of points on which doctors disagreed; and the central authority that might have repressed serious divergences was wanting in the period of moral weakness that the Church went through, after the death of Boniface VIII. A plain man perplexed by such disagreements might naturally hold that any opinion maintained by a pious and orthodox writer must be a tolerably safe one to follow; and thus weak consciences might be subtly tempted to seek the support of authority for some desired relaxation of a moral rule. It does not, however, appear that this danger assumed formidable proportions until after the Reformation, when, in the struggle made by the Catholic Church to recover its hold on the world, the principle of obedience to authority was forced into keen, balanced, and prolonged conflict with the principle of reliance on private judgment. To the Jesuits, the foremost champions of the Counter-Reformation, it seemed fundamentally important for the cause of authority that laymen generally should be trained to submit their judgment to that of their ecclesiastical guides; as a means to this end it seemed indispensable that the confessional should be made attractive by accommodating ecclesiastico-moral law to worldly needs; and the theory of "Probabilism" supplied a plausible method for effecting this accommodation. The theory proceeded thus:—A layman could not

The Jesuits.

be expected to examine minutely into a point on which the learned differed; therefore he could not fairly be blamed for following any opinion that rested on the authority of even a single doctor; therefore his confessor must be authorised to hold him guiltless if any such "probable" opinion could be produced in his favour; nay, it was his duty to suggest such an opinion, even though opposed to his own, if it would relieve the conscience under his charge from a depressing burden. The results to which this Probabilism, applied with an earnest desire to avoid dangerous rigour, led in the 17th century were revealed to the world in the immortal *Lettres Provinciales* of Pascal.

§ 12. The Reformation. In tracing the development of casuistry we have been carried beyond the great crisis through which Western Christianity passed in the 16th century. The Reformation which Luther initiated may be viewed on several sides, even if we consider only its ethical principles and effects, apart from the political and social aims and tendencies with which it was connected in different European countries. It maintained the simplicity of Apostolic Christianity against the elaborate system of a corrupt hierarchy, the teaching of Scripture alone against the commentaries of the Fathers and the traditions of the Church, the right of private judgment against the dictation of ecclesiastical authority, the individual responsibility of every human soul before God in opposition to the papal control over purgatorial punishments, which had led to the revolting degradation of venal indulgences. Reviving the original antithesis between Christianity and Jewish legalism, it maintained the inwardness of faith to be the sole way to eternal life, in contrast to the outwardness of works; returning to Augustine, and expressing his spirit in a new formula, to resist the Neo-Pelagianism that had gradually developed itself within the apparent Augustinianism of the Church, it affirmed the total corruption of human nature, as contrasted with that "congruity" by which, according to the schoolmen, divine grace was to be earned; renewing the fervent humility of St. Paul, it enforced the universal and absolute imperativeness of all Christian duties, and the inevitable unworthiness of all Christian obedience, in opposition to the theory that "condign" merit might be gained by "supererogatory" conformity to evangelical "counsels." It will be seen that these changes, however profoundly important, were, ethically considered, either negative or quite general, relating to the tone and attitude of mind in which all duty should be done. As regards all positive matter of duty and virtue, and most of the prohibitive code for ordinary men, the tradition of Christian teaching was carried on substantially unchanged in the discourses and writings of the Reformed Churches; only, as the monastic life was discarded altogether, the moral ideal of conduct for Christians generally was relieved from a depressing comparison with what was before regarded as a more excellent way. Even the old method of casuistry was maintained[1] during the 16th and 17th centuries; though scriptural texts, interpreted and supplemented by the light of natural reason, now furnished the sole principles on which cases of conscience were decided.

Transition to modern ethical Philosophy.

In the 17th century, however, the interest of this quasi-legal treatment of morality gradually faded; and the ethical

[1] As the chief English casuists we may mention Perkins, Hall, Sanderson, as well as the more eminent Jeremy Taylor, whose *Ductor Dubitantium* appeared 1660.

studies of educated minds were occupied with the attempt, renewed after so many centuries, to find an independent philosophical basis for the moral code. The renewal of this attempt was only indirectly due to the Reformation; it is rather to be connected with that enthusiastic study of the remains of old pagan culture that spread from Italy over Europe in the 15th and 16th centuries; which, again, was partly the effect, partly the cause, of a widespread alienation from mediæval theology. To this "humanism" the Reformation seemed at first more hostile than the Roman hierarchy; indeed, the extent to which this latter had allowed itself to become paganised by the Renaissance was one of the points that especially roused the Reformers' indignation. Not the less important is the indirect stimulus given by the Reformation towards the development of a moral philosophy independent alike of Catholic and Protestant assumptions. Scholasticism, while reviving philosophy as a handmaid to theology, had metamorphosed its method into one resembling that of its mistress: thus shackling the renascent intellectual activity which it stimulated and exercised, by the double bondage to Aristotle and to the Church. When the Reformation shook the traditional authority in one department, the blow was necessarily felt in the other. Not twenty years after Luther's defiance of the Pope, the startling thesis "that all that Aristotle taught was false" was prosperously maintained by the youthful Ramus before the University of Paris; [1] and not many years later the series of remarkable thinkers in Italy who heralded the dawn of modern physical science—Cardanus, Telesius, Patritius, Campanella, Bruno—began to propound their anti-Aristotelian views as to

[1] It is noteworthy that Luther had also spoken with sweeping disrespect of "the Philosopher."

the constitution of the universe, and the right method of investigating it. It was to be foreseen that a similar assertion of independence would make itself heard in ethics also; and, indeed, amid the clash of dogmatic convictions, the variations and aberrations of private judgment, that the multiplying divisions of Christendom exhibited after the Reformation, reflective persons would naturally be led to seek for an ethical method that—relying solely on the common reason and common moral experience of mankind—might claim universal acceptance from all sects. The chief results of this search, as prosecuted in England from the 17th century onward, will occupy our attention in the next chapter.

CHAPTER IV

MODERN, CHIEFLY ENGLISH, ETHICS

§ 1. Modern ethics before Hobbes. Bacon.

THE great writer with whose name we in England are accustomed especially to connect the transition from mediæval to modern thought—Francis Bacon—has given in his *Advancement of Learning* a brief sketch of moral philosophy, which contains much just criticism and pregnant suggestion, and deserves to be read by all students of the subject.[1] But Bacon's great task of reforming scientific

[1] See *Advancement of Learning*, Book II. ch. xx.-xxii. Bacon takes the "main and primitive division of moral knowledge" to be into (1) "the exemplar or platform of good," and (2) the "regiment or culture of the mind." It is in the latter branch that he finds the older moralists most markedly deficient; they have not treated fully and systematically of the "several characters and tempers of men's natures and dispositions," their different affections, and the occasions of these, and modes of influencing them. In respect of the "exemplar or platform of good," their work appears to him more satisfactory—if we discard their pagan extravagances as to the possible attainment of supreme felicity upon earth. They have well described, enforced, and defended the general forms of virtue and duty, and their particular species; and have excellently handled the "degrees and comparative nature of good." He thinks, however, that they might with advantage have "stayed a little longer on the inquiry concerning the roots of good and evil and the strings of these roots," and have "consulted with nature" somewhat more. For observation of nature shows us how "there is formed in everything a double nature of good; the one, as everything is total or substantive in itself; the other as it is a part or member of a larger

method was one which, as he conceived it, left morals on one side; and he never made any serious effort to reduce his ethical views to a coherent system, methodically reasoned on an independent basis. Thus the outline of which I have spoken was never filled in, and does not seem to have had any material effect in determining the subsequent development of ethical thought. The main stream of English ethics, so far as it flows independently of Revelational Theology,[1] begins with Hobbes and the replies that Hobbes provoked; and the temptation to establish an intellectual filiation between Hobbes and Bacon is one that the sober historian must resist. Indeed the starting-point of Hobbes's ethical speculation is mainly, I conceive, to be sought in a department remote from Bacon's meditations; namely, in the

body; whereof the latter is in degree the greater and the worthier." We see this exemplified even in the physical world; but it is on "man, if he degenerate not," that this "double nature of good" is more specially engraven; and "this being set down and strongly planted, doth judge and determine most of the controversies wherein moral philosophy is most conversant." Here the later views both of Cumberland and of Shaftesbury are to some extent anticipated. But Bacon expressly disclaims the construction of a complete moral system independently of revealed religion. "It must be confessed," he says, "that a great part of the law moral is of that perfection whereunto the light of nature cannot aspire"; for though this "light of nature" is "imprinted upon the spirit of man by an inward instinct, according to the law of conscience," it is only "sufficient to check the vice, not to inform the duty.

[1] I do not mean that this "independence of Revelational Theology" is complete in the case of all the thinkers whose doctrines are here summarised: indeed, I expressly state the contrary in the case of Clarke (see p. 179). But the part of Clarke's doctrine which I have expounded is—in its author's own view—worked out by a purely rational method, independently of any premises derived from revelation: and similarly, in dealing with other moralists who are also orthodox theologians, I have confined my attention entirely to such doctrines as are intended by their authors to rest on a purely rational basis.

The Law of Nature. current view of the Law of Nature, to which—in its political aspect especially—the new conditions of the troubled century preceding Hobbes had directed an unusual amount of attention. For the need of independent practical principles, which I have noted as largely due to the Reformation, was most strongly felt in the region of political relations; since the regulation of these was deeply disturbed, in a twofold way, by the religious wars of the 16th century: first, through the gravity and urgency of the doubts as to the rights of sovereigns and duties of subjects which the confessional divisions inevitably raised; and secondly, through the collapse of the real though imperfect regulative influence that had previously been exercised over Western Europe by the unity of Christendom. In the resulting chaotic condition of public law, several writers—both Catholic and Protestant—attempted to supply the void of regulative principles by developing that conception of the Law of Nature which the schoolmen had formed, partly by tradition from Cicero through Augustine, and partly from the recently revived study of Roman Jurisprudence. This conception, as it was presented in the system of Thomas Aquinas, was rather the wider notion which belongs to ethics than the narrower notion with which Jurisprudence or Politics is primarily concerned; the Law of Nature was defined to mean not merely the rules of mutual behaviour that men may rightly be coerced into obeying, but, more broadly, the rules that they ought to observe, so far as these are cognisable by the light of nature apart from revelation. The same absence of distinction between the provinces of Ethics and Jurisprudence is commonly found in the view of Natural Law given by writers on the subject before Grotius; and, though the required distinction is clearly taken in the epoch-making work *de Jure Belli et*

Grotius (1583-1645).

Pacis (1625), in which Grotius expounded the principles of Natural Law as applicable to international relations, still in the general account which he gives of Natural Law the wider ethical notion is retained. Thus when he defines "Jus Naturale" as the "dictate of Right Reason, indicating that an act, from its agreement or disagreement with man's rational and social nature, is morally disgraceful or morally necessary," the definition is clearly applicable, if not to the whole of the code of moral duty, at any rate to that larger part of it which relates to social conduct;[1] and not merely to the rules determining the imperative claims which individuals or communities may make on each other,—though it is with these latter that Grotius is specially concerned. In either case Natural Law, according to Grotius and other writers of the age, is a part of divine law that follows necessarily from the essential nature of man, who is distinguished among animals by his peculiar "appetite" for tranquil association with his fellows, and his tendency to act on general principles. It is therefore as unalterable, even by God Himself, as the truths of mathematics (although its effect may be overruled in any particular case by an express command of God); hence it is cognisable *a priori*, from the abstract consideration of human nature, though its existence may also be known *a posteriori* from its universal acceptance in human societies. By the Roman jurists, from whom the

[1] It is noteworthy that the words "ac sociali" are not found in the original text of the definition of Jus Naturale, given in Book I. ch. i. § 10 of Grotius's treatise. They were added by his editor, Barbeyrac, who held that a comparison of § 12 of the same chapter showed them to have been accidentally omitted. I rather doubt this, as I think that Grotius intended the phrase in § 10 to be applicable to moral duty generally, in accordance with what he says in § 9; but as the addition of the words "ac sociali" certainly makes the definition more in harmony with his general treatment of the subject, I have let them stand.

conception was taken, this law of nature was not usually conceived as actually having a substantive existence independent of positive codes; it was rather something that underlay existing law, and was to be looked for through it, though it might perhaps be expected ultimately to supersede it, and in the meanwhile represented an ideal standard, by which improvements in legislation were to be guided. Still, the language of the jurists, in some passages, clearly implied that a period of human history, in which men were governed by the law of nature alone, had existed prior to the institution of civil society:[1] it was known from Seneca (*Ep.* xc.) that the Stoic Poseidonius had identified this period with the mythical golden age; and the ideas thus derived from pagan sources easily coalesced, in the minds of mediæval thinkers, with ideas gathered from the narrative of Genesis. Thus there had come to be established and current a conception of a "state of nature," social in a sense, but not yet political, in which individuals or single families had lived side by side,—under none other than such "natural" laws as those prohibiting mutual injury, and mutual interference with each other's use of the goods of the earth that were common to all, giving parents authority over their children, imposing on wives a vow of fidelity to their husbands, and obliging all to the observance of compacts freely entered into. This conception Grotius took, and gave it additional force and solidity by using the principles of this Natural Law—so far as they seemed applicable —for the determination of international rights and duties;

[1] The most definite statement of this kind that I know is the following (*Inst. Just.* II. i. 2):—"Palam est vetustius esse jus naturale, quod cum ipso genere humano rerum natura prodidit. Civilia enim jura tunc esse cæperunt, cum et civitates condi et magistratus creari et leges scribi cæperunt."

since it was obvious that independent nations, regarded as corporate units, were still in the state of nature relatively to each other. It was not assumed that the principles of natural right were perfectly realised in the conduct of primitive independent individuals any more than by nations now; indeed, one point with which Grotius is especially concerned is the natural right of private war, arising out of the violation of more primary rights. Still, the definition of Natural Law above quoted implied a general tendency to observe it; and we may note that it was especially necessary for Grotius to assume such a general observance in the case of contracts; since it was by an "express or tacit pact" that the right of property (as distinct from the mere right to non-interference during use) was held by him to have been instituted. A similar "fundamental pact" had long been generally regarded as the normal origin of legitimate sovereignty.

The ideas above expressed were not, as I have said, in the main peculiar to Grotius. At the same time the rapid and remarkable success of his treatise would bring this view of Natural Right into prominence, and would suggest to penetrating minds such questions as—"What is man's ultimate reason for obeying these laws? Wherein does their agreement with his rational and social nature exactly consist? How far, and in what sense, is his nature really social?"

§ 2. Hobbes (1588-1679).

It was the answer which Hobbes gave to these fundamental questions that supplied the starting-point for independent ethical philosophy in England. Hobbes's psychology is in the first place frankly materialistic; he holds that man's sensations, imaginations, thoughts, emotions, are all mere "appearances" of motions in the "interior parts" of his body. Accordingly he regards pleasure as essentially motion "helping vital action," and pain as motion "hindering" it. There is no logical connection between this theory and the doctrine that appetite or desire has always pleasure (or the absence of pain) for its object; but a materialist, framing a system of psychology, is likely to give special attention to the active impulses arising out of bodily wants, whose obvious end is the preservation of the agent's organism; and this, together with a philosophic wish to simplify, may lead him to the conclusion that all human impulses are similarly self-regarding. This, at any rate, is Hobbes's cardinal doctrine in moral psychology, that each man's appetites or desires are naturally directed either to the preservation of his life, or to that heightening of it which he feels as pleasure;[1] including the aversions that are similarly directed "fromward" pain. Hobbes does not distinguish instinctive from deliberate pleasure-seeking; and he confidently resolves the most apparently unselfish emotions into phases of self-regard. Pity he finds to be grief for the calamity of others, arising from imagination of the like calamity befalling oneself; what we admire with seeming disinterestedness as beautiful (*pulchrum*) is really "pleasure

[1] He even apparently regards the organic motion which he calls "appetite" as indistinguishable from the heightened vital action of which the appearance is "delight or pleasure";—a strange confusion, since, though it may be plausibly maintained that desire is an inseparable element of what we call pleasure, it is evident that desire is often experienced without pleasure: as Hobbes himself says, "Appetite without the opinion of attaining" is "despair," and not delight. I have therefore in the text passed over this identification of desire and pleasure as a palpable inadvertence; but Hobbes's persuasion that the latter involves the former should be noted, as it appears again in his account of happiness or felicity; which he declares not to consist "in the repose of a mind satisfied," but in a "continual progress of the desire from one object to another; the attaining of the former being still but the way to the latter."

in promise"; when men are not immediately seeking present pleasure, they desire power as a means to future pleasure, and thus have a derivative delight in the exercise of power which prompts to what we call benevolent action. The vaunted social inclinations of men, when we consider them narrowly, resolve themselves either into desire for personal benefit to be obtained from or through others, or desire for reputation; "all society is either for gain or glory." No doubt men naturally require mutual help: "infants have need of others to help them to live, and those of riper years to help them to live well"; but so far as this need is concerned, it is "dominion" rather than society that a man would naturally seek if all fear were removed: apart from mutual fear, men would have no natural tendency to enter into political union with their fellows, and to accept the restrictions and positive obligations which such union involves. If any one doubts this natural unsociality of man, Hobbes bids him consider what opinion of his fellows his own actions imply: "when taking a journey he arms himself; when going to sleep he locks his doors; when even in his house he locks his chests; and this when he knows there be laws and public officers, armed, to revenge all injuries that shall be done him."

What, then, is the conduct that ought to be adopted, the reasonable course of conduct, for this egoistic, naturally unsocial being, living side by side with similar beings? In the first place, since all the voluntary actions of men tend to their own preservation or pleasure, it cannot be reasonable to aim at anything else;[1] in fact, nature rather than

[1] There is, however, a noticeable—though perhaps unconscious—discrepancy between Hobbes's theory of the ends that men naturally seek and his standard for determining their natural rights. This latter is never

reason fixes the end of human action, to which it is reason's function to show the means. Hence if we ask why it is reasonable for any individual to observe the rules of social behaviour that are commonly called moral, the answer is obvious that this is only indirectly reasonable, as a means to his own preservation or pleasure. It is not, however, in this, which is only the old Cyrenaic or Epicurean answer, that the distinctive point of Hobbism lies; but rather in the doctrine that even this indirect reasonableness of the most fundamental moral rules is entirely conditional on their general observance, which cannot be secured without the intervention of government. *E.g.* it is not reasonable for me to perform first my share of a contract, if I have "any reasonable suspicion" that the other party will not afterwards perform his; and such reasonable suspicion cannot be effectually excluded except in a state of society in which he is punished for non-performance. Thus the ordinary rules of social behaviour are only hypothetically obligatory until they are actualised by the erection of "a common power" that may "use the strength and means of all" to enforce on all the observance of rules tending to the common benefit. On the other hand, Hobbes yields to no one in maintaining the paramount importance of moral regulations. The rules prescribing justice or the performance of covenants, equity in judging between man and man, requital of benefits, sociability, forgiveness of wrong so far as security allows, the rules prohibiting contumely, pride, arrogance, and

Pleasure simply, but always Preservation—though on occasion he enlarges the notion of "preservation" into "preservation of life so as not to be weary of it." His view seems to be that in a state of nature most men would fight, rob, etc., "for delectation merely" or "for glory," and hence all men must be allowed an indefinite right to fight, rob, etc., "for preservation."

other subordinate precepts,—which may all be summed up in the simple formula, "Do not that to another which thou wouldest not have done to thyself,"[1]—he calls "immutable and eternal laws of nature"; meaning that though a man is not unconditionally bound to realise them in act, he is bound as a reasonable being to desire and aim at their realisation. For they must always be means to the attainment of peace, and the "first and fundamental law of nature"—so far as man's relations to his fellows are concerned[2]—is to "seek peace and follow it"; though if peace cannot be obtained, he may reasonably "seek and use all helps and advantages of war." It is equally opposed to nature's end of self-preservation (1) that an individual should render unreciprocated obedience to moral rules in the interest of others, and so "make himself a prey to others," and (2) that he should refuse to observe such rules when he has sufficient security that they will be observed by others, and so "seek not peace but war." For the state of nature, in which men must be supposed to have existed before government was instituted, and into which they would relapse if it were abolished, is indeed a

[1] It is clear that Hobbes does not distinguish this formula from the well-known "golden rule" of the Gospel,—cf. *Leviathan*, ch. xv. p. 79, and ch. xvii. p. 85,—whereas the formula above quoted is, of course, the golden rule taken only in its negative application, as prescribing abstinences, not positive services. It is, perhaps, even more remarkable that Puffendorf, quoting Hobbes, should not have observed the difference between the two formulæ.—Cf. *De Jure Naturæ et Gentium*, II. ch. iii. § 13.

[2] Hobbes takes the term "Law of Nature" in its widest ethical sense, and expressly recognises that "things tending to the destruction of particular men, such as drunkenness and all parts of intemperance," are "amongst those things which the Law of Nature has forbidden"; but he is only concerned to expound the laws regulative of social conduct, and tending "to the conservation of men in multitudes."

state free from moral restraints; but it is therefore utterly miserable. It is a state in which, owing to well-grounded mutual fear, every man has a right to everything, "even to one another's body," for it may conduce to his preservation; or, as Hobbes also expresses it, a state in which "right and wrong, justice and injustice, have no place";[1] but it is therefore also a state of war in which every man's hand is against his neighbour's,—a state so wretched and perilous that it is the first dictate of rational self-love to emerge from it into the peace of an ordered commonwealth. Such a commonwealth may arise either by "institution," through compact of the subjects with each other to obey as sovereign a defined individual or assembly acting as one, or by "acquisition" through force, followed by a surrender of the vanquished to the victor at discretion; but in either case the authority of the sovereign must be unquestioned and unlimited. The sovereign is itself bound by the Law of Nature to seek the good of the people, which cannot be separated from its own good; but it is responsible to God alone for its fulfilment of this duty. Its commands are the final measure of right and wrong for the outward conduct of its subjects, and ought to be absolutely obeyed by every one, so long as it affords him protection, and does not threaten serious harm to him personally; since to dispute its dictates would be the first step towards anarchy, the

[1] Hobbes does not recognise any formal contradiction between the two statements; because he defines Right (substantive) = Liberty = absence of external impediments; but he practically means by "a right" what most people ordinarily mean by it, *i.e.* a rightful liberty, a liberty claimed and approved by the individual's reason. In any case the statement that "the notions of right and wrong have no place" in the state of nature is too wide for his real meaning; for he would admit that intemperance is prohibited by the Law of Nature in this state. See preceding note.

one paramount peril outweighing all particular defects in legislation and administration.

It is easy to understand how, in the crisis of 1640,—when the ethico-political system of Hobbes first took written shape, —a peace-loving philosopher, weary of the din of warring sects, should regard the claims of individual conscience as essentially anarchical, and the most threatening danger to social wellbeing ; but however strong might be men's yearning for order, a view of social duty, in which the only fixed positions were selfishness everywhere and unlimited power somewhere, could not but appear offensively paradoxical. Nevertheless, offensive or not, there was an originality, a force, an apparent coherence in Hobbism which rendered it undeniably impressive ; in fact, we find that for two generations the efforts to construct morality on a philosophical basis take more or less the form of answers to Hobbes. From an ethical point of view Hobbism divides itself naturally into two parts, which are combined by Hobbes's peculiar political doctrines into a coherent whole, but are not otherwise necessarily connected. Its theoretical basis is the principle of egoism,—viz. that it is natural, and so reasonable, for each individual to aim solely at his own preservation or pleasure; while, for the practical determination of the particulars of duty it makes social morality entirely dependent on positive law and institution. It thus affirmed the relativity of good and evil in a double sense ;— good and evil, for any individual citizen, may from one point of view be defined as the objects respectively of his desire and aversion ; from another point of view, they may be said to be determined for him by his sovereign. It is the latter part or aspect of the system which is primarily attacked by the first generation of writers that replied to Hobbes. This attack, or rather the counter-exposition of orthodox doctrine, is conducted on different methods by the Cambridge moralists and by Cumberland respectively. The former, regarding morality primarily as a body of knowledge of right and wrong, good and evil, rather than a mere code of rules, insist on its absolute character, independent of any legislative will, and its intuitive certainty. The latter is content with the legal view of morality, but endeavours to establish the validity of the laws of nature by basing them on the single supreme principle of rational regard for the "common good of all," and showing them, as so based, to be adequately supported by Divine sanctions.

§ 3. The Cambridge Moralists. Cudworth (1617-1688).

Cudworth was the most distinguished of the little group of thinkers at Cambridge in the 17th century, commonly known as the "Cambridge Platonists," who, embracing Platonic principles seen through a Neo-Platonic medium, but also influenced by the new thought of Descartes, endeavoured to blend rational theology with religious philosophy. In his treatise on *Eternal and Immutable Morality* (which was not published till more than forty years after his death in 1688), his main aim is to uphold the "essential and eternal distinctions of good and evil" as independent of mere arbitrary Will, whether human or divine. He maintains this thesis not only against Hobbes's view of good and evil as determined by the sovereign; but equally against the doctrine of Duns Scotus and Occam, and certain later theologians who regarded all morality as dependent upon the mere will and positive appointment of God. According to Cudworth, the distinctions of good and evil have an objective reality, cognisable by reason no less than the relations of space or number: the knowledge of them comes no doubt to the human mind from the Divine; but it is from the Divine

Reason, in whose light man imperfectly participates, not merely from the Divine Will as such. Ethical, like mathematical, truth relates properly and primarily not to sensible particulars, but to the intelligible and universal essences of things, which are as immutable as the Eternal mind whose existence is inseparable from theirs: ethical propositions, therefore, are as unchangeably valid for the direction of the conduct of rational beings as the truths of geometry are. Cudworth does not take note of the sense in which Hobbes, in spite of his relativism, does yet maintain laws of nature to be eternal and immutable; nor does his refutation of Hobbism—which he treats as a "novantique philosophy," a mere revival of the relativism and atomism[1] of Protagoras—appear to me generally penetrating or effective. His main polemical point is the *argumentum ad hominem*, by which he tries to show that Hobbes's atomic materialism involves the conception of an objective physical world, the object not of passive sense that varies from man to man, but of the active intellect that is the same in all; there is therefore, he urges, an inconsistency in refusing to admit a similar exercise of intellect in morals, and an objective world of right and wrong, which the mind by its normal activity clearly apprehends.

Cudworth, in the work above mentioned, gives no systematic exposition of the ethical principles which he holds to be thus intuitively apprehended. But we may supply this deficiency from the *Enchiridion Ethicum* of Henry More, another thinker of the same school. More gives a list of twenty-three *Noemata Moralia*, the truth of which will, he says, be immediately manifest. Some of these admit of a

More (1614-1687).

[1] Cudworth misspends some labour in proving that Protagoras—not Democritus—is the author of Atomism as well as Relativism.

purely egoistic application, and appear to be so understood by the author;—as, *e.g.*, that goods differ in quality as well as duration; that the superior good is always to be preferred, and the lesser evil; that the absence of a given amount of good is preferable to the presence of equivalent evil; that future good or evil is to be regarded as much as present, if equally certain, and nearly as much if very probable. Whatever may be thought of these axioms, it is evident that the serious controversy between Hobbism and modern Platonism related not to principles of this kind, but to others which demand from the individual a (real or apparent) sacrifice for his fellows. Such are the evangelical principle of "doing as you would be done by," the principle of justice, or "giving every man his own, and letting him enjoy it without interference," and especially what More states as the abstract formula of benevolence, that "if it be good that one man should be supplied with the means of living well and happily, it is mathematically certain that it is doubly good that two should be so supplied, and so on." The mere statement of such formulæ, however, does not fully meet the issue raised by Hobbes: granting that it is for the common benefit that more rather than fewer members of the community should be benefited,—which is, indeed, almost an identical proposition,—the question still remains what motive an individual has to conform to this or any other social principle, when it conflicts with his natural desires and private interest. To this question Cudworth gives no explicit reply, and the answer of More is hardly clear. On the one hand he maintains that these principles express an absolute good, which is to be called intellectual because its essence and truth are defined and apprehended by the intellect. We might infer from this that the intellect, so judging, is itself the proper and complete determinant of the will, and that man, as a rational being, ought to aim at the realisation of absolute good for its own sake: and this inference would also be suggested by More's definition of virtue as an "intellectual force of the soul by which she has such complete mastery over animal impulses and bodily passions, that in each action she can easily seek what is absolutely and simply best." But it does not seem to be really More's view. He explains that though absolute good is discerned by the intellect, the "sweetness and flavour" of it is apprehended, not by the intellect proper, but by what he calls a "boniform faculty"; and it is in this sweetness and flavour that the motive to virtuous conduct lies; ethics is the "art of living well and happily," and true happiness lies in "the pleasure which the soul derives from the sense of virtue." In short, More's Platonism appears to be really as hedonistic as Hobbism in its conception of the ultimate spring of moral action; only the feeling to which it appeals as ultimate motive is of a kind that only a mind of exceptional moral refinement can habitually feel with the decisive intensity required.

§ 4. Morality as a Code of Nature.

It is to be observed that though More lays down the abstract principle of regarding one's neighbour's good as much as one's own with the full breadth with which Christianity inculcates it—and though the highest form of the "boniform faculty" is the love of God and one's neighbour—yet when he afterwards comes to discuss and classify virtues he is too much under the influence of Platonic-Aristotelian thought to give a distinct place to benevolence, except under the old form of liberality. In this respect his system presents a striking contrast to Cumberland's, whose treatise *De Legibus Naturæ* (1672),

Cumberland (1632-1718).

though written like More's in Latin, is yet in its ethical matter thoroughly modern. Cumberland is a thinker both original and comprehensive, who has furnished material to more than one better-known moralist; but his academic prolixity and discursiveness, his academic language, and a want of clearness of view in spite of an elaborate display of exact and complete demonstration, have doomed his work to oblivion. At any rate he is noteworthy as having been the first to lay down that "the common good of all" is the supreme end and standard, in subordination to which all other rules and virtues are to be determined. So far he may be fairly called the precursor of the later utilitarianism. His fundamental principle and supreme "Law of Nature," in which all other laws of nature are implicitly included, is thus stated: "The greatest possible benevolence[1] of every rational agent towards all the rest constitutes the happiest state of each and all, so far as depends on their own power, and is necessarily required for their happiness; accordingly Common Good will be the Supreme Law." It is, however, important to notice that in his "good" is included not merely happiness, in the ordinary sense, but "perfection"; and he does not even define perfection so as strictly to exclude from it the notion of moral perfection or virtue, and thus save his explanation of morality from an obvious logical circle. A notion so incompletely determined could hardly be used for deducing particular moral rules with any precision; but in fact Cumberland does not attempt this; his supreme principle is not designed to rectify, but merely to support and systematise, common morality. This principle, as was said, is conceived as strictly a law, and therefore

[1] He explains that he means by this *effective* benevolence, not a languid and lifeless principle that does not take effect in outward acts.

referred to a law-giver, God, and provided with a sanction in the effects of its observance or violation on the agent's happiness. That the divine will is expressed by it, Cumberland, "not being so fortunate as to possess innate ideas," tries to prove by a long inductive examination of the evidences of man's essential sociality exhibited in his physical and mental constitution. His account of the sanction, again, is sufficiently comprehensive, including both the internal and the external rewards of virtue and punishments of vice; and he, like later utilitarians, explains moral obligation to lie primarily in the force exercised on the will by these sanctions. He considers, however, that while this egoistic motive is indispensable, and is the normal spring of action in the earlier stages of man's moral obedience, yet rational beings tend to rise from this to the nobler motives of love to God, regard for His honour, and disinterested affection for the common good. At the same time it is difficult to put together in a clear and consistent view his different statements as to the connection between the good of the individual and universal good, and as to the manner in which the rational apprehension of either or both goods operates in determining volition.

Locke (1632-1704).

The clearness which we seek in vain from Cumberland is found to the fullest extent in a more famous writer, whose *Essay on the Human Understanding* (1690) was already planned when Cumberland's treatise appeared. And yet Locke's ethical opinions have been widely misunderstood; since from a confusion between "innate ideas" and "intuitions," which has been common in recent ethical discussion, it has been supposed that the founder of English empiricism must necessarily have been hostile to "intuitional" ethics. But this is a complete misapprehension, so far as the determination of moral rules is concerned; though it is no doubt true that Locke rejects the view that the mere apprehension by the reason of the obligatoriness of certain rules is, or ought to be, a sufficient motive to their performance, apart from the foreseen consequences to the individual of observing or neglecting them. He agrees, in fact, with Hobbes in interpreting "good" and "evil" as "nothing but pleasure and pain or that which occasions or procures pleasure and pain"; and he defines "Moral good and evil" as "only the conformity or disagreement of our voluntary actions to some law, whereby good and evil is drawn on us from the will and power of the lawmaker." But none the less he agrees entirely with Hobbes's opponents in holding ethical rules to be actually obligatory independently of political society, and capable of being scientifically constructed on principles intuitively known: though he does not regard these principles as implanted in the human mind at birth. The aggregate of such rules he conceives as the law of God,—carefully distinguishing it, not only from civil law, but from the law of opinion or reputation, the varying moral standard by which men actually distribute praise and blame,—and being divine he assumes it to be sanctioned by adequate rewards and punishments. He does not, indeed, speak of the scientific ascertainment of this code as having been completely effected, but he affirms its possibility in language remarkably strong and decisive. "The idea," he says, "of a Supreme Being, infinite in power, goodness, and wisdom, whose workmanship we are, and upon whom we depend, and the idea of ourselves, as understanding rational beings, being such as are clear in us, would, I suppose, if duly considered and pursued, afford such foundations of our duty and rules of action as might place morality among the sciences capable of demonstration; wherein, I doubt not, but from self-evident propositions, by necessary consequences as incontestible as those in mathematics, the measures of right and wrong might be made out." As Locke cannot consistently mean by God's "goodness" anything but the disposition to give pleasure, it might be inferred that the ultimate standard of right rules of action ought to be the common happiness of the beings affected by the action; but Locke does not explicitly adopt this standard. In the passage from which I have just quoted, the propositions which he gives as instances or intuitive moral truths—"no government allows absolute liberty," and "where there is no property there is no injustice"—have no evident connection with general happiness; so again in his treatise on "Civil Government," where he expounds that part of the code of nature which appears to him important in determining the source and limits of governmental power, his *rationale* of the rules laid down is not utilitarian, except in a latent or secondary way. His conception of the Law of Nature is, in the main, that which has come to him immediately from Grotius and his disciple Puffendorf, more remotely from the Stoics and the Roman jurists; though one or two important modifications are due to his own reflection. That all men are originally free and equal; that one ought not to harm another, but rather aid in preserving him, so far as his own preservation is not thereby impeded; that compacts ought to be kept; that parents have a power to control and direct their children, corresponding to their duty of maturing and training them, but only till they come to the age of reason; that the goods of the earth are common to all in the first instance, but become the private property of one who has "mixed his labour" with them,[1] if there is "enough and as good left in common for others"—these principles appear to Locke intelligible and plain to any rational being who will contemplate the relations of men, as originally created, to each other and to God, without any explicit reference to general happiness as the supreme end. God, he argues, has made men similar in nature and faculties, *therefore* they are to be regarded as mutually independent; He has made them to last during His pleasure, *therefore* every one is bound to preserve his own life and that of others; and so forth. Not that Locke is averse to arguments showing the tendency of moral rules to promote general happiness: he has no doubt that they have this tendency, and he uses such arguments to some extent; but this line of reasoning is not fundamental in his system. Hence if his view be called in any sense utilitarian in respect of its method of determining right action, and not merely in respect of the motive it accepts as normal, it ought to be added that the utilitarianism is for the most part latent and unconscious.[2]

[1] This is, perhaps, the most important innovation of Locke's; in the view of Grotius, as we saw, the right of private property was held to depend on an express or tacit compact.

[2] I think that Locke's relation to utilitarianism is exactly characterised by some phrases of Puffendorf in which the latter is speaking of his own method. "In assigning," he says, "the cause and reason [for a law of nature] we are wont to have recourse, not to the benefit proceeding from it, but to the general nature in which it is founded." For example, if we are to give a reason why one man ought "not to hurt another, we do not usually say because abstaining from mutual violence is profitable (although it is so indeed in the highest degree), but because the person is another man, that is, an animal related to us by nature whom it would be criminal to harm." It may, I think, be inferred from the manner in which Locke mentions Puffendorf in his essay on education that he was in substantial agreement with his view of the Law of Nature.

§ 5. Clarke (1675-1729).

Fifteen years after the publication of Locke's treatises on Civil Government (1705), an impressive attempt was made by Clarke to "place morality among the sciences capable of demonstration, from self-evident propositions as incontestible as those in mathematics"; but it was made on the lines of Cudworth's reasoning rather than of Locke's; as it maintained against Hobbes and Locke,[1] that the cognition of self-evident practical propositions is in itself, independently of pleasure and pain, a sufficient motive to a rational being as such for acting in accordance with them. The aim of the lectures in which Clarke's system was expounded was to prove the "reasonableness and certainty" of the Christian revelation: and, with this view, to exhibit on the one hand the eternal and immutable obligations of morality "incumbent on men from the very nature and reason of things themselves," and on the other hand the impossibility of "defending" these obligations "to any effectual purpose," or enforcing them with any sufficient strength, without the belief in immortality and future rewards and punishments. This doubleness of aim—which, as we shall see, complicates Clarke's task rather seriously—must always be kept in view in examining his system. He is anxious to show both that moral rules are binding independently of the sanctions that divine legislation has attached to them, and also that such rules are laws of God, with adequate sanctions attached to their observance and violation; the two propositions are, in his view, necessarily connected, since only from the absolute bindingness of justice on all rational wills are we able to infer with philosophic certainty that God, being necessarily just, will

[1] It should be observed that Clarke's polemic is formally directed against Hobbes alone; he does not, so far as I am aware, ever define his relation to Locke.

punish ill desert and reward good desert. In examining the first, and more strictly ethical, portion of his argument, it is convenient to distinguish two questions: (1) What are the self-evident and immutable principles of morality? and (2) What is their relation to the individual's will? His general account of the manner in which moral principles are apprehended is that, from the "necessary and eternal different relations that different things bear to one another," result "fitness and unfitness of the application of different things or different relations one to another"—a "fitness or suitableness of certain circumstances to certain persons, and unsuitableness of others, according to the nature of things and the qualification of persons"; and that this fitness and unfitness are as intuitively evident to the reason contemplating these relations, as the equality and inequality of mathematical quantities. This general conception he illustrates by exhibiting the self-evidence of the four chief rules of righteousness; *i.e.* the rules of (1) Piety towards God, (2) Equity and (3) Benevolence towards our fellows, and (4) the rule of duty towards a man's own self, which he calls Sobriety. The last of these rules, as defined by Clarke, is manifestly not primary and independent in its obligation, since it inculcates the preservation of life and the control of passions and appetites, *with a view to the performance of duty*, which is therefore assumed to be already determined; and in the exposition of the Rule of Piety he hardly attempts the precision which his mathematical analogy suggests.[1] It is rather

[1] The "fitness" or "congruity" which he here tries to exhibit is the "congruity" between (*a*) admiration, awe, fear, hope, and other human feelings, and (*b*) the divine attributes of Eternity, Infinity, Omniscience, Power and Justice, Mercy, etc. But the indefinite qualitative correspondence between human emotions and divine attributes is as unlike as possible to the exact quantitative rela-

in the rules of Equity and Universal Benevolence—which, in Clarke's view, sum up social duty—that the force and significance of this analogy appears. The principle of Equity —that "whatever I judge reasonable or unreasonable for another to do for me, that by the same judgment I declare reasonable or unreasonable that I in the like case should do for him"—has undoubtedly a certain resemblance to a mathematical axiom: and the same may be said of the principle that a greater good is to be preferred to a less, whether it be my good or another's [1]—which we have already noted, in a slightly different form, among More's *Noemata Moralia.*

If the self-evidence, in some sense, of these propositions be granted, it remains to consider how far the intuitive cognition of them is or ought to be decisive in determining the individual's volition. On this point a careful examination of Clarke's language shows that the position which he is really prepared to maintain is by no means either so clear or so uncompromising as the general tenor of his language implies. At first sight he seems to lay down, without qualification, that a rational creature, as such, must act in conformity with its cognition of moral truth: through

tion which we apprehend between the terms of a mathematical comparison.

[1] I have elsewhere observed (*Methods of Ethics*, Book III. ch. xiii. § 4) that this principle, as stated by Clarke, is not free from the charge of tautology; but I regard this charge as only affecting the form, not the substance, of his proposition. It is, I think, a more serious objection to the completeness of Clarke's exposition, that the rules of Equity and Benevolence, as stated by himself, hardly exemplify his general account of self-evident moral truth; for the relations contemplated in these rules are relations of *similarity:* whereas what, after his general account of moral truth, we expect him to show us—and what for practical purposes we need to be shown—is how *differences* of treatment of human beings correspond to differences in their circumstances and relations.

this cognition we are enabled to affirm with certainty that God, the supreme Reason governing the universe, will order the destinies of His creatures in conformity to justice and benevolence, and make men happy unless they have deserved to be miserable ; and on similar grounds we can equally affirm that "were not men most unnaturally corrupted by perverse and unaccountably false opinions and monstrous evil customs and habits . . . it would be impossible that universal equity should not be practised by all mankind"—as impossible as that they should not believe that two and two make four. Nay, Clarke often presses the analogy between ethics and mathematics so far as to use phrases which not only overlook the essential distinction between what is and what ought to be, but even overleap this distinction extravagantly ; as, *e.g.*, in saying that the man who "wilfully acts contrary to justice wills things to be what they are not and cannot be." What he really means is less paradoxically stated in the general proposition that "originally and in reality it is as natural and (morally speaking) necessary that the will should be determined in every action by the reason of the thing and the right of the case, as it is natural and (absolutely speaking) necessary that the understanding should submit to a demonstrated truth." From these and similar passages we should infer that if a man deviates from the rules of Equity and Universal Benevolence, under the seductions of pleasure and pain, it is not, in Clarke's view, that he has solid reasons for so deviating, but that he is partly under the influence of irrational impulses. But when he comes afterwards to argue the need of future rewards and punishments we find that his claim on behalf of morality is startlingly reduced. He now only contends that "virtue deserves to be chosen for its own sake, and vice to be avoided, though a man was sure for his own particular neither to gain nor lose anything by the practice of either." He fully admits that the question is altered when vice is attended by pleasure and profit to the vicious man, virtue by loss and calamity; and even that it is "not truly reasonable that men by adhering to virtue should part with their lives, if thereby they deprived themselves of all possibility of receiving any advantage from their adherence." That is, he admits implicitly a reasonableness from the individual's point of view in the preference of Self-interest to Virtue, if the empirically known conditions of human life are alone taken into account; though from an abstract or universal point of view it is reasonable to prefer Virtue to Interest. The contradiction between the two kinds of reasonableness was no doubt convenient for showing the need of theology to defend the truths of ethics; but as Clarke's theological system also requires ethical truth to be irrefragably established apart from theology—in order that the moral attributes of the Deity may be philosophically known—this contradiction was a serious source of weakness: it exhibited a conflict among the intuitions of the practical reason, for which no parallel could be found in the mathematical intuitions with which Clarke compared them.

Thus, on the whole, the impressive earnestness with which Clarke enforced the doctrine of rational morality only rendered more manifest the difficulty of establishing ethics on an independent philosophical basis; so long at least as the psychological egoism of Hobbes was not definitely assailed and overthrown. Until this was done, the utmost demonstration of the abstract reasonableness of social duty only leaves us with an irreconcilable antagonism between the view of abstract reason and the self-love which is allowed to be normal in man's appetitive nature. Let us grant that there is as much intellectual absurdity in acting unjustly as in denying that two and two make four; still, if a man has to choose between absurdity and unhappiness, he will naturally prefer the former; and Clarke, as we have seen, is not really prepared to maintain that such preference is irrational.

§ 6. Shaftesbury (1671-1713). It remained to try another psychological basis for ethical construction; instead of presenting the principle of social duty as abstract reason, liable to conflict to any extent with natural self-love, it might be possible, by exhibiting the naturalness of man's social affections, to demonstrate a normal harmony between these and his reflective self-regard. This is the line of thought which Shaftesbury may be said to have initiated. Not, of course, that he is original in insisting on the fact of natural affections binding men to their fellows; Cumberland, to say nothing of earlier writers, had dwelt on this at some length; and Clarke had used it to supplement his exposition of the abstract reasonableness of universal benevolence. But no moralist before Shaftesbury had made this the cardinal point in his system; no one had yet definitely transferred the centre of ethical interest from the Reason, conceived as apprehending either abstract moral distinctions or laws of divine legislation, to the emotional impulses that prompt to social duty; no one had undertaken to distinguish clearly, by careful analysis of experience, the disinterested and self-regarding elements of our appetitive nature, or to prove inductively their perfect harmony. In his *Inquiry concerning Virtue and Merit* (1711)[1] he begins by attacking the egoistic interpretation

[1] The treatise was printed first in 1699; but its influence must be dated from its republication in the second volume of the *Characteristics*, which appeared in 1711.

of good which Hobbes had put forward; and which, as we have seen, was not necessarily excluded by the doctrine of rational intuitions of duty. This interpretation, he says, would be only true if we considered man as a wholly unrelated individual. Such a being we might doubtless call "good," if his impulses and dispositions were harmonized and adapted to the attainment of his own felicity.[1] But a man we must and do consider in relation to a larger system of which he forms a part, and so we only call him "good" when his impulses and dispositions are so graduated and balanced as to promote the good of this larger whole. Again, we do not attribute goodness to such a being merely because his outward acts have beneficial results; when we speak of a man as good, we mean that his dispositions or affections are such as tend of themselves, without external constraint, to promote the good or happiness of human society. Hobbes's moral man, who, if let loose from governmental control, would straightway spread ruin among his fellows, is not what we commonly agree to call good. Goodness, then, in a "sensible creature" implies primarily disinterested affections, whose direct object is the good of

[1] In the greater part of his argument Shaftesbury interprets the "good" of the individual hedonistically, as equivalent to pleasure, satisfaction, delight, enjoyment. But it is to be observed that the conception of "Good" with which he begins is not definitely hedonistic; "interest or good" is at first taken to mean the "right state of a creature," that "is by nature forwarded and by himself affectionately sought"; and in one passage he seems to conceive of a "planetary system" as having an end or good. Still, when the application of the term is narrowed to human beings, he slides—almost unconsciously—into a purely hedonistic interpretation of it. Indeed, he defines Philosophy itself as "the study of happiness" (*Moralists*, Part III. § 3). I may add that he never, so far as I know, recognises any possibility of conflict between the good or happiness of the human species, and the good of the "system of the universe."

others; but Shaftesbury does not hold that such benevolent social impulses are always good, and that no other impulses are necessary to constitute a creature good. On the contrary, he is careful to point out how particular benevolent affections—*e.g.* pity or parental love—may be so "over great" as to detract from the force and natural operation of other kind affections, and even so extensive as to defeat themselves and miss the attainment of their own ends; and how, again, a deficiency in the impulses that tend to the preservation of the individual may be injurious to the species, and therefore vicious. Goodness, in short, depends upon the co-existence of impulses of both kinds, each in its proper measure relatively to the rest, so as to maintain a just proportionment, balance, and harmony of the different elements,—tendency to promote the good of mankind being taken as the criterion of the right degrees and proportions. This being established, the main aim of Shaftesbury's argument is to prove that in human beings the same balancing and blending of private and social affections, which tends naturally to public good, is also conducive to the happiness of the individual in whom it exists. He distinguishes three classes of impulses: (1) "Natural affections," which he defines to be "such as are founded in love, complacency, goodwill, and sympathy with the kind"; (2) "Self-affections," which include love of life, resentment of injury, bodily appetite, interest or "desire of those conveniencies by which we are well provided for and maintained," emulation or love of praise, indolence or love of ease and rest; and (3) "Unnatural affections," under which head come not only all malevolent impulses except resentment, but also impulses due to superstition, barbarous custom, or depraved appetite, and even certain "self-passions," when exorbitant and monstrous in degree.[1] Taking the first class, he dwells on their importance as sources of happiness to the individual who experiences them; pleasures of mind being superior to those of body, and the exercise of benevolent affections yielding the richest harvest of mental satisfaction, in (1) the pleasurableness of the benevolent emotion itself, (2) the sympathetic enjoyment of the happiness of others, and (3) the pleasure arising from a consciousness of their love and esteem. He points out what a large place the social affections occupy in human life,—being indeed an indispensable element even of what are vaguely thought of as the sensual enjoyments of the voluptuary; and concludes that "to have these natural and good affections in full strength is to have the chief means and power of self-enjoyment; to want them is certain misery and ill." Thus though to a superficial view these disinterested impulses, aiming at others' good, appear to lead a man away from his own good, in reality they are found to lead him to it. On the other hand, the "self-affections" or "self-passions," which, as conceived by Shaftesbury, constitute "self-love," appear to aim directly at the individual's good; but it is only if kept within strict limits that they really promote it. To show this he dwells on the painfulness of anger, the palpable loss of pleasure on the whole through excessive indulgence of sensual appetites, the restlessness and disquiet that attend covetousness and immoderate love of praise, the mischief of various kinds incurred by excessive sloth. Even love of life may exist in

[1] The terminology of the classification is not altogether defensible, as, according to Shaftesbury's own view, the "self-affections" were as "natural" as the social affections: the latter, however, may be said to be in a special sense "natural" as directed towards nature's *largest* end, the good of the species or kind

excess and tend to the unhappiness of the creature that indulges it. On the whole, therefore, he concludes that the point of indulgence at which these self-passions or self-affections begin to be mischievous to the individual coincides with that at which they begin to be mischievous to society; while up to this point they are conducive both to public and to private good. He does not, however, attempt to prove the exact coincidence of the two points by any close or cogent reasoning.

That the "unnatural affections" should be excluded altogether from a well-balanced mind is implied in the very conception of them; since they are defined as affections that tend neither to public nor to private good. It might, however, be urged that even purely malevolent desires (which he has chiefly in view here) carry a kind of pleasure with them, so that where they are strong, their satisfaction might seem to constitute an element of the individual's happiness too important to be discarded. But this view Shaftesbury regards as quite erroneous. "To love and to be kind," he says, ". . . is itself original joy, depending on no preceding pain or uneasiness, and producing nothing but satisfaction merely. On the other side, animosity, hatred, and bitterness is original misery and torment, producing no other pleasure or satisfaction than as the unnatural desire is for the instant satisfied by something which appeases it. How strong soever this pleasure may appear, it only the more implies the misery of the state that produces it." If we add to this the painfulness of the consciousness of the ill-will of others, it seems to him abundantly clear, that "to have these horrid, monstrous, and unnatural affections is to be miserable in the highest degree"; and thus we are led again to the general conclusion that the same balance, order, economy of affections which tends to the public good, tends also to the good of the individual.

So far I have made no reference to the doctrine of a "moral sense," which is sometimes represented as Shaftesbury's cardinal tenet; but in fact this doctrine, though characteristic and important, is not exactly necessary to his main argument; it is the crown rather than the keystone of his ethical structure. Even a man who had no moral sense would, in Shaftesbury's view, always find it his interest to maintain in himself precisely that balance of social and self-regarding affections that is most conducive to the good of the human species: and such a being, if he existed, might properly be said to have "goodness," though not virtue. But such a man, Shaftesbury holds, is not really to be found. In a "rational creature," not only "the outward beings that offer themselves to the sense are objects of affection; but the very actions themselves, and the affections of pity, kindness, gratitude, and their contrarys, being brought before the mind by reflection, become objects." So that, by means of this reflected sense, there arises another kind of affection towards the very affections[1] themselves; a love of goodness for its own sake and on account of its own natural beauty and worth, and aversion to its opposite. It is impossible, he thinks, to conceive a rational creature entirely devoid of this moral or "reflex" sensibility; which accordingly furnishes an additional impulse to good conduct—by which any deficiency in the balance of social and self-regarding affections may be supplemented and corrected—

[1] Shaftesbury sometimes speaks of "affections and actions," sometimes of "affections" alone, as the proper objects of moral likings and aversions; his view being, I conceive, that it is not the outward act in itself that arouses moral sensibility, but the act as a manifestation of sentiment.

and an additional gratification to be taken into account in the reckoning which proves the coincidence of private and public good. For the operation of the moral sense, when uncorrupted, is conceived by Shaftesbury to be always in harmony with rational judgment as to what is or is not conducive to the good of the human species, though it does not necessarily involve the explicit formation of such a judgment; and he holds that "no speculative opinion is capable immediately and directly to exclude or destroy the moral sense." It may, however, be to a great extent lost by "custom or licentiousness of practice": and it may, in time, be profoundly perverted by a false religion that bids us honour and esteem a deity with immoral attributes.

The appearance of Shaftesbury's *Characteristics* marks a turning-point in the history of English ethical thought. With the generation of moralists that followed, the consideration of abstract rational principles falls into the background, and its place is taken by empirical study of the human mind, observation of the actual play of its various impulses and sentiments. This empirical psychology had not indeed been neglected by previous writers. More, among others, had imitated Descartes in a discussion of the passions, and Locke's essay had given a still stronger impulse in the same direction; still, Shaftesbury is the first moralist who distinctly takes psychological experience as the basis of ethics. His suggestions were developed by Hutcheson into one of the most elaborate systems of moral philosophy which we possess; and through Hutcheson, if not directly, they influenced Hume's speculations, and are thus connected with later utilitarianism. Moreover, the substance of Shaftesbury's main argument was adopted by Butler, though it could not pass the scrutiny of that powerful and cautious intellect without receiving important modifications and additions. On the other hand, the ethical optimism of Shaftesbury, being rather broadly impressive than exactly reasoned, and being connected with a natural theology that implied the Christian scheme to be superfluous—and hinted it to be worse,—challenged attack equally from orthodox divines and from cynical freethinkers. Of these latter Mandeville, the author of *The Fable of the Bees, or Private Vices Public Benefits* (1724), was a conspicuous if not a typical specimen. He can hardly be called a "moralist"; and though it is impossible to deny him a considerable share of philosophical penetration, his anti-moral paradoxes have not even apparent coherence. He is convinced that virtue (where it is more than a mere pretence) is purely artificial; but he is not quite certain whether it is a useless trammel of appetites and passions that are advantageous to society, or a device creditable to the politicians who introduced it by playing upon the "pride and vanity" of the "silly creature man." The view, however, to which he gave audacious expression, that moral regulation is something alien to the natural man and imposed on him from without, seems to have been very current in the polite society of his time; as may be inferred both from Berkeley's *Alciphron* and from Butler's more famous sermons. **Mandeville.**

§ 7. Butler (1692-1752). The view of "human nature" against which Butler preached was not exactly Mandeville's, nor was it properly to be called Hobbist, although Butler fairly treats it as having a philosophical basis in Hobbes's psychology. It was, so to say, Hobbism turned inside out—rendered licentious and anarchical instead of constructive. Hobbes had said, "the natural state of man is non-moral, unregulated; moral rules are means to the end of peace, which is a means to the end of self-preservation." On this view morality, so far as Hobbes deals with it, though conventional and dependent for its actuality on the social compact which establishes government, is actually binding on man as a reasonable being. But the quasi-theistic assumption that what is natural must be reasonable probably remained in the minds of most persons who became convinced that unrestrained egoism is natural; and the combination of the two beliefs tended to produce results which, though not perhaps practically subversive of peace, were at any rate dangerous to social wellbeing. To meet this view Butler does not content himself, as he is sometimes carelessly supposed to do, with simply insisting on the natural claim to authority of the conscience which his opponents repudiated as artificial; he also uses a more subtle and effective argument *ad hominem*. He first follows Shaftesbury in exhibiting the social affections as no less natural than the appetites and desires which tend more directly to self-preservation; then going further and reviving the Stoic view of the *prima naturæ*, the first objects of natural appetites, he argues that pleasure is not the primary aim even of the impulses which Shaftesbury allowed to be "self-affections"; but rather a result which follows upon their attaining their natural ends. We have, in fact, to distinguish Self-love, the "general desire that every man hath of his own happiness" or pleasure, from the particular affections, passions, and appetites directed towards objects other than pleasure, in the satisfaction of which pleasure consists. The latter are "necessarily presupposed" as distinct impulses in "the very idea of an interested pursuit"; since, if there were no such pre-existing desires, there would be no pleasure for self-love to aim at. Thus, *e.g.*, the object of hunger is the eating of food, not the pleasure of eating it;

hunger is, therefore, strictly speaking, no more "interested" than benevolence; for, granting that sensual pleasures are an element in the happiness at which self-love aims, the same at least may be said for the pleasures of love and sympathy. That bodily appetites (or other particular desires) are not forms of self-love, is further shown by the fact that every one of them may in certain circumstances come into conflict with it. Indeed, it is common enough for men to sacrifice to passion what they know to be their true interests; at the same time we do not consider such conduct "natural" in man as a rational being; we rather regard it as natural for him to govern his transient impulses. Thus the notion of natural unregulated egoism turns out to be a psychological chimæra; for (1) man's primary impulses cannot be sweepingly called egoistic in any sense, since none of them aim immediately at the individual's pleasure, while the obvious tendencies of some are as clearly towards social wellbeing as those of others are towards self-preservation; and (2) a man cannot be consistently egoistic without being continually self-regulative. Indeed, we may say that an egoist must be doubly self-regulative, since rational self-love ought to restrain not only other impulses, but itself also; for as happiness is made up of feelings that result from the satisfaction of impulses other than self-love, any over-development of the latter, enfeebling these other impulses, must proportionally diminish the happiness at which self-love aims.

Human nature, on its practical side, then, in Butler's view—more distinctly and explicitly than in Shaftesbury's—is conceived to be not merely a system of impulses, in which a certain balance and harmony has to be maintained in order that it may be in a good condition, but a system in which some springs of action are naturally governing and regulative, while others are naturally submissive to regulation. As regards the latter, Butler maintains with Shaftesbury that all impulses which can properly be called natural —all which belong to the original plan and constitution of human nature—have a certain legitimate sphere of operation. This is true even of the impulses to inflict harm; among which he distinguishes (1) merely instinctive resentment, which he regards as a useful aid to self-defence against sudden mischief, however caused, from (2) deliberate resentment, of which the proper object is wrong and injustice as distinct from mere harm. When properly limited such deliberate resentment is an impulse socially useful, and even indispensable for the effective administration of Justice; for though "it were much to be wished" that men would prosecute offenders from "reason and cool reflection," experience shows that they will not. "Resentment being out of the case, there is not, properly speaking, any such thing as direct ill-will in one man towards another"; *e.g.* envy is merely desire of superiority taking a bad means to its end. In short, all our natural appetites, passions, and affections—however distinct, in their immediate ends, from both Self-love and Benevolence—have within due limits a tendency to promote both public and private good; though one set of them, including the bodily appetites, tend primarily to the good of the individual; while others, such as "desire of esteem, love of society as distinct from affection to the good of it, indignation against successful vice," tend primarily to public good.

So much for the natural springs of action that need regulation. It is more difficult to ascertain Butler's view of the naturally regulative principles. The language of his first sermon would rather suggest that there are three such principles—Self-love, Benevolence, and Conscience; the two former being subordinately regulative of the two groups of impulses that have a primary tendency to private and to public good respectively; while conscience is supremely regulative over all. But on looking closer at Butler's language it will be seen that what he contemplates under the notion of benevolence is not definitely a desire for general good as such, but rather kind affection for particular individuals—"if there is in mankind any disposition to friendship; if there be any such thing as compassion, as the paternal or filial affections; if there be any affection in human nature, the object and end of which is the good of another, this is benevolence." Possibly he doubted the existence of public benevolence, or regard to the happiness of mankind in general, as distinct on the one hand from particular kind affections,[1] and on the other hand from conscience; more certainly, at the time of writing the sermons, he had not definitely abandoned the view of Shaftesbury that the good or happiness of society as a whole is the ultimate end of conduct approved by conscience—"that mankind is a community," he says, "that we all stand in a relation to each other, that there is a public end and interest of society which each particular is obliged to promote, is the sum of morals."[2] At any rate he does not—like Hutcheson—distinctly recognise a calm regard for general happiness as a normal governing principle, parallel to the calm regard for private happiness which he calls self-love.

There remain, then, Conscience and "Reasonable Self-love" as the two authorities in the polity of the soul. With

[1] Hume, as we shall see, explicitly denied the existence of "public benevolence" as an *ordinary* human emotion. See p. 211.

[2] Sermon IX. (but see note to Sermon XII.)

regard to these Butler's real view is not (as is widely supposed) that self-love is naturally subordinate to conscience—at least if we consider the theoretical rather than the practical relation between the two. He treats them as independent principles, and so far co-ordinate in authority that it is not "according to nature" that either should be overruled. "Reasonable self-love and conscience are the chief or superior principles in the nature of man; because an action may be suitable to this nature, though all other principles be violated; but becomes unsuitable if either of those are."[1] He even goes so far as to "let it be allowed" that "if there ever should be, as it is impossible there ever should be, any inconsistence between them," conscience would have to give way; since "our ideas of happiness and misery are of all our ideas the nearest and most important to us . . . though virtue or moral rectitude does indeed consist in affection to and pursuit of what is right and good as such; yet, when we sit down in a cool hour, we can neither justify to ourselves this or any other pursuit, till we are convinced that it will be for our happiness, or at least not contrary to it."[2] That the ultimate appeal must be to the individual's interest was similarly assumed in Shaftesbury's argument, though it is not formally stated by him; notwithstanding all his emphasis on the disinterested impulses to Virtue, still, when he raises the questions, "What *obligation* there is to Virtue, or what *reason* to embrace it?" it never occurs to him to answer them from any other than an egoistic point of view; his "obligation" is the obligation of self-interest; his "reasons" are entirely addressed to self-love. Butler, however, considers that his own view corrects Shaftesbury's by taking due note of the authority of con-

[1] At the end of Sermon III. [2] Sermon XI.

science; and that this correction is fundamentally important in dealing with the case of a "sceptic not convinced of the happy tendency of virtue" in this world. He thinks that if the natural authoritativeness of conscience is recognised, even such a sceptic cannot reasonably doubt that duty is to be preferred to worldly interest—independently of the sanctions of revealed religion; since the dictates of conscience are clear and certain, while the calculations of self-interest lead to merely probable conclusions; and where two authorities conflict "the more certain obligation must entirely supersede and destroy the less certain."

Butler's ethical construction, then, is based upon what we may call a guarded optimism: it is reasonable, he holds, to assume that the two inner authorities under which we find ourselves placed by nature are harmonious, not conflicting, until proof to the contrary is given; and it is impossible that such proof should be given, owing to the inevitable uncertainty of egoistic calculation. It may be added that a further psychological reason for anticipating the ultimate coincidence of Virtue with the Happiness of the virtuous agent is found by him in the "discernment of good and ill desert," which by an "unquestionable natural association" accompanies our discernment of moral good and evil.

Butler's express statement of the duality of the regulative principles in human nature constitutes an important step in ethical speculation; since it brings into clear view the most fundamental difference between the ethical thought of modern England and that of the old Greco-Roman world, —a difference all the more striking because Butler's general formula of "living according to nature" is taken from

Stoicism, and his view of human nature as an ordered polity of impulses is distinctly Platonic. But in Platonism and Stoicism, and in Greek moral philosophy generally, but one regulative and governing faculty is recognised under the name of Reason—however the regulation of Reason may be understood; in the modern ethical view, when it has worked itself clear, there are found to be two,—Universal Reason and Egoistic Reason, or Conscience and Self-love. This dualism, as has been noticed, appears confusedly in Clarke's account of "reasonable" conduct, and implicitly in Shaftesbury's account of the obligation to Virtue; but its clear recognition by Butler is perhaps most nearly anticipated in Wollaston's *Religion of Nature Delineated* (1722). Here, for the first time, we find "moral good" and "natural good" or "happiness" treated separately as two essentially distinct objects of rational pursuit and investigation; the harmony between them being regarded as matter of religious faith, not moral knowledge. Wollaston's theory of moral evil as consisting in the practical contradiction of a true proposition, closely resembles the most paradoxical part of Clarke's doctrine, and was not likely to approve itself to the strong common sense of Butler; but his statement of happiness or pleasure as a "justly desirable" end at which every rational being "ought" to aim corresponds exactly to Butler's conception of self-love as a naturally governing impulse; while the "moral arithmetic" with which he compares pleasures and pains, and endeavours to make the notion of happiness quantitatively precise, is an anticipation of Benthamism.

Wollaston (1659-1724).

If we ask for a justification of the dual authority of Conscience and Reasonable Self-love—beyond the mere fact of their natural claims to authority—we turn to an aspect of Butler's thought which is but imperfectly developed or disclosed. As regards the reasonableness of self-love, indeed, he scarcely recognises the need of any explanation: he merely remarks that it "belongs to man as a reasonable creature, reflecting on his own interest or happiness," to make that happiness an ultimate end; and that, therefore, "interest, one's own happiness, is a manifest obligation." The reasonableness of conscience is a different matter: here he has before him the work of such moralists as Clarke, who had endeavoured elaborately to exhibit moral principles as rational intuitions or axioms, analogous to the intuitions or axioms of mathematics: and this line of reasoning Butler admits as valid, though he does not follow it. He agrees with Clarke that "there is a moral fitness and unfitness in actions, prior to all will, which determines the Divine Conduct"; that "moral duties arise out of the nature of the case," and "moral precepts are precepts of which we see the reason"; so that "vice is contrary to the nature and reason of things" in a sense quite different from that in which it is "a violation and breaking in upon our own nature." Still, he never makes any attempt to exhibit this abstract reasonableness in the moral rules to which he refers: his method is to ascertain by psychological reflection what dictates conscience lays down, not to reduce these dictates to self-evident intuitions or moral axioms. This method brings him ultimately to recognise a marked divergence between the directions of the moral faculty and the conclusions to which a simple consideration of what is most conducive to general happiness might lead. I say "ultimately," because it is interesting to note how, in the development of Butler's ethical view, there gradually emerges that opposition between "intuitional" and "utilitarian" morality which has filled so large a space in more recent ethical discussion. This opposition is quite latent in earlier writers; Clarke finds himself in perfect agreement with Cumberland; and Shaftesbury conceives the moral sense, in a normal state, as immediately approving actions seen to be conducive to the good or happiness of the species. And in a passage before quoted from Butler's ninth sermon ("Upon Forgiveness of Injuries") the practical divergence between Conscience and Benevolence is still ignored; it is, however, suggested, though in a tentative way, in a note to Sermon XII. ("Upon the Love of our Neighbour"); but it is very explicitly and emphatically stated in the Dissertation on Virtue appended to the *Analogy*, published in 1736—ten years after the sermons. He there affirms that "benevolence and the want of it, singly considered, are in no sort the whole of virtue and vice"; for "we are constituted so as to condemn falsehood, unprovoked violence, injustice, and to approve of benevolence to some preferably to others, abstracted from all consideration which conduct is likeliest to produce an over-balance of happiness or misery." He even characterises the opposite opinion as a "mistake, than which none can be conceived more terrible. For it is certain that some of the most shocking instances of injustice, adultery, murder, perjury, and even of persecution, may, in many supposable cases, not have the appearance of being likely to produce an overbalance of misery in the present state; perhaps sometimes may have the contrary appearance."

§ 8. Shaftesbury's doctrine developed and systematised.

Butler is not certain that any author has designed to assert that complete coincidence between Virtue and Benevolence which he disputes in the passages above quoted; but he thinks that "some of great and distinguished merit have expressed themselves in a manner which may occasion some danger to careless readers" of falling into the terrible mistake that he signalises. Probably we may assume Shaftesbury to be one of the authors here referred to; almost certainly we may assume another to be Hutcheson, who in his *Inquiry Concerning the Original of our Ideas of Virtue* had definitely identified virtue with benevolence. The identification is slightly qualified in Hutcheson's posthumously published *System of Moral Philosophy* (1755); in which the general view of Shaftesbury is more fully developed, with several new psychological distinctions, including the separation of "calm" benevolence—as well as, after Butler, "calm self-love"—from the "turbulent" passions, selfish or social. Hutcheson also follows Butler in laying stress on the "regulating and controlling function" of the moral sense; but he still regards "kind affections"[1] as the principal objects of moral approbation—the "calm" and "extensive" affections being preferred to the turbulent and narrow. The most excellent disposition, he holds, which "naturally gains the highest approbation" is *either* the "calm, stable, universal goodwill to all" by which a man is determined "to desire the highest happiness of the greatest possible system of sensitive beings," *or* the desire and love of moral excellence, which in man is inseparable from the universal goodwill that it chiefly approves. These two principles cannot conflict, and therefore there is no practical need of determining which is highest: Hutcheson is disposed to treat them as co-ordinate. Only in a secondary sense is approval due to certain "abilities and dispositions

Hutcheson (1694-1747).

[1] Butler, on the other hand, defines the object of the moral faculty as "actions"—including intentions and tendencies to act—as distinct from mere passive feelings, so far as these are out of our power.

immediately connected with virtuous affections," as candour, veracity, fortitude, sense of honour; while in a lower grade still are placed sciences and arts along with even bodily skills and gifts; indeed, the approbation we give to these is not strictly moral, but is referred to the "sense of decency or dignity," which (as well as the sense of honour) is to be distinguished from the moral sense. Calm self-love Hutcheson regards as not in itself an object either of moral approbation or disapprobation; the "actions which flow solely from self-love, and yet evidence no want of benevolence, having no hurtful effects upon others, seem perfectly indifferent in a moral sense": at the same time he enters into a careful analysis of the elements of happiness,[1] in order to show that a true regard for private interest always coincides with the moral sense and with benevolence. While thus maintaining Shaftesbury's "harmony" between public and private good, Hutcheson is still more careful to establish the strict disinterestedness of benevolent affections. Shaftesbury had conclusively shown that these were not in the vulgar sense selfish; but the very stress which he lays on the pleasure inseparable from their exercise suggests a subtle egoistic theory which he does not expressly exclude, since it may be said that this "intrinsic reward" constitutes the real motive of the benevolent man. To this Hutcheson replies that no doubt the exquisite delight of the emotion of love is a motive to sustain and develop it; but this pleasure cannot be directly obtained, any more than other pleasures, by merely desiring it; it can only be sought by

[1] It is worth noticing that Hutcheson's express definition of the object of self-love includes "perfection" as well as "happiness"; but in the working out of his system he considers private good exclusively as happiness or pleasure.

the indirect process of cultivating and indulging the disinterested desire for others' good, which is thus shown to be distinct from the desire for the pleasure of benevolence. He points to the fact that the imminence of death often intensifies instead of diminishing a man's desire for the welfare of those he loves, as a crucial experiment proving the disinterestedness of love; adding, as confirmatory evidence, that the sympathy and admiration commonly felt for self-sacrifice depends on the belief that it is something different from refined self-seeking.

It remains to consider how, from the doctrine that affection is the proper object of approbation, we are to deduce moral rules or "natural laws" prescribing or prohibiting outward acts. It is obvious that all actions conducive to the general good will deserve our highest approbation if done from disinterested benevolence; but how if they are not so done? In answering this question, Hutcheson avails himself of a scholastic distinction between "material" and "formal" goodness. "An action," he says, "is *materially* good when in fact it tends to the interest of the system, so far as we can judge of its tendency, or to the good of some part consistent with that of the system, whatever were the affections of the agent. An action is *formally* good when it flowed from good affection in a just proportion." On the pivot of this distinction Hutcheson turns round from the point of view of Shaftesbury to that of later utilitarianism. As regards "material" goodness of actions, he adopts explicitly and unreservedly the formula afterwards taken as fundamental by Bentham; holding that "that action is best which procures the greatest happiness for the greatest numbers, and the worst which in a like manner occasions misery." Accordingly his treatment of external rights and duties, though decidedly inferior in methodical clearness and precision, does not differ fundamentally from that of Paley or Bentham; only he lays greater stress on the immediate conduciveness of actions to the happiness of individuals, and more often refers in a merely supplementary or restrictive way to their tendencies in respect of general happiness. It may be noticed, too, that he still accepts the "social compact" as the natural mode of constituting government, and regards the obligations of subjects to civil obedience as normally dependent on a tacit contract; though he is careful to state that consent is not absolutely necessary to the just establishment of beneficent government, nor the source of an irrevocable obligation to obey a pernicious one.

§ 9. Moral sentiments and sympathy. Hume (1711-1776).

An important step further in political utilitarianism was taken by Hume. Hume concedes that "if we trace government to its first origin in the woods and deserts," we must allow that "nothing but their own consent could at first associate men together," and "subject multitudes to the command of one." But the present duty of allegiance to government cannot be based on this ancient agreement of savages: and history shows that almost all historical governments "have been founded originally either on usurpation or conquest or both," and "that in the few cases where consent may seem to have taken place it was commonly so irregular, so confined, or so much intermixed with either fraud or violence that it cannot have any great authority." No doubt old established governments are commonly supported on the willing consent of the governed; but the latter "imagine not that their consent gives a title," or that they are free to withhold it: "it never was pleaded as an excuse for a rebel that the first act he performed, after he came to years of discretion, was to levy war against the sovereign of the state." Fidelity to compact cannot therefore be the actual basis of the duty of allegiance to government as generally recognised; and if it be still urged that it is nevertheless the *right* basis, Hume answers that "both allegiance and fidelity stand precisely on the same foundation," viz. the "apparent interests and necessities of human society," so that "we gain nothing by resolving the one into the other": our sense of obligation to both alike is founded on a perception of their paramount utility to society. It is in this derivation of the sense of moral obligation that the fundamental difference lies between Hutcheson's ethical doctrine and Hume's.[1] The former, while accepting con-

[1] Hume's ethical view was first expounded in his *Treatise on Human Nature* (1739); but the final statement of it is to be found in his *Inquiry into the Principles of Morals* (1751). As the earlier *Treatise* was expressly repudiated by its author, I have in the main confined my attention to the later work, which, in Hume's own opinion, was of all his writings "incomparably the best." In respect, however, of the duty of allegiance to government, it seemed desirable to supplement it by the *Essay of the Original Contract*, published 1752. I think, also, that Hume's view as to the origin of Justice cannot easily be understood from the later treatise alone. In the *Treatise on Human Nature* he agrees broadly with Hobbes as to the original connection of Justice with Self-interest, and holds, like Hobbes, that its obligations are conditional on the existence of an established social order which it is the individual's interest to maintain. Where he separates from Hobbes is, firstly, on the question of the *origin* of this established order,—he treats Hobbes's "state of nature" as a philosophical fiction, holding that the observance of Justice is not to be referred to an express compact, but to a gradually attained convention similar in kind to that by which Language and Currency must be conceived to have come into existence. Secondly, distinguishing the "moral obligation" of justice, or the "sentiment of right and wrong" in just and unjust acts, from the motive of self-interest that originally prompted to the observance of the rules of justice, he refers the former to Sympathy, which makes injustice displease us even when it is too remote to affect our interests; and he

duciveness to happiness as the criterion of "material goodness," had adhered to Shaftesbury's view that dispositions, not results of action, were the proper object of moral approval; at the same time, while giving to benevolence the first place in his account of personal merit, he had shrunk from the paradox of treating it as the sole virtue, and had added a rather undefined and unexplained train of qualities,—veracity, fortitude, activity, industry, sagacity, —immediately approved in various degrees by the "moral sense" or the "sense of dignity." This naturally suggested to a mind like Hume's, anxious to apply the experimental method to psychology, the problem of reducing to some common principle the approbations given to these different elements of personal merit. That Reason alone could furnish such a principle—as Cudworth, Clarke, and others had maintained—Hume emphatically denied. A "very accurate reason or judgment" is doubtless often requisite to instruct us adequately in the pernicious or useful tendency of qualities or actions: but reason "is not alone sufficient to produce any moral blame or approbation." The essence of a crime, he contends, never consists in any relation discovered by reason:—*e.g.* when we condemn ingratitude, it is not the mere "contrariety" between good and evil that is the ground of our disapproval; otherwise we should

regards this sympathy as a necessary supplement to self-interest in a large and numerous society. In the *Inquiry*, the original derivation of Justice from Self-interest is kept in the background; but a careful reader will perceive that Hume had not discarded it. He had doubtless come to attach more importance to the operation of sympathy: but he still regards the sphere of justice as limited by its indirect relation to self-interest,—*e.g.* he expressly says that we should not, properly speaking, lie under any restraint of justice with regard to rational beings who were so much weaker than ourselves that we had no reason to fear their resentment.

equally disapprove of returning good for evil. When, after ascertaining by reason the circumstances and consequences of any act, the mind passes to a moral decision on it, it does not proceed to discover any new fact or relation: what happens is that from the contemplation of the circumstances and relations already known, the mind feels a sentiment of esteem or contempt, approbation or blame: just as natural beauty, though it depends on the proportion, relation, and position of parts, "is not in any of the parts or members" of the beautiful object, but "results from the whole" when presented to an intelligent mind, gifted with the requisite refined sensibility.

What kind of feeling, then, is the real root of moral approbation? Philosophers have endeavoured to find this root entirely in self-love. But this view, Hume holds, is easy to disprove by "crucial experiments" on the play of our moral sentiments: thus "we frequently bestow praise on virtuous actions, performed in very distant ages and remote countries," and "a brave deed performed by an adversary commands our approbation," though "its consequences may be acknowledged prejudical to our particular interest." In short, a fellow-feeling with the happiness and misery of others must be admitted as a "principle in human nature, beyond which we cannot hope to find any principle more general"; and this sympathy furnishes a complete explanation of the approbation given to the different qualities that make up our common notion of personal merit. Hume endeavours to establish this inductively by a survey of the qualities, commonly praised as virtues, which he finds to be always either useful or immediately agreeable, either to the virtuous agent himself or to others. He maintains that "reflections on public interest and utility" are "the *sole* source of the moral approbation paid to fidelity, justice, veracity, integrity," and other important virtues, as well as the sole foundation of the duty of allegiance: taking pains to show, in the leading case of Justice, that the obligation of its rules depends entirely on the actual balance of impulses in human nature and "the particular state and condition in which men are placed." For "reverse in any considerable circumstance the condition of men: produce extreme abundance or extreme necessity; implant in the human breast perfect moderation and humanity, or perfect rapaciousness and malice, by rendering justice totally useless, you thereby totally destroy its essence, and suspend its obligation upon mankind." Similarly, "if we examine the particular laws by which justice is directed and property determined," we shall find that public utility is their only basis and justification. "Who sees not, for instance, that whatever is produced or improved by a man's art or industry ought for ever to be secured to him, in order to give encouragement to such *useful* habits and accomplishments? That the property ought also to descend to children and relations, for the same *useful* purpose? That it may be alienated by consent, in order to beget that commerce and intercourse that is so *beneficial* to human society? and that all contracts and promises ought carefully to be fulfilled, in order to secure mutual trust and confidence, by which the general *interest* of mankind is so much promoted?" Nay, if this consideration be left out of account, "nothing can appear more whimsical, unnatural, and even superstitious than all or most of the laws of justice or of property." In fact, the particular rules are really sometimes arbitrary; for sometimes when the interests of society require some rule, they do not determine what particular rule should be laid down: "in that case, the slightest analogies are laid hold of, in order to prevent that indifference and ambiguity which would be the source of perpetual dissension." Similarly,—and in no other way,—we can justify the variations that we find in civil laws "which extend, restrain, modify, and alter the rules of natural justice according to the particular convenience of each community." Hume admits that a doubt may arise concerning his theory from the undeniable fact that we blame injustice when we are not "conscious of any immediate reflection on the pernicious consequences of it": but considers that this may be explained as an effect of "education and acquired habits." He also remarks that in some cases "by associations of ideas" the general rules by which we praise and blame are "extended beyond the principle" of utility, whence they first arise.[1]

But though utility, in Hume's view, is the sole foundation of several important virtues, and the source of a considerable part of the merit ascribed to others, it is not the sole basis of moral sentiments.[2] There are other mental qualities, such as cheerfulness, courtesy, modesty, which "without any utility or tendency to further good," charm the beholder and excite his approbation, through his sympathy with the immediate pleasure they give, either to the person possessed of them or to others. Even so eminently "useful" a quality

[1] It is, however, noteworthy that Hume gives much less scope to this explanation by "associations of ideas" in his later treatise than in his earlier one.

[2] Writers who represent Hume as "making utility the standard of right and wrong" appear not to have observed that Hume never employs the term "utility" in the wider sense of "conduciveness to happiness," which has commonly been attached to it in ethical discussion since Paley and Bentham. He always employs it in the narrower sense of "tendency to *ulterior* good"; distinguishing the "useful" from the "immediately agreeable," as it is still distinguished in ordinary discourse.

as Benevolence is partly approved from its immediate agreeableness; as is shown by the "kind way of blame" in which we say that a person is "too good" when he "carries his attention for others beyond the proper bounds." As the benevolence is in this case the reverse of useful, we cannot forbear to censure: but its "engaging tenderness so seizes the heart" that we censure in a manner which "at bottom implies more esteem than many panegyrics."[1] Again, the usefulness that is a source of approbation need not necessarily be public utility; indeed the most subtle and original part of Hume's argument for his general theory is that which deals with qualities praised as immediately useful to their possessor. The most cynical man of the world, he says, with whatever "sullen incredulity" he may repudiate virtue as a hollow pretence, cannot really refuse his approbation to "discretion, caution, enterprise, industry, frugality, economy, good sense, prudence, discernment"; nor again, to "temperance, sobriety, patience, perseverance, considerateness, secrecy, order, insinuation, address, presence of mind, quickness of conception, facility of expression." It is evident that the merit of these qualities in our eyes is chiefly due to our perception of their tendency to serve the interests of the person possessed of them, so that the cynic in praising them is really exhibiting the unselfish sympathy of which he doubts the existence.

[1] It is noteworthy that the sympathy manifested in this "kind blame" is conceived by Hume to be sympathy with the benevolent feeling of the agent rather than with the immediate pleasure given to the object of the benevolence. A more penetrating analysis of this phenomenon might have led him to the view, afterwards taken by Adam Smith, that in such cases the spectator's sympathy with the benevolent agent is rather sympathy with his active impulse than with the pleasure his benevolent emotion affords him.

So far the moral faculty has been considered as contemplative rather than active; and this, indeed, is the point of view from which Hume mainly regards it. He does not attempt, like Hutcheson, to develop a scheme of external duties; nor to determine the rank in moral worth of the different qualities that moral sentiment approves. We may observe, too, that on the question of the disinterestedness, strictly speaking, of virtuous conduct Hume's view did not seem quite clear. It is noteworthy that in his earlier treatise he denies the very existence in ordinary human beings of the "calm, stable, universal goodwill" which Hutcheson treats as the normally supreme motive. "In general, it may be affirmed that there is no such passion in human minds as the love of mankind, merely as such, independent of personal qualities, or services, or of relation to oneself;[1] public benevolence, therefore, or a regard for the interests of mankind, cannot be the original motive to Justice." Nor does he expressly retract this view in his later treatise; but he speaks of moral approbation as derived from "humanity and benevolence," and expressly recognises, after Butler, that there is a strictly disinterested element in our benevolent impulses (as also in hunger, thirst, love of fame, and other passions). On the other hand, he does not seem to think that moral sentiment or "taste" can "become a motive to action," except as it "gives pleasure or pain, and thereby constitutes happiness or misery." It is difficult to make these views quite consistent; but at any rate Hume emphatically maintains—as we should expect—that "*reason* is no motive to action," except so far as it "directs the impulse received from appetite or inclination"; and he does not definitely recognise—in his later treatise at

[1] *Treatise on Human Nature*, Part II. § 1.

least—any "obligation" to virtue, except that of the agent's interest or happiness. He attempts, however, to show, in a summary way, that all the duties which his theory of morals recommends are also "the true interest of the individual," —taking into account the importance to his happiness of "peaceful reflection on one's own conduct."

But even if we consider the moral consciousness merely as a particular kind of pleasurable emotion, there is an obvious question suggested by Hume's theory, to which he gives no adequate answer. If the essence of "moral taste" is sympathy with the pleasure of others, why is not this specific feeling excited by other things besides virtue that tend to cause such pleasure? On this point Hume contents himself with the unsatisfactory remark that "there are a numerous set of passions and sentiments, of which thinking rational beings are by the original constitution of nature the only proper objects." Moreover, the vagueness of his own conception of moral approbation is shown by the list of "useful and agreeable" qualities which he considers worthy of approbation; in which merely intellectual gifts are indiscriminately mixed with properly moral excellences.[1] It is, therefore, natural that he should leave the specific quality of the moral sentiments a fact still needing explanation. An original and ingenious solution of this problem was offered by his friend and contemporary

[1] See the list of qualities useful to their possessor, quoted on p. 210. In earlier editions of the *Inquiry*, Hume expressly included all approved qualities under the general notion of "virtue." In later editions he avoided this strain on usage by substituting or adding "merit" in several passages,—allowing that some of the laudable qualities which he mentions would be more commonly called "talents," but still maintaining that "there is little distinction made in our internal estimation" of "virtues" and "talents."

Adam Smith, in his *Theory of Moral Sentiments* (1759). Adam Smith, like Hume, regards sympathy as the ultimate element into which moral sentiments may be analysed, and holds that there is no ground for assuming a peculiar "moral sense": nor does he dispute the actuality or importance of that sympathetic pleasure in the happy effects of virtue, on which Hume laid stress. He even believes that "after the strictest examination, it will be found" to be "universally the case" that "no qualities of the mind are approved of as virtuous, but such as are useful or agreeable, either to the person himself or to others." But while recognising that "Nature has so happily adjusted our sentiments of approbation to the conveniency both of the individual and of society," he still holds that these sentiments do not arise "originally and essentially" from any perception of utility; though no doubt such perception "enhances and enlivens" them,—and, in the important cases of "prudence, justice, and benevolence," our sense of the agreeable effects of virtue constitutes "always a considerable, frequently the greater part of our approbation." Still "it seems impossible that we should have no other reason for praising a man than that for which we commend a chest of drawers"; and it will be found on examination that "the usefulness of any disposition of mind is seldom the first ground of approbation, and that the sentiment of approbation always involves in it a sense of propriety quite distinct from the perception of utility."

Adam Smith (1723-1790)

This sense of propriety, then, is the most essential and universal element of our moral judgments. Primarily, such judgments are passed on the character and conduct of others; and in this case the sense of propriety, in its simplest form, arises from direct sympathy or "fellow-feeling" with the passions of others, which a spectator feels from imagining himself in their situation.[1] The consciousness of an accord of feeling with another human being is always pleasurable, even when the feeling that excites sympathy—and consequently the sympathetic feeling itself, so far as it reproduces this—is painful: and the sense of such accord is the essence of what we call "approbation" of the feeling and of the expressions and actions in which it takes effect. "To approve of the passions of others as suitable to their objects is the same thing as to sympathise with them, . . . the man whose sympathy keeps time to my grief cannot but admit the reasonableness of my sorrow." Similarly, a spectator disapproves of a passion as excessive, when it is exhibited in a degree to which his sympathy cannot reach; and as defective—though this is less common—when it appears to fall short of what would accord with the spectator's sympathetic imagination. To the obvious objection that we often approve without sympathising, it is replied that in such cases we are conscious that we should sympathise if we were in a normal condition and gave due attention to the matter; just as we may approve of a jest and of the laughter of the company, even when we do not ourselves laugh, being in a grave humour; because we are sensible that on most occasions we should join in such laughter. It is to be noted that the "point of propriety" is differently situated in different passions, as sometimes excess and sometimes defect is more disagreeable to the spectator.

[1] This sympathy Adam Smith treats as an original fact of human nature, due to a spontaneous play of imagination. He acutely remarks that we are thus sometimes brought to feel for another an emotion which has no counterpart in his own feeling:—as when we pity madmen who are perfectly gay and cheerful, and commiserate the dead for being laid in the "cold grave," a prey to corruption.

To obtain actually the accord of feeling that we desire, some effort is often required both on the part of the spectator to enter into the sentiments of the person principally concerned, and also on the part of the person principally concerned to "bring down his emotions"—or at least their outward expression—to "what the spectator can go along with." To persons who exhibit the latter effort in a degree which surprises as well as pleases, we attribute the "awful and respectable virtues of self-denial and self-government"; while the "amiable virtue of humanity" consists in that degree of sympathy "which surprises by its exquisite and unexpected delicacy and tenderness." In the case, however, of this amiable virtue, the spectator sympathises not merely with the emotion of the humane person, but with (1) the pleasure that humanity gives to its object, and (2) the gratitude that it excites.

It is to this last operation of sympathy that our sense of *merit* in virtuous actions is due. We attribute merit to an act or an agent, when it or he appears to be the "proper and approved object of gratitude"; that is, when we as "indifferent bystanders" sympathise with the gratitude which the act excites—or would normally excite—in the persons benefited by it. But we do not heartily sympathise with gratitude, unless we also sympathise with the motives of the action that excites it: hence the sense of merit "seems to be a compounded sentiment, made up of two distinct emotions," (1) a direct sympathy with the sentiments of the agent, and (2) an indirect sympathy with the gratitude of those who receive the benefit of his actions,—the latter being the predominant element. Similarly the sense of demerit is made up of a direct antipathy to the feelings of the misdoer and an indirect sympathy with the resentment of the sufferer. This sympathetic indignation, impelling us to approve and demand the punishment of an injury done to another, is the primary constituent of what we call the sense of justice; reflections on the importance of such punishment for the preservation of social order are only a secondary and supplementary source of this sentiment.

So far we have been considering the origin and foundation of our judgments concerning the sentiments and conduct of others. When, however, such judgments are passed on our own conduct, a further complication of the fundamental element is required to explain them. In the process of conscience I "divide myself, as it were, into two persons," and endeavour to enter into the feelings of an imaginary spectator looking at my conduct. Real spectators are liable to praise and blame wrongly, from incomplete knowledge of our actions and motives; but esteem and admiration mistakenly bestowed afford a very incomplete and superficial satisfaction; and when they are mistakenly withheld, we gain real comfort by appealing to a "supposed well-informed and impartial spectator." Thus a desire of being "praiseworthy" is developed, distinct from our desire of praise; and similarly a dread of blameworthiness distinct from dread of blame. It is to be remarked, however, that our sensitiveness to mistaken blame is ordinarily greater than our capacity of deriving satisfaction from mistaken praise; partly because we know that a frank confession would destroy mistaken praise, while we have no similar means of getting rid of mistaken blame: accordingly, in this latter case the ideal spectator, the "man within the breast," seems sometimes to be "astonished and confounded by the violence and clamour of the man without." On the other hand, it ought to be recognised that "the man within the breast requires often to be awakened and put in mind of his duty by the presence of the real spectator"; and when the real spectator at hand is indulgent and partial, while impartial ones are at a distance, the propriety of moral sentiments is apt to be corrupted. Hence the low state of international morality, and of the morality of party-warfare, as compared with ordinary private morality.

Again, the report of the "man within the breast" is liable to be perverted from truth by the internal influence of passion and self-regard, as well as by the opinions of the "man without." But against such self-deceit a valuable remedy has been provided by Nature in the "general rules of morality"; which are not to be regarded as original intuitions, but as "ultimately founded upon experience of what, in particular instances, our moral faculties, our natural sense of merit and propriety, approve or disapprove of." Regard for these general rules is what is properly called a sense of duty; and without this regard "there is no man whose conduct can be much depended upon," owing to "the inequalities of humour to which all men are subject." Adam Smith, indeed, goes so far as to say that this regard for general rules "is the only principle by which the bulk of mankind are capable of directing their actions"; but it is somewhat difficult to reconcile this with his general theory —especially as, in the case of most virtues, the general rules are said to be "in many respects so loose and inaccurate," that our conduct should rather be directed "by a certain taste" than by precise maxims. The rules of Justice, however, he holds to be "accurate in the highest degree," so that they "determine with the greatest exactness any external action which it requires.' He further takes care to assure us that the general rules of morality are "justly to be regarded as the laws of the Deity," and that the voice of "the man within the breast, the supposed impartial spectator," if we listen to it with "diligent and reverential attention," will "never deceive us": but it can hardly be said that his theory affords any cogent arguments for these conclusions.[1]

§ 10. Moral Sentiments compounded by Association.

The theories of Hume and Adam Smith taken together anticipate, to an important extent, the explanations of the origin of moral sentiments which have been more recently current in the utilitarian school. But both of them err in underrating the complexity of the moral sentiments, and in not recognising that, however these sentiments may have originated, they are now, as introspectively examined, different from mere sympathy with the feelings and impulses of others; they are compounds that cannot be directly analysed into the simple element of sympathy, however complicated and combined. In these respects both Hume's and Adam Smith's methods of explanation compare unfavourably with that of Hartley, whose *Observations on Man* (1749) come in time before Hume's *Inquiry*. Hartley's importance lies mainly in his original and comprehensive application of the laws of association of ideas to the explanation of all our more complex and refined emotions; he shows elaborately how, by the repeated and combined effects of such association, the pleasures and pains of "(1) imagination, (2) ambition, (3) self-interest, (4) sympathy, (5) theopathy, and (6) the moral sense" are developed out of the elementary pleasures and pains of sensation. He was

Hartley (1705-1757).

[1] It is especially difficult to reconcile these statements with what Adam Smith elsewhere says of the variations of moral sentiments from age to age and from country to country, and of the destructive influence exercised on "good morals" by particular usages.

not indeed the first among English writers to draw attention to the importance of association in modifying mental phenomena; some of its more striking effects were noticed by Locke, and its operation was made a cardinal point in the metaphysical doctrine of Hume; who also referred to the principle slightly in his account of justice and other "artificial" virtues. And some years earlier, Gay,[1] admitting Hutcheson's proof of the present disinterestedness of moral and benevolent impulses, had maintained that these (like the desires of knowledge or fame, the delight of reading, hunting, and planting, etc.) were derived from self-love by "the power of association." But a thorough and systematic application of the principle to ethical psychology is first found in Hartley's work; he also was the first definitely to conceive association as producing, instead of mere cohesion of mental phenomena, a quasi-chemical combination of them into a compound apparently different from its elements. His theory is primarily physiological, and assumes the complete correspondence of mind and body; he explains how "compound vibratiuncles" in the "medullary substance" are formed from the original vibrations that arise in the organ of sense; and how, correspondingly, the repetition of sensations, contemporaneously or in immediate succession, tends to produce cohering groups of the "miniatures" or traces of the original feelings, which thus coalesce into emotions and ideas really complex but apparently simple. Each of the six classes of pleasures and pains before mentioned is both later and more complex than those which precede it in the list, being due to the combined operation of the preceding classes; accordingly

[1] In an essay prefixed to Law's translation of King's *Origin of Evil* (1731).

the pleasures of the moral sense, being the latest, are of all the most complex. In the first stage of their growth they consist mainly of the pleasing and displeasing associations of the language which children hear applied to virtues and vices respectively; with these are gradually blended traces of the (non-moral) satisfactions derived by a man from his own virtues and those of others. Sociality and benevolence, when they have been developed, add their quota; and a further contribution is furnished by the æsthetic gratification derived from "the great suitableness of all the virtues to each other and to the beauty, order, and perfection of the world." Again, from the hopes continually felt of rewards hereafter for the performance of duty, ideal pleasure tends to connect itself with the notion of duty without any express recollection of these hopes; and finally, religious emotion adds another element to the "general mixed pleasing idea and consciousness" which arise in us when we reflect on our own virtuous affections or actions. A similar blending of pains causes the sense of guilt and anxiety that arises when we reflect on our vices.

Hartley's sensationalism, however, is very far from leading him to exalt the corporeal pleasures; indeed, the fact that they are, in his view, the foundation of all the rest is considered by him as an argument for their inferiority; since "that which is prior in the order of nature is always less perfect and principal than that which is posterior." Similarly the inferiority of the pleasures of imagination, excited by the beauties of nature and art, and by the sciences, is argued from the fact that they are "in general the first of our intellectual pleasures" and "manifestly intended to generate and augment the higher orders." On the whole, he concludes that no one aiming at his own greatest happiness ought to make the sensible pleasures, or those of imagination or ambition, a paramount object; a fuller measure of those inferior pleasures will be attained if the pursuit of them is subordinated to the precepts of sympathy, piety, and the moral sense. So far the argument in favour of religion and morality seems to rest frankly on an egoistic basis. But Hartley further maintains that to make even rational self-interest a primary object of pursuit, would tend to damp and extinguish the higher pleasures of the love of God and our neighbour: its proper function in human development is to put us on "begetting in ourselves the dispositions of Benevolence, Piety, and the Moral Sense." Accordingly our ideal aim—though probably unattainable in this life—should be to carry this subordination of self-interest further and further till we arrive at "perfect self-annihilation and the pure love of God"; so that reasonable self-love may receive its fullest satisfaction by its own extinction. For the pleasures of sympathy, theopathy, and the moral sense, unlike the inferior kinds, may be pursued without danger of excess and without mutual conflict. Piety and Rational Benevolence mutually support each other: "it must be the will of an infinitely benevolent being that we should cultivate universal unlimited benevolence"; on the other hand "benevolence can never be free from partiality and selfishness till we take our station in the Divine Nature and view everything from thence": again, the pleasures of sympathy are "approved of and enforced entirely" by the moral sense, of which they are one principal source.

So far Hartley's practical doctrine appears to be broadly coincident with that of Shaftesbury or Hutcheson; and he expressly says that "benevolence being a primary pursuit," it follows that we are to "direct every action so as to produce the greatest happiness and the least misery in our power"; this is the "rule of social behaviour which universal unlimited benevolence inculcates." But notwithstanding his unhesitating acceptance of this rule, Hartley is far from anticipating the method of later utilitarianism. Owing to the difficulties and perplexities that attend the calculation of the consequences of our actions, we must, he thinks, largely substitute for this general rule several others less general: such as (besides obedience to Scripture) regard to our own moral sense and that of others, and to our "natural motions of goodwill and compassion"; preference of persons in near relations to strangers, and of benevolent and religious persons to the rest of mankind; regard for veracity; and obedience to the civil magistrate. These subordinate rules are chiefly to direct us in deliberate acts; while on sudden emergencies, which exclude deliberation, the moral sentiments should be our guides. But what method of decision is to be applied when any two or more of these maxims conflict, as they are *primâ facie* likely to do, Hartley does not make clear; he only suggests vaguely that they are to "moderate and restrain," to "influence and interpret" one another: nor does his derivation of the moral sense appear to afford adequate grounds for that confidence in its utterances which he seems to feel.

Psychology and Ethics.

On the whole we must say that, though Hartley is obviously in earnest in his attempt to determine the rule of life, the systematic vigour which still gives an interest to his psychology, in spite of its defects of style and treatment, is not applied by him to the question of the criterion or standard of right conduct; on this point his exposition is blurred by a vague and shallow optimism that prevents him from facing the difficulties of the problem. A somewhat similar inferiority has been noted in Adam Smith's work, when he passes from psychological analysis to ethical construction. It would seem that the intellectual energy of this period of English ethical thought had a general tendency to take a psychological rather than a strictly ethical turn. In Hume's case, indeed, the absorption of ethics into psychology is sometimes so complete as to lead him to a confusing use of language; thus in one or two passages he insists with apparent emphasis on the "reality of moral distinctions"; but a closer examination shows that he means no more by this than the real existence of the likes and dislikes that human beings feel for each other's qualities. The fact is, that amid the observations and analyses of feelings which became prominent in the line of ethical thought initiated by Shaftesbury, the fundamental questions "What is right?" and "Why?" tended to drop somewhat into the background—not without manifest danger to morality. For the binding force of moral rules becomes evanescent if we admit—as even Hutcheson seems not unwilling to do—that the "sense" of them may naturally vary from man to man as the palate does; and it is only another way of putting Hume's doctrine, that reason is not concerned with the ends of action, to say that the mere existence of a moral sentiment is in itself no reason for obeying it. A reaction, in one form or another, against the tendency to dissolve ethics into psychology was inevitable; and it was obvious that this reaction might take place in either of the two lines of thought, which, having been peacefully allied in Clarke and Cumberland, had become distinctly opposed to each other in Butler and Hutcheson. It might either fall back on the moral principles commonly accepted, and, affirming their objective validity, endeavour to exhibit them as a coherent and complete set of ultimate ethical truths; or it might take the utility or conduciveness to pleasure, to which Hume had referred for the origin of moral sentiments, as an ultimate standard by which these sentiments might be judged and corrected. The former is the line adopted with substantial agreement by Price, Reid, Stewart, and other members of the Intuitional school, still represented among us by able writers; the latter method, with considerably more divergence of view and treatment, was employed independently and almost simultaneously by Paley and Bentham in both ethics and politics, and is at the present time current under the name of Utilitarianism.

§ 11. Later Intuitionism. Price (1723-1791).

Price's *Review of the Chief Questions and Difficulties of Morals* was published in 1757, two years before Adam Smith's treatise. In regarding moral ideas as derived from the "intuition of truth or immediate discernment of the nature of things by the understanding," Price revives the general view of Cudworth and Clarke; but with several specific differences which it is important to notice, as they find their explanation in the intervening development of ethical thought, which we have been employed in considering. Firstly, his conception of "right" and "wrong" as "single ideas" incapable of definition or analysis—the notions "right," "fit," "ought," "duty," "obligation," being coincident or identical—at least avoids the confusions into which Clarke and Wollaston had been led by pressing the analogy between ethical and mathematical or physical truth. Secondly, the emotional element of the moral consciousness, on which attention had been concentrated by Shaftesbury and his followers, is henceforth distinctly recognised as accompanying the intellectual intuition, though it is carefully subordinated to it. While right and wrong, in Price's view, are "real objective qualities" of actions, moral "beauty and deformity" are subjective ideas; representing feelings which are partly the necessary effects of the perceptions of right and wrong in rational beings as such, partly due to an "implanted sense" or varying emotional susceptibility. Thus, both reason and sense or instinct cooperate in the impulse to virtuous conduct, though the rational element is primary and paramount. Price further follows Butler in expressly distinguishing the perception of merit and demerit in agents, as another accompaniment of perception of right and wrong in their actions; the former cognition, however, is only a peculiar species of the latter, since, to perceive merit in any one is to perceive that it is right to reward him. He is careful,—as Reid also is,—to state that the merit of the agent depends entirely on the intention or "formal rightness" of his act; a man is not blameworthy for unintended evil, though he may of course be blamed for any wilful neglect which has caused him to be ignorant of his real duty. When we turn to the subject matter of virtue, we find that Price, in comparison with More or Clarke, is decidedly laxer in accepting and stating his ethical first principles; chiefly on account of the new opposition to the view of Shaftesbury and Hutcheson, by which his controversial position is complicated. What Price is specially concerned to show is the existence of ultimate moral principles *besides* the principle of universal benevolence. Not that he repudiates the obligation either of this latter principle or of the principle of rational self-love: on the contrary he takes pains to exhibit the self-evidence of both the one and the other. "There is not anything," he says, "of which we have more undeniably an intuitive perception, than that it is 'right to pursue and promote happiness,' whether for ourselves or for others." But he agrees with Butler that gratitude, veracity, fulfilment of promises, and justice are obligatory independently of their conduciveness to happiness: and—grappling with the task, which Butler's caution had avoided, of working out our common moral consciousness of these duties into a body of express truth intuitively apprehended—he is led by the difficulty of the task to appeal to Common Sense rather than Reason as the judge of moral evidence. Thus in maintaining the obligation of veracity he does not exactly seek to show the self-evidence of the abstract proposition "that truth ought to be spoken"; he rather argues, by an inductive reference to common moral opinion, that "we cannot avoid pronouncing that there is an intrinsic rectitude in sincerity." Similarly in expounding justice,—"that part of virtue which regards property,"—he seems prepared to accept *en bloc* as ultimate jural truths the traditional principles of Roman jurisprudence, which refer the right of property to "first possession, labour, succession, and donation." He thus partially and half-unconsciously anticipates, in the department of ethics, the general change in philosophic method which we associate with the name of Reid—the founder of the Philosophy of Common Sense. Finally, Price, writing after the demonstration by Shaftesbury and Butler of the actuality of disinterested impulses in human nature, is bolder and clearer than Cudworth or Clarke in insisting that right actions are to be chosen because they are right by virtuous agents, —even going so far as to lay down that an act loses its moral worth in proportion as it is done from natural inclination.

§ 12. Reid (1710-1796). On this latter point Reid, in his *Essays on the Active Powers of the Human Mind* (1788), states a conclusion more in harmony with common sense, only maintaining that "no act can be morally good in which regard for what is right has not *some* influence." This is partly due to the fact that Reid's moral psychology is, more distinctly than Price's, developed on the lines laid down by Butler. With Butler he recognises as fundamental the distinction between (1) rational and governing principles of action, and (2) non-rational impulses which need regulation; at the same time holding that the latter, so far as they are natural, have a legitimate sphere of operation, tend to the good of the individual and of society, and are indeed indispensable supplements to the rational principles in such beings as men. Among these non-rational springs of action he distinguishes between (1) "mechanical" instincts and habits, that operate "without will, intention, or thought," and those (2) "animal[1] principles" which "operate upon the will and intention but do not suppose any exercise of judgment or reason" in the determination of the ends towards which they impel. The original animal principles in man he classifies, with more precision than Butler, as (*a*) Appetites —distinguished as being "periodical and accompanied with an uneasy sensation"; (*b*) Desires (in the narrower sense), of which the chief are desire of power or superiority, desire of esteem, and desire of knowledge; and (*c*) Affections or emotions directed towards persons, both benevolent and malevolent. The common characteristics of benevolent affections are agreeable emotion and desire of good to their objects; similarly malevolent affections involve "vexation and disquiet" along with a desire to hurt; still Reid follows Butler in recognising the legitimacy and utility of

[1] The term is singular and infelicitous, since it is made to include such affections as pity, public spirit, and "esteem for the wise and good," which we have no ground for attributing to brutes.

both sudden and deliberate resentment within their proper sphere, as of all other original and natural impulses. "Acquired desires," on the other hand, are generally "not only useless, but hurtful and even disgraceful." Reid follows Butler again in his acceptance of that duality of governing principles which we have noticed as a cardinal point in the latter's doctrine. He considers "regard for one's good on the whole" (Butler's self-love) and "sense of duty" (Butler's conscience) as two essentially distinct and co-ordinate rational principles, though naturally often comprehended under the one term, Reason. The rationality of the former principle he takes pains to explain and establish; in opposition to Hume's doctrine that it is no part of the function of reason to determine the ends which we ought to pursue, or the preference due to one end over another. He urges that the notion of "good[1] on the whole" is one which only a reasoning being can form, involving as it does abstraction from the objects of all particular desires, and comparison of past and future with present feelings; and maintains that it is a contradiction to suppose a rational being to have the notion of its Good on the Whole without a desire for it, and that such a desire must naturally regulate all particular appetites and passions. It cannot reasonably be subordinated even to the moral faculty; in fact, a man who believes that virtue is contrary to his happiness on the whole—which cannot really be the case in a morally governed world—is reduced to the "miserable dilemma whether it is better to

[1] It is to be observed that whereas Price and Stewart (after Butler) identify the object of self-love with happiness or pleasure, Reid conceives this "good" more vaguely as including perfection *and* happiness; though he sometimes uses "good" and happiness as convertible terms, and seems practically to have the latter in view in all that he says of self-love.

be a fool or a knave." As regards the moral faculty itself, Reid's statement coincides in the main with Price's; it is both intellectual and active, not merely perceiving the "rightness" or "moral obligation" of actions (which Reid conceives as a simple unanalysable relation between act and agent), but also impelling the will to the performance of what is seen to be right. Both thinkers hold that this perception of right and wrong in actions is accompanied by a perception of merit and demerit in agents, and also by a specific emotion; but whereas Price conceives this emotion chiefly as pleasure or pain, analogous to that produced in the mind by physical beauty or deformity, Reid regards it chiefly as benevolent affection, esteem, and sympathy (or their opposites), for the virtuous (or vicious) agent. This "pleasurable good-will," when the moral judgment relates to a man's own actions, becomes "the testimony of a good conscience—the purest and most valuable of all human enjoyments." Reid is careful to observe that the moral faculty is not "innate" except in germ; it stands in need of "education, training, exercise (for which society is indispensable), and habit," to enable it to attain moral truth. He does not with Price object to its being called the "moral sense," provided we understand by this a source not merely of feelings or notions, but of "ultimate truths." Here he omits to notice the important question whether the premises of moral reasoning are universal or individual judgments; as to which the use of the term "sense" seems rather to suggest the second alternative. Indeed, he seems himself to be undecided on this question; since, though he generally represents ethical method as deductive, he also speaks of the "original judgment that this action is right and that wrong."

The truth is that the construction of a scientific method of ethics is a matter of little practical moment to Reid; since he holds that, "in order to know what is right and what is wrong in human conduct, we need only listen to the dictates of conscience when the mind is calm and unruffled."[1] Accordingly, though he offers a list of first principles, by deduction from which men's common moral opinions may be confirmed, he does not present it with any claim to completeness. Besides maxims relating to virtue in general,—such as (1) that there is a right and wrong in conduct, but (2) only in voluntary conduct, and that we ought (3) to take pains to learn our duty, and (4) fortify ourselves against temptations to deviate from it,—Reid states five fundamental axioms.[2] The first of these is merely the principle of rational self-love, "that we ought to prefer a greater to a lesser good, though more distant, and a less evil to a greater,"—the mention of which seems rather inconsistent with Reid's distinct separation of the "moral faculty" from "self-love." The third is the general rule of benevolence stated in the somewhat vague Stoical formula, that "no one is born for himself only." The fourth, again, is the merely formal principle that "right and wrong must be the same to all in all circumstances," which belongs equally to all systems of objective morality; while the fifth prescribes the religious duty of "veneration or submission to God." Thus, the only principle that even appears to offer definite guidance as to social duty is the second: "that so far as the intention of nature appears in the constitution of man, we ought to act

[1] He does, however, expressly recognise that the conscience of an individual may err, and holds that in this case he is morally right in acting in accordance with his erroneous judgment.

[2] *Essays on the Active Powers*, V. ch. i.

according to that intention"; but the uselessness[1] of this for deductive purposes becomes manifest as soon as we try to apply it to practice.

It is obvious that these maxims, taken together, will carry us but a little way towards methodising the dictates of a plain man's conscience. Nor is their deficiency materially supplemented by a discussion on Justice which Reid adds in a subsequent chapter.[2] He argues with vigour against Hume (1) that different kinds of injury to which Justice is opposed—injuries to person or family, restriction of liberty, attacks on reputation, breach of contract—are perceived intuitively to be violations of natural rights, without conscious reference to the public good; and (2) that though the right of property is "not innate but acquired," it is a necessary consequence of the natural right to life—which implies a right to the means of life,—and of the natural right to liberty—which implies a right to the fruits of innocent labour. But he makes no effort to exhibit clear and precise axioms of Justice, by which the determination of these rights in concrete cases may be decided, without reference to public utility as an ultimate standard.

A similar incompleteness in the statement of ethical principles is found—at least in the department of social duty[3]—if we turn to the work of Reid's most influential dis- § 13. Dugald Stewart (1753-1828).

[1] *E.g.*, Reid proposes to apply this principle in favour of monogamy, arguing from the proportion of males and females born; without explaining why, if the intention of nature hence inferred excludes occasional polygamy, it does not also exclude occasional celibacy.

[2] *L.c.*, ch. v.

[3] Stewart classifies duties under three heads,—duties which respect the Deity, duties which respect our fellow-creatures, and duties which respect ourselves. Under the third head he discusses chiefly the internal sources and conditions of happiness; especially the influence on happiness of temper, opinions, imagination, and habits.

ciple, Dugald Stewart, whose *Philosophy of the Active and Moral Powers of Man* (1828) contains the general view of Butler and Reid,—and to some extent of Price,—expounded with more systematic fulness and precision, with more grace and finish of style, and with some minor improvements in moral psychology, but without any important original additions or modifications.[1] He lays stress on the obligation of justice as distinct from benevolence, yet in defining justice he does not get beyond the general notion of impartiality, which must equally find a place in any ethical system that establishes moral rules of universal application, whether on the utilitarian or any other principle. Afterwards, no doubt, distinguishing "integrity or honesty" as a branch of justice, he lays down the moral axiom "that the labourer is entitled to the fruit of his own labour" as the principle on which complete rights of property are founded; maintaining that occupancy alone would only confer a transient right of possession during use. But the only other principles which he discusses are veracity and fidelity to promises; and in treat-

[1] Among these it may be noticed that Stewart corrects Reid by distinguishing emulation or the desire of superiority on the one hand from the desire of power, and on the other hand from the malevolent affection of envy with which it is sometimes accompanied. Reid seems to have confounded it alternately with one or other of these two distinct impulses. Also, he is more definite and consistent than Reid in conceiving as "happiness" that "good on the whole" of the individual which he takes to be the object of the "rational and governing principle of action," which he consents after Butler to call self-love —though he offers some just criticism on the term. Also his account of the moral faculty is, in style and treatment, decidedly superior to Reid's: it is not, indeed, penetrating or profound; but it is a lucid, comprehensive, and judicious attempt to put together the elements of truth in the views of preceding writers, including Shaftesbury and Adam Smith, into a harmonious and coherent statement of the results of impartial reflection on the moral consciousness.

ing of these what he chiefly aims at showing is that there is in the human mind, independently of calculations of utility, a natural and instinctive love of truth, a natural impulse to sincerity in our mutual communications, and correspondingly a natural faith in testimony and a natural expectation that promises will be kept; and that there is "something pleasing and amiable" in veracity, and a recognised injustice in bad faith, abstracting from all regard to ulterior consequences. He does not attempt to state in either case a principle which is at once manifestly and absolutely binding, and sufficiently precise to give practical guidance.[1]

On the whole, then, it must be said that neither Reid nor Stewart offers more than a very meagre and tentative contribution to that ethical science by which, as they maintain, the received rules of morality may be rationally deduced from self-evident first principles. A more ambitious, but hardly more successful, attempt in the same direction was made by Whewell in his *Elements of Morality* **Whewell** (1846). Whewell's general moral view differs from that of **(1794-1866).** his Scotch predecessors chiefly in a point where we may trace the influence of Kant—viz., in his rejection of self-love as an independent rational and governing principle, and his consequent refusal to admit happiness, apart from duty, as a reasonable end for the individual. The moral reason, thus left in sole supremacy, is represented as enunciating five ultimate principles,—those of benevolence, justice, truth, purity, and order. With a little straining these are made to correspond to five chief divisions of Jus:

[1] Stewart seems to have been partly influenced by a desire to avoid the "hackneyed topics of practical morality"; but it is difficult to see how an ethical science which rests on common sense in the manner that Reid's and Stewart's does can consistently affect this dignified contempt of particulars.

viz., personal security,—benevolence being opposed to the ill-will that commonly causes personal injuries,—property, contract, marriage, and government; while the first, second, and fourth principles regulate respectively the three chief classes of human motives,—affections, mental desires, and appetites. Thus the list, with the addition of two general principles, "earnestness" and "moral purpose," has a certain air of systematic completeness. When, however, we look closer, we find that the principle of order, or obedience to government, is not seriously intended to imply the political absolutism which it seems to express, and which English common sense emphatically repudiates; while the formula of justice is given in the tautological or perfectly indefinite proposition "that every man ought to have his own." Whewell, indeed, explains that this latter formula must be practically interpreted by positive law, though he inconsistently speaks as if it supplied a standard for judging laws to be right or wrong. The principle of purity, again, "that the lower parts of our nature ought to be subject to the higher," merely particularises that supremacy of reason over sensuous rational impulses which is involved in the very notion of reasoned morality as applied to a being whose impulses are liable to deviate from rational duty. Thus, in short, if we ask for a clear and definite fundamental intuition, distinct from regard for happiness, we find really nothing in Whewell's doctrine except the single rule of veracity (including fidelity to promises); and even of this the axiomatic character becomes evanescent on closer inspection, since it is not maintained that the rule is practically unqualified, but only that it is practically undesirable to formulate its qualifications.

It does not fall within the plan of this work to enter into

controversy with writers still living, who maintain a doctrine of moral intuitions which, speaking broadly, may be affiliated to that of Butler and Reid. But it must, I think, be admitted that the doctrine of the intuitional school, down to the middle of the present century, had been developed with less care and consistency than might have been expected, in its statement of the fundamental axioms or intuitively known premises of moral reasoning. And if the controversy which this school conducted with the utilitarianism of Paley and Bentham had turned principally on the determination of the matter of duty, there can be little doubt that it would have been forced into more serious and systematic effort to define precisely and completely the principles and method on which we are to reason deductively to practical conclusions.[1] But in fact the difference between intuitionists and utilitarians as to the method of determining the particulars of the moral code was complicated with a more fundamental disagreement as to the very meaning of "moral obligation." This Paley and Bentham (after Locke) interpreted as merely the effect on the will of the prospective pleasures or pains attached to the observance or violation of moral rules; at the same time, holding with Hutcheson that "general happiness" is the final end and standard of these rules, they endeavoured to make the notion of general happiness clear and precise

Controversy between Intuitional and Utilitarian Schools.

[1] We may observe that some recent writers, who would generally be included in this school, avoid in different ways the difficulty of constructing a code of external conduct: *e.g.*, Dr. Martineau considers that moral intuition is primarily concerned not with outward acts but with the comparative excellence of conflicting motives; others hold that what is intuitively perceived is the rightness or wrongness of individual acts,—a view which obviously renders ethical reasoning practically superfluous.

by defining it to consist in "excess of pleasure over pain," —pleasures and pains being regarded as "differing in nothing but continuance or intensity." Their doctrine gained an attractive air of simplicity by thus using a single apparently clear notion—pleasure and its negative quantity pain—to answer both the fundamental questions of morals, "What is right?" and "Why should I do it?" But since there is no logical connection between the answers that have thus come to be considered as one doctrine, this apparent unity and simplicity has really hidden fundamental disagreements, and caused no little confusion in recent ethical debate.

§ 14. Utilitarianism. The originality—such as it is—of Paley's system (as of Bentham's) lies in its method of working out details rather than in its principles of construction. Paley expressly acknowledges his obligations to the original and suggestive, **Tucker.** though diffuse and whimsical, work of Abraham Tucker (*Light of Nature Pursued*, 1768-74). In this treatise we find "every man's own satisfaction"—or, more strictly, the "prospect or expectance of satisfaction"—"the spring that actuates all his motives," connected with "general good, the root whereout all our rules of conduct and sentiments of honour are to branch," by means of natural theology demonstrating the "unniggardly goodness of the author of nature." Tucker recognises that new inclinations arise by "translation," *i.e.*, that we acquire a liking to things from their having frequently promoted other desires; in particular, that the "moral senses" are thus formed, and also benevolence, which he conceives as a "pleasure of benefiting," prompting us to perform good offices because we like them. But it remains true, he thinks, that a man's own happiness—in the sense of an aggregate of pleasures and satisfactions—is the ultimate end of his actions; and he is careful to explain that satisfaction or pleasure is "one and the same in kind, however much it may vary in degree . . . whether a man is pleased with hearing music, seeing prospects, tasting dainties, performing laudable actions, or making agreeable reflections," and again that by "general good" he means "quantity of happiness," to which "every pleasure that we do to our neighbour is an addition." Here we have all the chief characteristics of Paley's utilitarianism: (1) purely quantitative estimate of pleasure; (2) criterion of moral rules, conduciveness to general pleasure; (3) universal motive, private pleasure; (4) connection between motive and rules, the Will of an omnipotent and benevolent being. There is, however, in Tucker's theological link between private and general happiness a peculiar ingenuity which Paley's common sense has avoided. He argues that men having no free will have really no desert; therefore the divine equity must ultimately distribute happiness in equal shares to all; therefore I must ultimately increase my own happiness most by conduct that adds most to the general fund which Providence administers.

But in fact a simple outline of Paley's ethical view may be found more than a generation earlier in the following passages from Gay's dissertation prefixed to Law's translation of King's *Origin of Evil* (1731):—"The idea of virtue is the conformity to a rule of life, directing the actions of all rational creatures with respect to each other's happiness; to which every one is always obliged. . . . Obligation is the necessity of doing or omitting something in order to be happy. . . . Full and complete obligation, which will extend to all cases, can only be that arising from the authority of God. . . . The will of God [so far as it directs behaviour to others] is the immediate rule or criterion of virtue . . . but it is evident from the nature of God that He could have no other design in creating mankind than their happiness; and therefore that He wills their happiness; therefore that my behaviour so far as it may be a means to the happiness of mankind should be such; so that happiness of mankind may be said to be the criterion of virtue once removed."

Paley (1743-1805). The first construction, however, of a tolerably complete system on this basis is to be found in Paley's *Principles of Moral and Political Philosophy* (1785). He begins by defining "obligation" to mean the being "urged by a violent motive resulting from the command of another"; in the case of moral obligation, the command proceeds from God, and the motive lies in the expectation of being rewarded and punished after this life. The commands of God are to be ascertained "from Scripture and the light of nature combined." Paley, however, holds that Scripture is given less to teach morality than to illustrate it by example and enforce it by new sanctions and greater certainty; and that the light of nature makes it clear that God wills the happiness of His creatures. Hence, his method in deciding moral questions is chiefly that of estimating the tendency of actions to promote or diminish the general happiness. To meet the obvious objections to this method, based on the immediate happiness caused by admitted crimes (such as "knocking a rich villain on the head"), he lays stress on the necessity of general rules in any kind of legislation;[1] while, by urging the importance of forming and maintaining good habits, he partly evades the difficulty of calculating the consequences of particular actions. In this way the utilitarian method is

[1] It must be allowed that Paley's application of this argument is somewhat loosely reasoned, and does not sufficiently distinguish the consequences of a single act of beneficent manslaughter from the consequences of a general permission to commit such acts.

freed from the subversive tendencies which Butler and others had discerned in it; as used by Paley, it merely explains the current moral and jural distinctions, exhibits the obvious basis of expediency which supports most of the received rules of law and morality, and furnishes a simple solution, in harmony with common sense, of some perplexing casuistical questions. Thus, *e.g.*, "natural rights" become rights of which the general observance would be useful apart from the institution of civil government; as distinguished from the no less binding "adventitious rights," the utility of which depends upon this institution. Private property is in this sense "natural," from its obvious advantages in encouraging labour, skill, preservative care; though actual rights of property depend on the general utility of conforming to the law of the land by which they are determined. Thus, again, many perplexities respecting the duties of veracity and good faith are solved, so as to avoid jesuitical laxities no less than superstitious scruples, by basing the obligation of such duties on the utilities—general and particular—of satisfying expectations deliberately produced. So, too, the general utilitarian basis of the established sexual morality is effectively expounded. We observe, however, that Paley's method is often mixed with reasonings that belong to an alien and older manner of thought; as when he supports the claim of the poor to charity by referring to the intention of mankind "when they agreed to a separation of the common fund," or when he infers that monogamy is a part of the divine design from the equal numbers of males and females born. In other cases his statement of utilitarian considerations is fragmentary and unmethodical, and tends to degenerate into loose exhortation on rather trite topics.

In unity, consistency, and thoroughness of method,

§ 15. Bentham and his School (1748-1842).

Bentham's utilitarianism has a decided superiority over Paley's. He throughout considers actions solely in respect of their pleasurable and painful consequences, expected or actual; and he fully recognises the need of making an exhaustive and systematic register of these consequences, free from the influences of common moral opinion, as expressed in the "eulogistic" and "dyslogistic" terms in ordinary use. And since the effects by which alone he estimates conduct are all empirically ascertainable—being such pleasures and pains as most men feel and all can observe to be felt,—all political or moral inferences drawn by Bentham's method lie open at every point to the test of practical experience. Every one, Bentham thinks, can tell what value he sets on the pleasures of alimentation, sex, the senses generally, wealth, power, curiosity, sympathy, antipathy (malevolence), the goodwill of individuals or of society at large, and on the corresponding pains, as well as the pains of labour and organic disorders;[1] and he can pretty well guess the rate at which they are valued by others; therefore if it be once granted that all actions are determined by pleasures and pains, and are to be judged by the same standard, the art both of legislation and of private conduct is apparently settled on a broad, simple, and clear empirical basis. If we are investigating the good or bad tendency of an act, we are to "begin with any person of those whose interests seem immediately affected by it, and take an account of the value of each distinguishable pleasure or pain which appears to be produced by it in the first

[1] This list gives twelve out of the fourteen classes in which Bentham arranges the springs of action, omitting the religious sanction (mentioned afterwards), and the pleasures and pains of self-interest, which include all the other classes except sympathy and antipathy.

instance"; we are to consider both the intensity and the duration of these feelings, and also their certainty and uncertainty,[1] but not any supposed difference of quality as distinct from intensity; for "quantity of pleasure being equal, pushpin is as good as poetry." We are then to consider the "fecundity" and "purity" of these primary effects; that is, their tendency to be followed by feelings of the same kind, and their tendency not to be followed by feelings of an opposite kind: then, if we sum up the values of all the pleasures and pains thus scrutinised, the balance on the side of pleasure or pain will give us the total good or bad tendency of the act with respect to the particular individual selected. Then we are to repeat the process in respect to every other individual "whose interests appear to be concerned"; and thus we shall arrive at the general good or bad tendency of the act. Bentham does not, indeed, expect that "this process should be strictly pursued previously to every moral judgment"; but he holds that "it may always be kept in view," and that the more we approximate to it, the more exact our ethical reasoning will become.

Suppose now that it has been thus determined what action, in any given circumstances, would be best in its tendency: we have next to inquire what motives a man has to do it. To obtain an instructive answer to this question, we have to classify pleasures and pains from a different point of view, "in the character of efficient causes or means"; or, to use Bentham's chief name for them in this relation, as "sanc-

[1] Bentham adds "propinquity or remoteness"; but I can hardly suppose him to mean that the date of a pleasure affects its value rationally estimated, except so far as increase of remoteness necessarily involves some increase of uncertainty.

tions "[1] of the rules of conduct to which they prompt men to conform. Men are actually induced to obey useful rules by the expectation of pleasures and pains for themselves either (1) from the ordinary course of nature "not purposely modified by the interposition of any will," human or divine, or (2) from the action of judges or magistrates appointed to execute the will of the sovereign, or (3) from the action of chance persons in the community, "according to each man's spontaneous disposition"; that is, in Bentham's terminology, by the "physical," the "political," and the "moral[2] or popular" sanction. To these he adds the "religious sanction," *i.e.* those pains and pleasures which are to be expected from the "immediate hand of a superior invisible being"; and at first sight the recognition of these supra-mundane consequences may seem to lift Bentham's system from that plain and palpable basis of mundane experience which constitutes its special claim to our attention. But the truth is that he does not seriously take account of religious hopes

[1] Bentham uses this term to include both pleasures and pains; but it is to be observed that Austin and (I believe) the whole school of jurists who have followed him restrict the term to pains—these being the kind of motives with which the legislator and judge are almost exclusively concerned.

[2] In Bentham's earliest classification of sanctions—in the *Principles of Morals and Legislation*—he does not expressly recognise the pleasures and pains of the moral sentiments. According to his definition they might be included under the head of "physical" sanctions; but we may probably infer that he considered these feelings—when separated on the one hand from regard for reputation and its consequences, and on the other hand from the hope of reward and the fear of punishment hereafter—as a comparatively unimportant weight in the balance of ordinary motives. Still in a later letter to Dumont (1821) he appears to refer separately to what are ordinarily called moral sentiments as "sympathetic and antipathetic sanctions."—Cf. *Princ. of Mor. and Leg.* (*Works*, vol. i.), p. 14, *note*.

and fears, except as motives actually operating on human minds, which therefore admit of being observed and measured as much as any other motives. He does not himself use the will of an omnipotent and benevolent being as a means of logically connecting individual and general happiness. He thus undoubtedly simplifies his system, and avoids the disputable inferences from nature and Scripture in which Paley's position is involved; but this gain is dearly purchased. For the question immediately arises, How then are the sanctions of the moral rules which it will most conduce to the general happiness for men to observe, shown to be always adequate in the case of all the individuals whose observance is required? To this question Bentham nowhere attempts to give a complete answer in any treatise published by himself. In his earliest book he expressly admits that "the only interest which a man is at all times sure to find adequate motives for consulting are his own," and does not go on to affirm that a completer knowledge of consequences would show him always adequate motives for aiming at general happiness. And in many parts of his vast work, in the region of legislative and constitutional theory, he rather seems to assume that the interests of some men will continually conflict with those of their fellows, unless we alter the balance of prudential calculation by a careful readjustment of penalties: but obviously on this assumption it cannot be maintained that a man will always gain his own greatest happiness by "maximising" general happiness, until legislative and constitutional reform has been perfected. Perhaps we may suppose Bentham, in his earlier period, to have held that, as a practical philanthropist, it was not his business to dwell on the occasional and partial conflict that occurs between private and general happiness in the present imperfect state of the world's arrangements; but rather to impress forcibly on men to how great an extent their happiness is actually promoted by what conduces to the general happiness; to show how honesty is normally the best policy, how voluntary services to others are a profitable investment in a sort of bank of general good-will, how erroneous in every way is the estimate of pains and pleasures by which the acts of practically selfish and vicious men are determined.[1] Still, in the *Deontology* published by Bowring from Bentham's MSS. after his death, it is distinctly assumed that, in actual human life as empirically known, the conduct most conducive to general happiness *always* coincides with that which conduces most to the happiness of the agent; and that "vice may be defined as a miscalculation of chances" from a purely mundane point of view. And it seems probable that this must be accepted as Bentham's real doctrine, in his later days; since he certainly held that the "constantly proper end of action on the part of every individual at the moment of action is his real greatest happiness from that moment to the end of life," without retracting his unqualified acceptance of the "greatest happiness of the greatest number" as a "plain but true standard for whatever is right and wrong in the field of morals;"[2] and the assumption just mentioned is required to reconcile these two convictions, if the empirical basis on which his whole reasoning proceeds is maintained. But since it is at least very difficult, in the actual conditions of human society, to give adequate empirical proof of this universal harmony of interests, it is not surprising that several of Bentham's disciples should have endeavoured to

[1] These topics are prominent in the *Deontology*.

[2] See Bentham's *Works*, vol. x. (*Life*), pp. 560, 561 and p. 79.

avoid this mode of supplying the gap in his system. One section of the school, represented by John Austin, apparently returned to Paley's position, and treated utilitarian morality[1] as a code of divine legislation; others, with Grote, were content to abate the severity of the claims made by "general happiness" on the individual, and to consider utilitarian duty as practically limited by reciprocity; while on the opposite side, an unqualified subordination of private to general happiness was advocated by J. S. Mill, who has probably done more than any other member of the school to spread and popularise utilitarianism in both ethics and politics.

§ 16. J. S. Mill (1806-1873).

The manner, however, in which Mill, in his short treatise on *Utilitarianism* (1861) endeavours to induce the individual to take general happiness as his ultimate end, is somewhat complicated and perplexing. To begin: he holds —with Hume and Bentham—that "questions of ultimate ends do not admit of proof, in the ordinary sense of the term"; he thinks, however, that "considerations may be presented, capable of determining the intellect to give its assent to the doctrine." The considerations that he actually presents (in ch. iv.) are briefly these: (1) What each man desires is pleasure (or absence of pain[2]) to himself, and he desires this always in proportion to the magnitude of the pleasure; (2) the only possible proof that anything is desirable is that people do actually desire it; (3) each

[1] It should be observed that Austin, after Bentham, ordinarily uses the term "moral" to connote what he more distinctly calls "positive morality," the code of rules supported by common opinion in any society.

[2] For brevity, it is often convenient in discussing Utilitarianism to refer expressly to pleasure only—pain being understood to be included as the negative quantity of pleasure.

person's happiness is therefore desirable or a good to himself; (4) the general happiness is therefore a good to the aggregate of all persons. If the aggregate could perform a really collective act of volition, these considerations might perhaps induce it to aim in this volition at general happiness; but they seem hardly adapted to convince an individual that he ought to take the "greatest amount of happiness altogether"—instead of the greatest amount of his own happiness—as the standard and supreme "directive rule" of his private conduct. Nor, to do Mill justice, does he seem to rely on such arguments for this purpose; for when he expressly raises the question (in ch. iii.) "What is the source of the obligation" of utilitarian morality? his reply consists entirely in a statement of "sanctions," in Bentham's sense—*i.e.* of private pleasures to be gained and pains to be avoided by the agent who aims at general happiness. In his analysis of these motives, however, he lays special stress on a sanction of which Bentham omitted to take note: the "feeling of unity with his fellow-creatures," which makes it a "natural want" of an individual of "properly cultivated moral nature" that his aims should be in harmony with theirs. This feeling, he says, is "in most individuals much inferior in strength to their selfish feelings, and is often wanting altogether"; but it presents itself to the minds of those who have it as "an attribute which it would not be well for them to be without"; and "this conviction is the ultimate sanction of the greatest-happiness morality." In affirming that individuals who have this feeling are convinced that it would not "be well for them to be without it," Mill does not exactly mean that they are convinced that they always attain their own happiness in proportion as they promote the general happiness; on the contrary, he holds that in the present "imperfect state of the world's arrangements" a man often can and does "best serve the happiness of others by the absolute sacrifice of his own." But he considers that the "conscious ability to do without happiness gives the best prospect of realising such happiness as is attainable"; as it raises the person above the chances of life, and frees him from excess of anxiety concerning its evils.

This curious blending of Stoic and Epicurean elements —Epicureanism furnishing the definition of the individual's good, and the Stoic mood being found to give the best prospect of attaining it—may be connected with another position which Mill maintains in opposition to Bentham: the recognition of differences of quality in pleasures distinct from and overriding differences of quantity. This recognition of quality has some efficacy in reconciling common sense to the adoption of Pleasure as a criterion of Duty; but the advantage is gained at the expense of consistency: since it is hard to see in what sense a man who of two alternative pleasures chooses the less pleasant on the ground of its superiority in quality can be affirmed to take "*greatest*" happiness or pleasure as his standard of preference. But even after the introduction of this alien element, it cannot be said that Mill's utilitarianism includes an adequate proof that persons of all natures and temperaments will obtain even the best chance of private happiness in this life by determining always to aim at general happiness; indeed he hardly attempts or professes to furnish such a proof.

On the whole, it would perhaps be now generally admitted that while the demand for adequate sanctions is one which the utilitarianism of Bentham or Mill cannot legitimately repel as irrelevant, it is yet one which it cannot completely meet without abandoning its purely empirical basis. It may, however, be pointed out that there are various ways in which a utilitarian system of morality may be used, without deciding whether the sanctions attached to it are always adequate. (1) It may be presented as practical guidance to all who choose "general good" as their ultimate end, whether they do so on religious grounds or through the predominance in their minds of impartial sympathy, or because their conscience acts in harmony with utilitarian principles, or for any combination of these or any other reasons; or (2) it may be offered as a code to be obeyed not absolutely, but only so far as the coincidence of private and general interest may in any case be judged to extend; or again (3) it may be proposed as a standard by which men may reasonably agree to praise and blame the conduct of others, even though they may not always think fit to act on it themselves. We may regard morality as a kind of supplementary legislation, supported by public opinion, which we may expect the public, when duly enlightened, to frame in accordance with the public interest.

From the point of view last mentioned, a new question arises as to the relation of private to general happiness, which must be carefully distinguished from that which we have been considering. Assuming that the promotion of general happiness is the ultimate end of morality, how far should the moralist and the educator aim at making benevolence the consciously predominant motive in the action of the individual; how far should he seek to develop the social impulses whose direct object is the happiness of others at the expense of impulses that may be called broadly "egoistic," —*i.e.* impulses that aim at personal satisfaction otherwise than through the happiness of others? On this question

Bentham's view is characteristically expressed in the saying that "for diet nothing but self-regarding affection will serve"; though "for a dessert benevolence is a very valuable addition." The teaching of Mill—under the influence, as will be presently noticed, of Comte, with whom, however, he materially disagrees—holds the balance differently, and more delicately, between practical "egoism" and "altruism." On the one hand, Mill[1] maintains that disinterested public spirit should be the prominent motive in the performance of all socially useful work, and that even hygienic precepts should be inculcated, not chiefly on grounds of prudence, but because "by squandering our health we disable ourselves from rendering services to our fellow-creatures." On the other hand, he considers that "life is not so rich in enjoyments that it can afford to forego the cultivation of all those that address themselves to the [so-called] egoistic propensities"; and that the function of moral *censure*—as distinct from moral *praise*—should be restricted to the prevention of conduct that positively harms others, or impedes their pursuit of their own happiness, or violates engagements expressly or tacitly undertaken by the agent. At the same time he extends the notion of "tacit undertaking" to include "all such positive good offices and disinterested services as the moral improvement of mankind has rendered customary," thus laying down a standard which in an improving society tends continually to grow more exacting. It follows from this doctrine as to the limits of legitimate censure that it should not be employed for the promotion of the happiness of the person censured; the "moral coercion

[1] The views summarised in this paragraph are found partly in Mill's essay on *Auguste Comte and Positivism* (Part II.), partly in his essay *On Liberty*.

of public opinion" is, in Mill's view, a form of social interference which society is only justified in using for its own protection. Mill admits that the mischief which a person does to himself may seriously affect those connected with him through sympathy or interest, and, in a minor degree, society at large: but he holds that this "inconvenience is one which society can afford to bear for the greater good of human freedom," except where there is "a definite damage, or definite risk of damage, either to an individual or to the public." For instance, we ought not to censure an ordinary citizen merely for being drunk; but if intemperance disables him from paying his debts or supporting his family, he is blameworthy; and a policeman is blameworthy if he is drunk on duty.

Associationism.

But though Mill holds that the moral sentiments ought to be deliberately and carefully regulated, in the way just described, so that their operation may be as conducive as possible to the general happiness, he does not simply identify moral sentiments with sympathy or rational benevolence; on the contrary, he considers that "the mind is not in a state conformable to utility unless it loves virtue as a thing desirable in itself" without conscious reference to its utility. Such love of virtue Mill holds to be in a sense natural, though not an ultimate and inexplicable fact of human nature: he explains it by the "law of association" of feelings and ideas, which, as we have seen, Hartley was the first to apply comprehensively in a psycho-physical theory of the development of mental phenomena.[1] This

[1] The importance of this principle was learnt by J. S. Mill from his father, James Mill, who in his *Analysis of the Human Mind* had developed with much vigour and clearness a view fundamentally similar to Hartley's, but unencumbered by the crudities of Hartley's physiology.

law, in Mill's view, operates in two ways, which it is important to distinguish. In the first place virtue, originally valued merely as conducive to non-moral pleasure or as protective against non-moral pains, comes through the influence of association to be an immediate source of pleasure, and of the pain of remorse if its rules are violated; it is therefore, to the morally developed mind, an object of desire for its own sake. So far, the performance of virtuous acts is only a particular mode of seeking one's own greatest pleasure. But Mill holds, further, that the acquired tendency to virtuous conduct may become so strong that the habit of willing it may continue, "even when the reward which the virtuous man receives from the consciousness of well-doing is anything but an equivalent for the sufferings he undergoes or the wishes he may have to renounce." It is in this way that the hero or martyr comes voluntarily to make an "absolute sacrifice of his own happiness" to promote the happiness of others; he cannot *desire* anything except in proportion as it is pleasant in prospect, but he may through habit *will* what is on the whole unpleasant—through the operation of the same law by which the miser first sought money as a means to comfort, but ends by sacrificing comfort to money. The moral sentiments which ultimately acquire this force are in Mill's view, as in Hartley's, derived from "very numerous and complex elements," so blended that the resulting feeling in most cases is "very unlike the sum of its elements." Their origin, in any ordinary individual, is no doubt partly artificial; as they are partly due to what Mr. Bain calls the "education of conscience under government or authority," which is liable to be misdirected, so that the moral impulses generated by it are sometimes absurd and mischievous. Sentiments of merely artificial origin, however, tend to yield, as intellectual culture goes on, to the "dissolving force of analysis": but so far as moral sentiments are in harmony with utilitarian rules they are sustained against this corrosive analysis by the permanent influence of the natural source from which they have partly sprung,—the "social feelings of mankind"; which are themselves compounded of (1) sympathy with the pleasures and pains of others, and (2) habits of consulting others' welfare from a consciousness of mutual need and implication of interests. The peculiar sentiment connected with our notions of justice and injustice Mill (after Adam Smith) explains as essentially resentment moralised by enlarged sympathy and intelligent self-interest; what we mean by injustice is harm done to an assignable individual by a breach of some rule for which we desire the violator to be punished, for the sake both of the person injured and of society at large, including ourselves. A view of the origin of moral sentiments, broadly similar to Mill's, is maintained by Mr. Bain, the chief living representative of the Associational Psychology, and by other writers of the same school. The combination of antecedents is somewhat differently given by different thinkers—Mr. Bain, in particular, laying special stress on the operation of purely disinterested sympathy;[1]—but they generally agree in representing the process of combination to be such as would make the moral promptings of any normal individual harmonise on the whole with the general interests of the community of which he is a member: so that the plain man's conscience may, on utilitarian principles, be regarded as a

[1] Mr. Bain considers this operation of sympathy to be a special case of the "tendency of every idea to act itself out, to become an actuality, not with a view to bring pleasure or ward off pain, but from an independent prompting of the mind."

useful though not infallible guide to conduct, especially where utilitarian calculations are difficult and uncertain.[1]

§ 17. Current Ethical Controversies.

Association and Evolution.

The general validity of this Associational explanation of conscience is, however, still a subject of dispute. It has been persistently controverted by writers of the intuitional school, who (unlike Hartley) have usually thought that this derivation of moral sentiments from more primitive feelings would be detrimental to the authority of the former. Their chief argument against this derivation has been based on the early period at which these sentiments are manifested

[1] An interesting form of the Associationist theory of the origin of moral sentiments is found in Mr. Herbert Spencer's *Data of Ethics* (§§ 44-47). In Mr. Spencer's view, "the essential trait in the moral consciousness" is the control of "the simpler and less ideal feelings by the more complex and more ideal." But this is also a cardinal trait of other restraints not properly called moral; and it is only gradually that properly moral restraint is "differentiated," in the course of evolution, from these other restraints. The impulses of savage men are at first restrained by a vague dread of the anger of other savages, living and dead—the dead being taken into account as the belief in ghosts develops—; out of this there are gradually evolved into distinctness the dread of judicial punishments, the dread of Divine vengeance, and the dread of social reprobation. It is from the restraints generated by these fears that the notion of moral "obligation" was originally derived: as the results dreaded in these cases, though "incidental rather than necessary," are more easy to conceive vividly than the "necessary natural" mischief wrought by bad actions, the representation of which is the proper source of strictly moral feeling and restraint. The latter, accordingly, develops more slowly than the restraints that emanate from political, religious, and social authorities, and under conditions of social union that only these other restraints could maintain: though having thus developed it comes to be quite independent, in conscious experience, of these other restraints. Mr. Spencer adds that the "element of coerciveness," imported into the strictly moral restraint from its association with political, religious, and social restraints, may be expected to fade as the properly "moral motive becomes distinct and predominant." Thus "the sense of duty or moral obligation is transitory and will diminish as fast as moralisation increases."

by children, which hardly, they urge, allows time for association to produce the effects ascribed to it. This argument has been met in recent times by the application to mind of a physiological theory of heredity, according to which changes produced in the mind or brain of a parent, by association of ideas or otherwise, tend to be inherited by his offspring; so that the development of the moral sense or any other faculty or susceptibility of existing man may be hypothetically carried back into the prehistoric life of the human race, without any change in the manner of derivation supposed. At present, however, this view of heredity is usually held in conjunction with Darwin's theory of natural selection; according to which different kinds of living things in the course of a series of generations come gradually to be endowed with organs, faculties, and habits tending to the preservation either of the individual or of the species under the conditions of life in which it is placed. This theory introduces into the history of the moral sentiments a new zoological factor; which, though in no way irreconcilable with the older psychological theory of their formation through coalescence of more primitive feelings, must yet be conceived as controlling and modifying the effects of the laws of association by favouring the existence of sentiments tending to the preservation of human life, and impeding the existence of those that have an opposite tendency.

Evolutional Ethics.

The view, however, of biological evolution which has recently become prevalent in consequence of the widespread acceptance of the Darwinian theory, has had effects on ethical thought of a still more fundamental kind. It has tended not merely to modify the Associational explanation of the growth of moral sentiments, but also to thrust aside the Benthamite criterion and method for determining the good and bad tendencies of actions; first, by substituting for "balance of pleasure over pain" some more objective biological conception—such as the "preservation of human society" or of the "human race," or, still more generally, "quantity of life"—as the end by conduciveness to which actions and characters are to be estimated; and secondly, by substituting for empirical utilitarian reasoning an attempt to deduce moral rules from biological or sociological laws. This latter procedure is sometimes called "establishing morality on a scientific basis."

The end which, in this deduction, furnishes the "scientific" criterion of moral rules is, as I have intimated, somewhat differently defined by different thinkers of the Evolutional school; but there is a more fundamental difference in their view of the relation of this objective end to happiness. By some Evolutionist writers happiness or pleasure seems to be regarded as a mere accompaniment—not scientifically important—of that preservation or expansion of life, which is regarded as the real ultimate end. Mr. Herbert Spencer, however, the most influential teacher of Evolutional Ethics, repudiates this view. He holds, indeed, that a survey of "universal conduct"—*i.e.* the actions of animate beings of all kinds—shows us "quantity of life, measured in breadth[1] as well as in length," as the end to which such actions tend to be more and more adjusted as the development of life proceeds; but he considers that conduct tending to the preservation of life is only good—and commonly judged to be so—on the assumption that life is attended with a "surplus of agreeable feeling." He does

[1] By differences of *breadth* Mr. Spencer means differences in the "quantities of change" that different living beings go through in the same time.

not expressly maintain that life is actually always so attended; still he appears to hold that, for ethical purposes, actions conducive to maximum quantity of life, and actions conducive to maximum quantity of agreeable feeling, may be taken to coincide. His readiness to assume this coincidence is perhaps due to the fact that he does not conceive an ethical system to be primarily concerned with the conduct of actual human beings: its primary business is to "formulate normal conduct in an ideal society,"—a society so ideal that in it normal conduct will produce "pleasure unalloyed by pain anywhere." In Mr. Spencer's view it is only conduct of which the effects are thus unmixed that can be called "absolutely right"; "conduct that has any concomitant of pain, or any painful consequence, is partially wrong": and as Ethical Science is primarily "a system of truths expressing the absolutely right," it is obvious that such truths cannot relate directly to the actions of actual men. The reasonings of "Absolute Ethics," then, are concerned with "ascertaining necessary relations" between actions and their consequences, and "deducing from necessary principles what conduct must be detrimental and what conduct must be beneficial" in an ideal society. When this deduction has been performed it belongs to an inferior mode of reasoning, which Mr. Spencer distinguishes as "Relative Ethics," to settle in a rough, empirical manner how far the rules of Absolute Ethics are to be taken as applicable to human beings here and now.

I am not aware that any other writer on Ethics, from the "evolution point of view," has adopted Mr. Spencer's doctrine as to the relations of Absolute and Relative Ethics. But there are other writers—of whom Mr. Leslie Stephen [1]

[1] In his *Science of Ethics* (1882).

may be taken as representative—who, while accepting happiness as the ultimate end of reasonable conduct, reject the Benthamite method of ascertaining empirically the conductiveness of actions to this end; and consider that a more "scientific criterion" of morality is obtained by investigating their conduciveness to the "efficiency" of the social organism,—efficiency, that is, for the purposes of its own preservation. In comparing this with the older utilitarian view, it is important not to exaggerate disagreement. Probably there is no moralist of any school who would deny the fundamental importance of rules and habits tending to the preservation of society; certainly there is no utilitarian—not being a pessimist—who would not regard the attainment of this result as the most indispensable function of morality, from a utilitarian point of view, and its main function in the earlier stages of moral development, when to live at all was a difficult task for human communities. The primary question at issue, therefore, is, whether we are to regard preservation as the sole end; whether we are to be content with the mere securing of existence for humanity generally, instead of seeking to make the secured existence more desirable,—whether, in short, the notion of "Well-being" is to be reduced to "Being with the promise of future being." If this question were settled in the affirmative it might then be further disputed how far the present condition of sociological knowledge is such as to render "conduciveness to the preservation of the social organism" a criterion completely applicable to the scientific reconstruction of morality.[1]

[1] The extent to which Sociology is to be regarded as already constituted is a point on which there would appear to be considerable difference of opinion among Evolutionists. Mr. Spencer regards it as

Optimism and Pessimism.

It is not easy to say how far the more or less optimistic view of the relation of Life to Happiness, which seems an essential part of both Mr. Spencer's and Mr. Stephen's ethical system, is shared by the increasing number of students who are devoting themselves to biological and sociological investigation. The prevalent opinion, however, would seem to be that life, normally and on the whole, is attended with a balance of pleasure over pain. The correctness of this opinion, however, is from time to time disputed by thoughtful arguments,—partly under the influence of the pessimistic philosophy of Germany, of which a brief account will be given later. The points on which pessimists lay stress are chiefly (1) the painfulness of the state of desire and unsatisfied longing which is yet a pervading and essential element of the process of life; (2) the indefinitely greater intensity of pain, especially organic pain, as compared with pleasure; and —as regards human beings in particular—(3) the irksomeness of the labour required from the great majority to secure even the imperfect degree of protection from disease and pain which is at present attained. A dogmatic conclusion, on these or other grounds, that human life is on the whole more painful than pleasurable, is perhaps rare in England; but it is a widespread opinion that the average of happiness attained by the masses, even in civilised communities, is deplorably low, and that the present aim of philanthropy should be rather to improve the quality of human life than to increase its quantity.

sufficiently established to be able to predict definitely an ideal society in the remote future. Mr. Stephen, on the other hand, declares that Sociology at present "consists of nothing more than a collection of unverified guesses and vague generalities, disguised under a more or less pretentious apparatus of quasi-scientific terminology."

The controversies that I have just briefly indicated, among empirical utilitarians, evolutional hedonists, or evolutionists pure and simple, are for the most part conducted on the basis of a general agreement to regard human life as essentially a part of the larger whole of animal life, and as something of which the goodness or badness is to be estimated on principles applicable—at least in some degree—to this larger whole. This basis, however, is emphatically repudiated by a school of thought which has recently become prominent; which holds that the good of man as a rational being depends essentially on the self-consciousness which distinguishes human life from the merely sentient existence of animals. The German sources from which this view has been mainly derived will be briefly described in a later section; in its English phase the doctrine has found its most elaborate and important expression in Green's *Prolegomena to Ethics*. According to Green the end or good of every man is the realisation of the faculties of his being as one of the many self-conscious subjects, "spirits" or "persons," in whom the one divine mind,—the one supreme subject implied in the existence of the world,—partially reproduces itself. Each such spirit or person, conscious of self as a combining intelligence, necessarily knows himself as something distinct from the world of nature which his combining intelligence constitutes: his existence, though in one aspect it is a part of this nature, is not merely natural; accordingly his aims and activities are not explicable by natural laws. As he is himself distinct from nature, so his true self-satisfaction or good cannot be found in the gratification of the wants and desires due to his animal organism, nor, indeed, in any conceivable series of pleasures that perish in the enjoyment: his true good

Transcendentalism.

T. H. Green (1836-1882).

must be permanent, as the self is which it satisfies; and it must be realised in a social life of self-conscious persons. A completely definite description of it cannot yet be given, since we cannot know what man's faculties are except from their realisation, which is as yet only partial: but a partial determination of it is to be found in the established moral code, which—though it is not to be regarded as absolutely and incontrovertibly valid—is yet unconditionally binding as against any conflicting impulse except that desire for the best in conduct, which is the spring of moral improvement. The one unconditional good is the good will; and "when we come to ask ourselves what are the essential forms in which the will for true good (which is the will to be good) must appear," our answer must "follow the lines of the Greek classification of virtues." Our conception must not, however, be restricted to virtue in the modern sense; it must include "art and science" as well as the "specifically moral virtues"; the good will is "the will to know what is true, to make what is beautiful, to endure pain and fear, to resist the allurements of pleasure, in the interest of some form of human society." Finally, we are told that "the idea of a true good does not admit of the distinction between good for self and good for others," and that it is not to be sought in "objects that admit of being competed for,"—though how exactly this is reconciled with the inclusion in the notion of the "realisation of scientific and artistic capacities" is not clearly explained.

§ 18. Free Will. In the account that I have given in this chapter of the development of English ethical thought from Hobbes to the present time, I have hitherto omitted to take note of the views held by different moralists on the question of Free Will. My reason for the omission is, that by several of the writers with whom I have been concerned, this difficult and obscure question is either not discussed at all, or treated in such a way as to minimise its ethical importance; and this latter mode of treatment is in harmony with my own view. In order to explain this comparative neglect to readers who may be disposed to take a different view, it is needful to distinguish three meanings in which "freedom" is attributed to the will or "inner self" of a human being—viz. (1) the general power of choosing among different alternatives of action without a motive, or against the resultant force of conflicting motives; (2) the power of choice between the promptings of reason and those of appetites (or other non-rational impulses) when the latter conflict with reason; (3) merely the quality of acting rationally in spite of conflicting impulses, however strong, the *non posse peccare* of the mediæval theologians. It is obvious that "freedom" in this third sense is something quite distinct from freedom in the first or second sense; and, indeed, is rather an ideal state after which the moral agent ought to aspire than a property which the human will can be said to possess. In the first sense, again, as distinct from the second, the assertion of "freedom" appears to have no ethical significance, except in so far as it introduces a general uncertainty into all our inferences respecting human conduct. Even in the second sense it hardly seems that the freedom of a man's will can be an element to be considered in examining what it is right or best for him to do (though of course the clearest convictions of duty will be fruitless if a man has not sufficient self-control to enable him to act on them); it is rather when we ask whether it is just to punish him for wrongdoing that it seems important to know whether he could have done otherwise. But the importance actually attached to this connection of Free Will with retributive Justice has been rather theological than strictly ethical, at least during a great part of the period with which we have been concerned; so that notwithstanding the prominence given to the question in the controversies of the Protestant divines of the 17th century, it does not appear that English moralists from Hobbes to Hume laid any stress on the relation of free will either to duty generally or to justice in particular. Neither the doctrine of Hobbes, that deliberation is a mere alternation of competing desires,—voluntary action immediately following the "last appetite,"—nor the hardly less decided Determinism of Locke, who held that the will is always moved by the greatest present uneasiness, appeared to either author to require any reconciliation with the belief in human responsibility. Even in Clarke's system, where Indeterminism is no doubt a cardinal notion, its importance is metaphysical rather than ethical; Clarke's view being that the apparently arbitrary particularity in the constitution of the physical universe is really only explicable by reference to creative free-will. In the ethical discussion of Shaftesbury and the "Sentimental" moralists generally, this question drops naturally out of sight; and the cautious Butler tries to exclude its perplexities as far as possible from the philosophy of practice. The position of the question, however, became materially different under the influence of the important reaction, initiated by Reid, against the whole manner of philosophising that had led finally to Hume. Not only did the conviction of Free Will occupy a prominent place among the beliefs of Common Sense which, in the view of the Scottish school, it was the business of philosophy to define and defend; it was also generally held by this school to be an absolutely essential point of ethical doctrine, and

Reid on Free Will.

inseparably connected with the judgment of good and ill desert which they maintained to be an essential element of the moral consciousness. In fact, the two main arguments on which Reid relies to prove Free Will are the universal consciousness of active power and the universal consciousness of accountability. In the first place, Reid urges, "we have a natural conviction that we act freely so early, universal, and necessary, that it must be the result of our constitution"; so that the supposition of its fallaciousness is "dishonourable to our Maker, and lays the foundation for universal scepticism." The force of this argument would seem to be weakened by Reid's admission that it is natural to rude nations to believe that sun, moon, sea, winds, have active power, whereas the progress of philosophy shows them to be dead and inactive: but Reid's view is that the universal notion of activity must find proper application somewhere, while reflection shows that it can only be properly applicable to the free human will,—a so-called agent whose acts are the necessary consequences of causes that lie outside his volition being, in fact, not an agent at all. That "acts are determined by the strongest motive" is, he contends, a proposition incapable of any proof that does not beg the question: if we measure the strength of a motive by the effect which it actually has on volition, it is doubtless easy to show that the strongest motive always prevails; but then we have assumed the very point at issue. If, on the other hand, we take our criterion from the agent's consciousness, and measure the strength of a motive by the felt difficulty of resisting it, then it must be admitted that impulses to action are sometimes successfully resisted, even when the agent feels it easier to yield than to resist. In fact, the ethically important competition of motives is that which takes place when an "animal motive," which as *felt* is strongest, impels in one direction, and a motive "strongest in the eye of reason" points the opposite way; *i.e.* when we have a conviction that it is our duty or our interest to resist appetite or passion, although more effort is required to resist than to yield. In such a conflict, though the flesh sometimes prevails against the spirit, it does not always prevail; moral freedom, then, is the power experience shows us to possess of *either* acting in accordance with our judgment as to what is best, *or* obeying the impulse felt to be the strongest.

A similar relation between rational and animal motives is implied, according to Reid, both in our general notion of responsibility and in the varying degrees of responsibility recognised in common moral judgments. An irresistible motive is generally admitted to take away guilt; no one is blamed for yielding to necessity, or thought to deserve punishment for what it was not in his power to prevent. Again, we commonly judge that the criminality of mischievous acts is materially diminished by their being done under the influence of violent pain or alarm, or even passion; and in this recognition of the limits of man's power of acting in resistance to feeling, the reality of his free agency within these limits is also implicitly recognised. For if all actions are equally necessary, if a man who betrays a State secret for a bribe is as much "compelled by an irresistible motive" as a man who betrays it on the rack, why should there be so profound a difference in our judgments of the two cases?

Since Reid's time the Freedom of the Will has, I think, been usually maintained by intuitional moralists, and usually on grounds broadly similar to those which I have just summarised: except so far as under the influence of Kant—operating either directly or as transmitted by Sir William

Hamilton and others—the argument from "consciousness of power" has been abandoned as really leading to an antinomy or conflict of opposite inconceivabilities, and the whole stress laid on the argument from consciousness of duty and desert. Utilitarian moralists, on the other hand, have usually been Determinists; and besides urging the difficulty of reconciling Free Will with the universality of causation as understood by all students of physical science, —a difficulty which the progress of science has pressed home with continually increasing force,—they have usually attempted to repel the argument from responsibility and desert by giving a somewhat new meaning to these current terms. The common judgment of ill-desert, according to the utilitarian Determinist, is merely the expression of natural resentment moralised by sympathy and enlightened self-regard: such resentment and the punishment to which it prompts are a proper and reasonable response to voluntary mischief—however little free the mischievous agent may have been—if, as is admitted, they tend to prevent similar mischief in future.[1] He allows that in a sense "ought" implies "can," and that only acts which it was "in a man's power" not to do are proper subjects of punishment or moral condemnation; but he explains "can" and "in his power" to imply only the absence of all insuperable obstacles except want of sufficient motive; it is just in such cases, he urges, that punishment and the expression of moral displeasure are required to supply the lacking motives to right conduct. He finds no difficulty in the fact that acts are commonly judged

Determinist Ethics.

[1] It should be observed, however, that some Determinists have dealt differently with the argument that necessity does away with ill-desert. They have admitted that punishment can only be legitimate if it be beneficial to the person punished; or they have held that the only lawful use of force is to restrain lawless force.

to be less culpable if done under the influence of violent fear or desire: for, as Bentham points out, the disposition manifested in such acts causes less alarm for the future than if the motive had been slighter. The Determinist, however, does not admit that current judgments of culpability, so far as they influence practice, are really in harmony with the doctrine of free will; and indeed it seems undeniable that we commonly agree in punishing negligence that has caused serious detriment without requiring proof that it was the result, directly or indirectly, of wilful disregard of duty; and that we do not consider rebellion or assassination less properly punishable, because they were prompted by disinterested patriotism, though we certainly consider their ill-desert less.

§ 19. French influence on English Ethics.

So far I have traced the course of English ethical speculation without bringing it into relation with contemporary European thought on the same subject. This course has seemed to me most convenient, because in fact almost all the systems described, from Hobbes downward, have been of essentially native growth, showing hardly any traces of foreign influence. We may observe that ethics is the only department in which this result appears. The physics and psychology of Descartes were much studied in England, and his metaphysical system was certainly the most important antecedent of Locke's; but Descartes hardly touched ethics proper. So again the controversy that Clarke conducted with Spinoza's doctrine, and afterwards personally with Leibnitz, was entirely confined to the metaphysical region. Catholic France was a school for Englishmen in many subjects, but not in morality; the great struggle between Jansenists and Jesuits had a very remote interest for us. It is not till the latter portion of the 18th century

that the impress of the French revolutionary philosophy begins to manifest itself on this side of the Channel; and even then its influence is not very marked in the region of ethical thought. It is true that Rousseau's bold and fervid exaltation of nature at the expense of civilisation, his praise of the happy ignorance, transparent manners, and simple virtues of uncultivated man as contrasted with the artificial, effete, corrupt product of modern society, had considerable effect in England as well as in France: and his eloquent proclamation of the inalienable sovereignty of the people as the principle of the only just and legitimate political order gave powerful aid to the development of the old English theory of the social compact in a revolutionary direction. Still, it is interesting to observe how even those English writers of the latter half of the 18th century, who were most powerfully affected by the movement of French political speculation, kept close to the old lines of English thought in laying down the ethical foundation on which they proposed to construct the new social order of rational and equal freedom: whether, like Price, they belonged to the intuitional school, or whether, like Priestley and Godwin, they accepted greatest happiness as the ultimate criterion of morality. Only in the derivation of Benthamism do we find that an important element is supplied by the works of a French writer, Helvetius; as Bentham himself was fully conscious.[1] It was Helvetius
from Helvetius that he learnt that, men being universally (1715-1771).
and solely governed by self-love, the so-called moral judgments are really the common judgments of any society as to

[1] It may be observed that Bentham's political doctrine first became widely known in the French paraphrase of Dumont; and that a certain portion of it—that relating to the *Principles of the Civil Code*—has never been given to the world in any other form.

its common interests; that it is therefore futile on the one hand to propose any standard of virtue, except that of conduciveness to general happiness, and on the other hand useless merely to lecture men on duty and scold them for vice; that the moralist's proper function is rather to exhibit the coincidence of virtue with private happiness; that, accordingly, though nature has bound men's interests together in many ways, and education by developing sympathy and the habit of mutual help may much extend the connection, still the most effective moralist is the legislator, who, by acting on self-love through legal sanctions, may mould human conduct as he chooses. These few simple doctrines give the ground plan of Bentham's indefatigable and life-long labours.

Comte (1798-1857).

So again, in the modified Benthamism of J. S. Mill, the influence of a French thinker, Auguste Comte (*Philosophie Positive*, 1829-42, and *Système de Politique Positive*, 1851-54), appears as the chief modifying element. This influence, so far as it has affected moral as distinct from political speculation, has been exercised primarily through the general conception of human progress, which, in Comte's view, consists in the ever-growing preponderance of the distinctively human attributes over the purely animal, social feelings being ranked highest among human attributes, and highest of all the most universalised phase of human affection, the devotion to humanity as a whole. Accordingly, it is the development of benevolence in man, and of the habit of "living for others," which Comte takes as the ultimate aim and standard of practice, rather than the mere increase of happiness. He holds, indeed, that the two are inseparable, and that the more *altruistic* any man's sentiments and habits of action can be made, the greater will be the happiness enjoyed by himself as well as by others. But he does not seriously trouble himself to argue with egoism, or to weigh carefully the amount of happiness that might be generally attained by the satisfaction of egoistic propensities duly regulated; a supreme unquestioning self-devotion, in which all personal calculations are suppressed, is an essential feature of his moral ideal. Such a view is almost diametrically opposed to Bentham's conception of normal human existence; the newer utilitarianism of Mill represents an endeavour to find the right middle path between the two extremes.

It is to be observed that, in Comte's view, devotion to humanity is the principle not merely of morality but of religion; *i.e.* it should not merely be practically predominant, but should be manifested and sustained by regular and partly symbolical forms of expression, private and public. This side of Comte's system, however, and the details of his ideal reconstruction of society, in which this religion plays an important part, have had but little influence either in England or elsewhere. On the other hand, his teaching on the subject of scientific method—especially on the method of Sociology or the Social Science, which he believed himself to have constructed, and of which he has a legitimate claim to be regarded as the chief founder—has had a profound and enduring effect on English ethical thought. In the utilitarianism of Paley and Bentham the proper rules of conduct, moral and legal, are determined by comparing the imaginary consequences of different modes of regulation on men and women, conceived as specimens of a substantially uniform and unchanging type. It is true that Bentham expressly recognises the varying influences of climate, race, religion, government, as considerations which it is important for the legislator to take into account; but his own work of social construction was almost entirely independent of such considerations, and his school generally appears to have been convinced of their competence to solve the most important ethical and political questions for human beings of all ages and countries, without regard to historic differences. But in the Comtian conception of social science, of which ethics and politics are the practical application, the knowledge of the laws of the evolution of society is of fundamental and continually increasing importance; humanity is regarded as having passed through a series of stages, in each of which a somewhat different set of laws and institutions, customs and habits, is normal and appropriate. Thus, present man is a being that can only be understood through a knowledge of his past history; and any effort to construct for him a moral and political ideal, by a purely abstract and unhistorical method, must be necessarily futile; whatever modifications may at any time be desirable in positive law and morality can only be determined by the aid of "social dynamics." This view extends far beyond the limits of Comte's special school or sect, and, indeed, seems to be very widely accepted among educated persons at the present day.

§ 20. German influence on English Ethics.

The influence of German—as of French—philosophy on English ethical thought has been comparatively unimportant until a recent period. In the 17th century, indeed, the treatise of Puffendorf on the *Law of Nature*, in which the general view of Grotius was restated with modifications—partly designed to effect a compromise with the new doctrine of Hobbes—seems to have been a good deal read at Oxford and elsewhere. Locke includes it among the books necessary to the complete education of a gentleman. But the subsequent development of the theory of conduct in Germany dropped almost entirely out of the cognisance of Englishmen; even the long dominant system ot Wolff (*d.* 1754), imposing in its elaborate and complete construction, was hardly known to our best informed writers. Nor does it appear that the greater fame and more commanding genius of Kant led to the careful study of his ethical system by English moralists, until it had been before the world for about fifty years.[1] His fundamental ethical doctrine, however, was early and eagerly embraced by one of the most remarkable and interesting among the leaders of English thought in the first part of this century,—the poet and philosopher Coleridge. Later, we find distinct traces of Kantian influence in Whewell and other writers of the intuitional school; and the continually increasing interest in the products of the German mind which Englishmen have shown during the last forty years has caused the works of Kant to be so widely known that the present work would be manifestly incomplete without an exposition of his ethical doctrines.

Kant (1724-1804).

The English moralist with whom Kant has most affinity is Price; in fact, Kantism, in the ethical thought of modern Europe, holds a place somewhat analogous to that occupied by the teaching of Price and Reid among ourselves. Kant,

[1] Kant's most valuable ethical treatises, the *Grundlegung zur Metaphysik der Sitten*, and the *Kritik der praktischen Vernunft*, were published in 1785 and 1788 respectively. In 1830 Sir James Mackintosh published in the *Encyclopædia Britannica* his *Dissertation on the Progress of Ethical Philosophy:* and the language in which this accomplished writer speaks of Kant's ethical doctrine indicates that it had not yet really found its way even to the cultivated intelligence of Englishmen. In 1836 Mr. Semple's translation of Kant's chief ethical writings initiated the new period of better acquaintance.

like these thinkers, holds that man as a rational being is unconditionally bound to conform to a certain rule of right, or "categorical imperative" of reason. Like Price, he holds that an action is not good unless done from a good motive, and that this motive must be essentially different from natural inclination of any kind; duty, to be duty, must be done for duty's sake. And he argues, with more subtlety than Price or Reid, that though a virtuous act is no doubt pleasant to the virtuous agent, and any violation of duty painful, this moral pleasure (or pain) cannot strictly be the motive to the act, because it follows instead of preceding the recognition of our obligation to do it.[1] With Price, again, he holds that rightness of intention and motive is not only an indispensable condition or element of the rightness of an action, but actually the sole determinant of its moral worth; but with more philosophical consistency he draws the inference—of which the English moralist does not seem to have dreamt—that there can be no separate rational principles for determining the "material" rightness of conduct, as distinct from its "formal" rightness; and therefore that all rules of duty, so far as universally binding, must admit of being exhibited as applications of the one general principle

[1] Singularly enough, the English writer who approaches most nearly to Kant on this point is the utilitarian Godwin, in his *Political Justice*. In Godwin's view, reason is the proper motive to acts conducive to general happiness: reason shows me that the happiness of a number of other men is of more value than my own; and the perception of this truth affords me at least *some* inducement to prefer the former to the latter. And supposing it to be replied that the motive is really the moral uneasiness involved in choosing the selfish alternative, Godwin answers that this uneasiness, though a "constant step" in the process of volition, is a merely "accidental" step,—"I feel pain in the neglect of an act of benevolence, because benevolence is judged by me to be conduct which it becomes me to adopt."

that duty ought to be done for duty's sake. The required demonstration is obtained as follows. The dictates of reason, Kant points out, must necessarily be addressed to all rational beings as such; hence, my intention cannot be right unless I am prepared to will the principle on which I act to be a universal law. We thus get the fundamental rule or imperative, "Act on a maxim which thou canst will to be law universal"; and this, Kant holds, will supply a sufficient criterion for determining all particular duties, since, "if we observe our state of mind at the time of any transgression of duty, we shall find that we really do not will that our maxim should be a universal law . . . our wish is that the opposite should remain a universal law, only we assume the liberty of making an exception in our own favour, or just for once only in favour of a passing inclination." The rule excludes wrong conduct with two degrees of stringency. Some kinds of immorality—such as making promises with the intention of breaking them—we cannot even conceive universalised; as soon as every one held himself free to break his promises no one would care to have promises made to them. Other maxims, such as that of leaving persons in distress to shift for themselves, we can easily conceive to be universal laws, but we cannot without contradiction will them to be such; for when we are ourselves in distress we cannot help desiring that others should help us.

Another important peculiarity of Kant's doctrine is his development of the connection between duty and free will. He holds that it is through our moral consciousness that we obtain a rational conviction that we are free; in the cognition that I ought to do what is right because it is right and not because I like it, it is implied that this purely rational volition is possible; that my action can be determined, not "mechanically," through the necessary operation of the natural stimuli of pleasurable and painful feelings, but in accordance with the laws of my true, reasonable self. The realisation of reason, or of human wills so far as rational, thus presents itself as the absolute end of duty; and we get, as a new form of the fundamental practical rule, "act so as to treat humanity, in thyself or any other, as an end always, and never as a means only." We may observe, too, that the notion of freedom connects ethics with jurisprudence in a simple and striking manner. The fundamental aim of jurisprudence is to realise external freedom by removing the hindrances imposed on each one's free action through the interferences of other wills. Ethics, on the other hand, is concerned with the realisation of internal freedom[1] by the resolute pursuit of rational ends in opposition to those of natural inclination. If we ask what precisely are the ends of reason—meaning by "end" a result which is sought to be produced by action—Kant's proposition that "all rational beings as such are ends in themselves for every rational being" hardly gives a clear answer. It might be interpreted to mean that the result to be practically sought is simply the development of the rationality of all rational beings—such as men—whom we find to be as yet imperfectly rational.

[1] I have tried in the text to get round the difficulty that I find in stating this part of Kant's doctrine distinctly and consistently; but I ought perhaps to explain frankly that his conception of Free Will seems to me to contain a confusion between two notions of freedom distinguished in § 18—(1) the Freedom that is only realised in right conduct, when reason successfully resists the seductions of appetite or passion, and (2) the Freedom to choose between right and wrong which is equally realised in either choice. It is Freedom in the latter sense, not in the former, that Libertarians have commonly regarded as inseparably connected with moral responsibility.

But this is not Kant's view. He holds, indeed, that each man should aim at making himself the most perfect possible instrument of reason, by cultivating both his natural faculties and his moral disposition; but he expressly denies that the perfection of others can be similarly prescribed as an end to each. It is, he says, "a contradiction to regard myself as in duty bound to promote the perfection of another; for it is just in this that the perfection of another man as a person consists, viz. that he is able *of himself* to set before him his own end according to his own notions of duty; and it is a contradiction to make it a duty for me to do something which no other but himself can do." In what practical sense, then, am I to make other rational beings my ends? Kant's answer is that what each is to aim at in the case of others is not Perfection but Happiness: he is to help others towards the attainment of those purely subjective ends that are determined for each not by reason but by natural inclination. For, Kant urges, "the ends of any subject which is an end in himself, ought as far as possible to be my ends also, if the conception of him as an end in himself is to have its full effect with me." Elsewhere he explains that to seek one's own happiness cannot be prescribed as a duty because it is an end to which every man is inevitably impelled by natural inclination: but that just because each inevitably desires his own happiness, and therefore desires that others should assist him in times of need, he is bound to make the happiness of others his ethical end, since he cannot *morally* demand aid from others without accepting the obligation of aiding them in like case. The exclusion of private happiness from the ends at which it is a duty to aim, at first sight strikingly contrasts with the view of Butler and Reid, that man, as a rational being, is under a "manifest obligation" to seek his own interest. The difference, however, is not really so great as it seems; since in his account of the *summum bonum* or Highest Good, Kant recognises by implication the reasonableness of the individual's regard for his private happiness: only, in Kant's view, it is not happiness simply which a truly reasonable self-love seeks, but happiness under the condition of being morally worthy of it. Though duty is to be done for duty's sake, and not as a means to the agent's happiness, still, Kant holds, we could not rationally do it if we did not hope thereby to attain happiness: since the highest good for man[1] is neither virtue nor happiness alone, but a moral world in which happiness is duly proportioned to merit. And Kant holds that we are bound by reason to conceive ourselves as necessarily belonging to such a world under the government of a wise author and ruler; since without such a world, "the glorious ideas of morality would be indeed objects of applause and admiration, but not springs of purpose and action." We must therefore postulate a cosmical order in which the demand for happiness as merited by duty finds satisfaction: and this involves a belief in God and a hereafter. But the certitude of this belief rests on an ethical basis alone. For, according to Kant's metaphysical doctrine, the world of nature, as known to each of us, is a mere complex of impressions on human sensibility, combined into a world of objects of possible experience by the self-conscious intelligence that conceives it; hence we can have no knowledge, as we can have no experience, of things as they are in themselves. Thus, though each of us, through his moral

[1] The absolutely highest good is the union of perfectly good or rational will with perfect blessedness, as in the Divine Existence as commonly conceived.

consciousness, knows himself to belong to a supersensible world, he knows nothing of the nature of that world; he knows *that* he is more than a mere phenomenon, but not *what* he is. Accordingly, though I can have a rational certainty that there is a God and a future life, my certitude, according to Kant, is not available for speculative knowledge: I do not theoretically know these beliefs to be true, but I must postulate them for practice, in order to fulfil rationally what I recognise as "categorically" commanded by the Practical Reason.

Post-Kantian Ethics.

Before Kant's death (1804) his works had begun to be read by the English thinker who, for more than a generation, was to stand as the chief representative in our island of German tendencies in philosophic thought.[1] But yet, when Coleridge's study of Kant began, the rapid and remarkable development of metaphysical view and method, of which the three chief stages are represented by Fichte, Schelling, and Hegel respectively, had already reached its second stage; the Subjective Idealism of Fichte had been developed in a series of treatises—and formally rejected by Kant—and the philosophy of Schelling was claiming the eager attention of all German students of metaphysics. One consequence of this was that the Kant partially assimilated by Coleridge was Kant seen through the medium of Schelling—a Kant who could not be believed "to have meant no more by his Noumenon or Thing in itself than his mere words express";[2] who, in fact, must be believed to have attained, through his practical convictions of duty and freedom, that

[1] This view of Coleridge is strikingly shown in an essay on him by J. S. Mill (1840), in which such phrases as "Coleridge and the Germans," the "Germano-Coleridgian doctrine," occur repeatedly.

[2] See Coleridge, *Biographia Literaria*, vol. i. pp. 145, 146.

speculative comprehension of the essential spirituality of human nature which his language appeared to repudiate. But though, viewed on its metaphysical side, the German influence obscurely communicated to the English mind through Coleridge was rather post-Kantian than Kantian, the same cannot be said of its strictly ethical side. The only German element discernible in the fragmentary ethical utterances of Coleridge is purely Kantian;[1] nor am I aware that any trace can be found elsewhere, in English ethical thought, of the peculiar doctrines of Fichte or Schelling, or of any post-Kantian German writer, until the influence of Hegel became manifest in the third quarter of the present century.[2]

Hegel (1770-1831). Hegel's ethical doctrine (expounded chiefly in his *Philosophie des Rechts*, 1821) shows a close affinity, and also a striking contrast, to Kant's. He holds, with Kant, that duty or good conduct consists in the conscious realisation of the free reasonable will, which is essentially the same in all rational beings. But in Kant's view the universal content of this will is only given in the formal condition of "only acting as one can desire all to act," which is to be subjectively applied by each rational agent to his own volition; whereas Hegel conceives the universal will as objectively presented to each man in the laws, institutions, and customary morality of the community of which he is a member. Thus, in his

[1] Thus in the *Friend*, vol. i. p. 340 (originally published 1809), he gives an unqualified adhesion to Kant's fundamental doctrine: "So act that thou mayst be able, without involving any contradiction, to will that the maxim of thy conduct should be the law of all intelligent Beings—is the one universal and sufficient principle and guide of morality."

[2] The manifestation of the Hegelian influence may be taken, I suppose, to begin with the publication of Mr. J. H. Stirling's remarkable book on the *Secret of Hegel* (1865).

view, not merely natural inclinations towards pleasures, or the desires for selfish happiness, require to be morally resisted; but even the prompting of the individual's conscience, the impulse to do what seems to him right, if it comes into conflict with the common sense of his community. It is true that Hegel regards the conscious effort to realise one's own conception of good as a higher stage of moral development than the mere conformity to the jural rules establishing property, maintaining contract, and allotting punishment to crime, in which the universal will is first expressed; since in such conformity this will is only accomplished accidentally by the outward concurrence of individual wills, and is not essentially realised in any of them. He holds, however, that this conscientious effort is self-deceived and futile, is even the very root of moral evil, unless it attains its realisation in harmony with the objective social relations in which the individual finds himself placed;—unless the individual recognises as his own essence the ethical substance presented to him in the family, in civil society, and finally in the state, the organisation of which is the highest manifestation of universal reason in the sphere of practice.

Hegelianism appears as a distinct element in English ethical thought at the present day;—the English Transcendentalism described in § 17 may be characterised as Kanto-Hegelian; but the direct influence of Hegel's system is perhaps less generally important than that indirectly exercised through the powerful stimulus which it has given to the study of the historical development of human thought and human society. According to Hegel, the essence of the universe is a process of thought from the abstract to the concrete; and a right understanding of this process gives the key for interpreting the evolution in time of European philosophy. So again, in his view, the history of mankind is a history of the necessary development of the free spirit through the different forms of political organisation: the first being that of the Oriental monarchy, in which freedom belongs to the monarch only; the second, that of the Greco-Roman republics, in which a select body of free citizens is sustained on a basis of slavery; while finally in the modern societies, sprung from the Teutonic invasion of the decaying Roman Empire, freedom is recognised as the natural right of all members of the community. The effect of the lectures (posthumously edited) in which Hegel's *Philosophy of History* and *History of Philosophy* were expounded has extended far beyond the limits of his special school; indeed, the present predominance of the historical method in all departments of the theory of practice is not a little due to their influence.

German Pessimism.

It was before[1] noticed that, in antithesis to the Evolutionistic Optimism of such writers as Spencer, a pessimistic view of animal life as a whole, and of human life as its highest development, has faintly manifested itself in recent English thought. In somewhat similar antithesis to the different kind of Evolutionistic Optimism, which belongs to the post-Kantian Idealism generally and the system of Hegel in particular, stands the pessimism of Schopenhauer.

Schopenhauer (1788-1860).

Taking from Kant the doctrine that the objective world of which we have experience is altogether constructed of elements supplied by human sensibility, combined according to laws of the experiencing mind, Schopenhauer diverges from Kantism in his conception of the Thing-in-itself that impresses our sensibility. In his view it is One Will that is

[1] *See* p. 258.

the innermost essence of every thing and of the totality of things. This Will, by its very nature, strives blindly to manifest and objectify itself; the mechanical and chemical forces of the inorganic world, the actions of living organisms from the lowest upwards, exhibit different stages of this objectification, which reaches its highest grade in organisms endowed with a brain, and therefore possessing consciousness. As manifested in living beings this Will may be more definitely conceived as the Will or striving to live: this instinctive impulse towards life is the deepest essence of all animal nature. But as this striving necessarily implies defect and discontent with the present condition, the life which it constitutes and maintains is essentially a suffering life; even the transient satisfactions by which it is chequered are really deliverances from pain and not positively good. This essential misery of life reaches its maximum in man, the most advanced manifestation of Will; and it will necessarily be increased by intellectual progress, even though this develops what Schopenhauer recognised as the purest human satisfaction—the restful contemplation of beauty. In this unhappy state of things the duty that philosophy points out to man is plainly the negation or denial of will; in this all true morality is summed up. Of such denial there are two stages: the lowest is that attained in ordinary virtue, which is essentially love and sympathy resting on a recognition of the real identity of any one ego with all others; the virtuous man represses and denies the egoism from which all injustice springs, and which is the affirmation of the will in one individual aggressively encroaching on the manifestation of the same will in another. But ordinary virtuous or sympathetic action is not yet free from the fundamental error of affirming the will to live: complete denial of this will is only attained by the ascetic self-mortification that turns away altogether from the illusory pleasures of life, repressing even the impulse that prompts to the propagation of the species.

Hartmann. Schopenhauer's primary argument for pessimism—based, as we have seen, on a consideration of the essential nature of Will—is confirmed, he tells us, by a careful and impartial observation of human experience. But the *a posteriori* proof of the misery of life has been more fully developed by a recent writer—E. von Hartmann—who, though of considerable originality, may be broadly regarded as a disciple of Schopenhauer, and who agrees with Schopenhauer in holding that the existence of the actual world is due to an irrational act of unconscious will.[1] Hartmann rejects Schopenhauer's doctrine that *all* pleasure is merely relief from pain: but he holds that the pleasures which arise from cessation of pains greatly preponderate over the pleasures not so conditioned, and are greatly inferior in intensity to the pains by which they are conditioned; that the fatigue of nerves caused by the prolongation of any kind of feeling tends to increase the painfulness of pain and to diminish the pleasantness of pleasure; that satisfaction is always brief, while dissatisfaction is as enduring as desire itself. Then, taking a survey of the chief directions of human effort, he urges that many emotions—as envy, chagrin, regret for the past, hatred—are purely or almost purely painful; that many states of life—as health, youth, freedom—are valued merely as implying absence of certain pains, while others—as labour and marriage—are recognised

[1] Hartmann, however, unlike Schopenhauer, conceives the "Unconscious" that is the ultimate ground of existence to be not merely Unconscious Will but Unconscious Intelligence also.

as evils chosen to avoid greater evils; that the common pursuit of riches, power, honour, etc., is illusory so far as the objects sought are conceived as ultimate ends; that many impulses leading to action—hunger, love of children, compassion, ambition—bring the agent clearly far more pain than pleasure, while many more cause a clear preponderance of pain on the whole, taking into account the feeling of patients as well as agents; that, finally, the only activities which bring an excess of pleasure—the cultivation of art and science—are capable of being really enjoyed by comparatively few, and these few persons whose superior intelligence specially exposes them to pain from other sources. These considerations lead Hartmann to the "indubitable conclusion" that the pain in the world now greatly exceeds the pleasure, not only on the whole, but in the case even of the most favourably circumstanced individuals. He then proceeds to argue that there is no prospect of material improvement in the future, but rather of increased misery: the progress of science brings little or no positive pleasure, and the partial increase in protection against pain that the human race may derive from it will be far more than outweighed by the increased consciousness of the predominance of pain, due to the development of human intelligence and sympathy. Hartmann's practical conclusion is that we should aim at the negation of the will to live, not each for himself, as Schopenhauer recommended, but universally, by working towards the end of the world-process and the annihilation of all so-called existence.

INDEX